When *Destiny Sings*

Judith Cuffe

POOLBEG

Published 2020
by Poolbeg Press Ltd
123 Grange Hill, Baldoyle
Dublin 13, Ireland
E-mail: poolbeg@poolbeg.com
www.poolbeg.com

© Poolbeg Press Ltd. 2020, copyright for editing, typesetting, layout, design, ebook

A catalogue record for this book is available from the British Library.

ISBN 978-1-78199-333-0

Typeset by Poolbeg Press Ltd

www.poolbeg.com

ABOUT THE AUTHOR

Judith Cuffe lives in County Wicklow, Ireland with her husband, three children and faithful writing companion, Wilbur, the dog. A book lover and a fan of the written word, she finally got round to following her dream and writing that book. *When Destiny Sings* is her first novel and she is currently working on a sequel. When she isn't writing, she can be found in the gym, hillwalking, following the latest fashions or ferrying the children around as Mum's Taxi. To find out more about Judith, follow her on Facebook (Judy in The Middle) and Instagram (@judy_middle), or on her website www.judyinthemiddle.com.

For Mal. Through
every evolution
and beyond.
For ever. x

Prologue

Now

She sat hunched in her car at the brow of the hill, overlooking the town, and tried to steady her breathing. She'd been so sure this was the right thing to do – what she needed to do – but now she was unsure. It was just as she'd left it, all those years before, and yet everything had changed. Time had moved on, but she hadn't. She wiped at the tears that sprang to her eyes, reminding her of how alone she was. It was twelve years since she'd seen this place, but the memories hit her hard in the chest. She'd sworn she'd never return. Her mother had made her promise when she said goodbye to her that day that she'd never come back. Not for anything.

"You have to be strong now, my love. I taught you to be strong, didn't I? I'll always be with you, watching over you, but there's nothing here for you now, nothing at all," she'd told her through the tears.

Then she'd taken a thick envelope from her bedside locker and pressed it into her hand, folding her fingers around it and securing it there with all the strength she had left.

She'd squeezed her mother close, attempting to transfer all of her love to her, believing that it might somehow

1

magically heal her, or perhaps she'd been trying to absorb energy – enough to see her through what her mother had asked. Holding her mother's ravaged body so tight she feared she'd crush the life from her, there and then, but she hadn't.

Eventually, her grip had loosened. Then she'd automatically done as instructed – packed her bags, meticulously folding everything into the suitcase as if going on a trip instead of embarking on a life transformation. Her limbs moved without instruction, her mother's words pushing her along. She'd stood at the bedroom door one last time.

"I can't." Her voice broke, her chest heaving.

"You can, my love, and you will. Look at me."

That final image would stay with her for ever: a weakened body, a mind still so sharp, filled with purpose.

All the way there, she'd wanted to turn back, to run home and tell her mother she was wrong and she wouldn't leave her. But she'd kept going – purchased the one-way ticket to Dublin. She'd sat woodenly on the bench waiting, taking out the piece of paper with the instructions written carefully in her mother's failing hand. Every so often, her own hand flew to the inside pocket of her denim jacket, checking to see that the envelope was still there, the entire episode not imagined.

And then she felt it. It was like a knife tearing through her heart, ripping apart her seams. As she stepped on the train, she inhaled sharply, a ragged noise escaping her lips, and she knew there was no point in going back now. Even though it seemed impossible, to this day, she could pinpoint the exact moment her mother drew her last breath, leaving this world behind. She was gone.

It was just her now; alone – an orphan with no links to the past. She wouldn't be around for the funeral, nor to witness the busybodies who'd come to *mourn* her mother's tragic death. She'd be far away by then, although she knew they'd be all talk about the selfish daughter who'd upped and disappeared in the night, leaving her mother to meet her Maker alone.

But now she needed to know why. Why had she been sent away at seventeen years of age to fend for herself? What had happened all those years ago? Nobody, certainly not her mother, had ever really told her of the life that came before her. Her own life had seemed so perfect until it wasn't. She'd been young, with a head so filled with thoughts of herself that the past hadn't seemed important and she'd never thought to ask. So, she'd left with the envelope of money and floated for twelve years on autopilot, surviving, not understanding the emptiness that constantly shrouded her.

She supposed she'd been lucky, really. She'd managed well enough on her own, burying the past and becoming someone new, but the past always catches up, doesn't it? It's always there, lurking in the shadows. And now it was time to revisit it – to unravel it, to unfurl the mess, straighten it out, so she might someday be able to move on. Even now, just sitting here on the hill, looking down at where it all began, well, it brought her a little comfort, as if she could feel them around her again, sense the person she once was.

Yes, her mother insisted that she should never return. Not for anything or anyone, ever. But she started the car engine and commenced the descent into the past, into Knockmore.

PART ONE

Ann Fitzgerald

Now

"Don't be late and remember my motto: dress for the life you want – not the life you have. Oh, hang on, that doesn't quite work for you!" Sophie laughed down the phone.

"I'll be there," Ann promised, hanging up.

She wished the life she had was one that would allow her to throw on leggings and a sweatshirt and stick her hair up into a messy bun. But that wouldn't do at all. Dom liked her to look her best.

"When you walk into a room, I want them to be able to smell the money," he told her once. "I want them to think Dom Fitzgerald's wife wants for nothing."

It was the stupidest thing she'd ever heard. It had almost started an argument until he'd laughed and told her to "Chill out." She hated that statement. He used it all the time, making her feel like she was the uptight one and he was so laid back that he got to say whatever he liked if it was followed with "chill out". Maybe she was uptight.

She stood in her walk-in wardrobe, staring blankly at the rows and rows of clothes hanging there, neatly lined up. She'd spent all of Sunday afternoon mundanely arranging them by category so that she had something ready for whatever occasion should arise and yet she still felt as though she had nothing to wear. Dress for the life you want. If only she knew what that was.

In the end, she settled on a pair of leather leggings – as a compromise – and flat over-the-knee boots that she could at least walk in. She pulled a cashmere sweater over her head and looked at herself in the mirror, running her hand over the star on the front. Mam used to love stars. She'd say that your entire future was already mapped out in them. All you had to do was believe that the best was yet to come. She hoped she was right. She didn't feel like she was living her best life lately, even though she had more than she could ever possibly need, and yet . . .

The last few months had been a whirlwind and she felt exhausted, though she knew she had no right to be. She'd gone from working a forty-hour week to . . . well, nothing. Dom had insisted she give up work after the wedding.

"There's no need for you to continue and we talked about this. I need you at home. I work long hours as it is and there won't be any point as soon as there are babies, and I'm sure there will be lots of them soon."

He'd kissed her then, reassuring her, and she'd been happy to go along with it, as old-fashioned as it seemed. Perhaps he was right. Besides, she didn't earn even a quarter of what he did, but she'd loved working, adored her independence, and she missed it.

"Are you out of your mind? I'd do anything to be able to give up work and go to the gym and shop all day. I'd be happy to swap with you, except for the baby bit, of course, and Dom, no and no."

Sophie was about as maternal as a teenage boy after an energy drink. But the truth was, Ann didn't feel ready to have kids yet either, especially not the five or so that were so clearly written in *his* stars. He came from a giant chaotic family, with more sweaty nieces and nephews than you could count. While she enjoyed the huge, plush family get-togethers – for about fifteen minutes, anyway – it was so different from what she was used to. Dom would go mad if he knew she was still taking the pill. He'd already started to wonder why he hadn't yet managed to "conquer the egg".

She wouldn't think about that today. Today, all she needed to do was buy a dress for his thirtieth birthday next week and finalise plans. She pulled on the cream woollen coat he'd bought her in London last year, grabbed her bag and ran out of the door. She liked living near town and hardly ever used the brand-new Mini that sat sadly unused in the driveway, surplus to requirements. She knew how it felt. She almost felt sorry for it, but instead, she chose to walk everywhere. It was the only thing she'd asked for when they were buying their first house, that it was close enough so that she could walk almost anywhere she needed.

They'd settled on Pembroke Street.

"It's a little pokey. Will do as a starter home," Dom told her.

"My God, it's huge," she'd said, looking around at the four bedrooms, all en suite.

The kitchen was high gloss and shining, perfectly primed for sticky handprints to maul the shimmering surfaces. The entire house was very modern, with more glass than walls. "Brimming with light," the estate agent had said, but to Ann it seemed cold. If it were up to her, she'd have bought something cosier. She hated open-plan, preferring the option to shut the door and curl up on a great big squashy sofa, or to sit in front of the fire on, dare she say it, carpet.

"This is how the houses are now. When we have kids,

we can buy rolls and rolls of carpet *and* a bigger house," Dom promised.

The house had previously been owned by two architects, who'd refurbished it to within an inch of its life. Once they'd finished it, they lived in it for a year and then sold it on, ready to purchase the next project awaiting bedazzlement. It seemed a strange way of life to her, never settling, always wanting more, but then again, everything about *this* way of life seemed unusual and try as she might, she wasn't sure she'd ever understand it.

"We've got it! I won the bidding war," Dom had told her triumphantly just weeks before the wedding.

She nearly died when he told her how much he'd paid for it. He was willing to go all the way to ensure it was his. But that was Dom, always wanting to win, at whatever cost.

"It's his height," Sophie told her. "Always the same. Short men always try to overcompensate."

"Ah, come on, Soph, he's not exactly Tom Cruise," Ann giggled.

"No, he's worse. He's Danny DeVito!"

They'd laughed about it, but lately she was beginning to think Sophie was right. He was an inch or so shorter than her and while it had never bothered her in the slightest, it always caused him concern.

"I nearly didn't ask you out because we're the same height," he'd told her after their second date.

She didn't want to burst his bubble, but it was glaringly obvious, especially when she wore heels, that she was winning in the height stakes.

"What made you change your mind?" she'd asked.

"Well, everyone else wanted you too, and I wasn't going to let them win, that's not the way I roll."

10

Ann had caused quite the stir when she'd first started in the accounts department five years ago, or so he told her, anyway. She'd been mortified, never purposely trying to impress with her looks, preferring to keep her professional appearance as understated as possible.

"Ah, Ann, you just don't get it. It takes us mere mortals hours to achieve the look that you wake up with," Sophie said when Ann told her she couldn't walk to the photocopier without being asked out for a drink after work.

Ann couldn't understand it. She always dressed so conservatively at work, rarely wore make-up and kept her hair tied up neatly.

"You, my friend, make those black pencil skirts and sweaters look like they came straight off the catwalk in Milan and not from Primark," Sophie said.

Ann brushed off the compliment, as she always did, much to Sophie's annoyance.

"Take the compliment, will you? Stop being so Irish. You're gorgeous."

Ann didn't know about that. Her mam had been stunning, all legs, tanned skin and blonde hair. Ann couldn't deny that lately when she looked in the mirror, it was all she could see staring back at her: her mam's face, her mam's smile.

"Just go with it. Go out for a drink. What's the worst that could happen?" Sophie encouraged.

So she had – with a few of them, anyway. But it was Dom who eventually won her over. It hadn't taken him long, either – three dates in and she was smitten. What he lacked in height he made up for in confidence. He was charming, attentive, persistent, successful, and he made her feel special. But most of all, she felt wanted. She hadn't felt that in a long time and she had to admit that it was hard not to get swept along by it all. It was like stepping into the pages of a society magazine, the type that lay open in the reception of Fitzgerald Stock Brokers. "One of the best places to work in Dublin," if you were young, full of energy, wanted to live the dream, and especially if your name was Dominic Fitzgerald.

It was his father's firm, but he shared the same work ethic as Bernard Fitzgerald, if not his towering height. Ann adored her father-in-law. He was a great big lug of a man who, like her, had arrived in the Big Smoke from another small Irish town many moons ago, forging a successful career for himself. He worked hard and played hard, but he was the salt of the earth, never giving in to the glittering lifestyle that his success could easily afford him.

Bernard Fitzgerald was very sought-after as an after-dinner speaker, commanding the room with his no-apologies attitude. Ann loved listening to his inspiring rags-to-riches tale, which always finished with the same sentiment: "It could all be gone tomorrow. Money won't wipe your tears, celebrate your glory, nor embrace you at night. Real success is family." To Bernard, it wasn't just a quote thrown out to secure a standing ovation, he meant it, and you could see it in the way he looked at his kids and his wife, Patricia.

Perhaps it was these values she'd glimpsed in Dom that had made her fall in love with him. But lately, she wasn't so sure if it was all gone tomorrow how her husband would feel. Dom appreciated the finer things in life far more than she did. He worked hard for it and had been incredibly successful in his own right, but she couldn't imagine Dom settling for a takeaway on a Saturday night and a bottle of wine from Lidl. It was always about the best restaurants, the finest clothes, the fastest cars, the on-trend holidays.

Dom was the type to twirl his wine dramatically, practically inserting his entire face into the glass, sniffing and savouring, and sometimes she just wanted to shout, "Drink the feckin' thing!" Ann wouldn't know a Chablis from a Merlot if it hit her in the face. She wasn't entirely sure that Dom did, either. At first she hadn't minded the "act", found it somewhat endearing, assumed he wanted to impress her, and she'd hardly even balked when he started calling her *Bella* and it had stuck. Eventually, she'd stopped correcting him and had started answering to it.

"Ann is just so plain," he'd said. "And you're anything but plain, Bella."

She was constantly asked were her parents Scandinavian. Her hair was almost white, her skin tanned to a rich brown, and yet she had the brightest blue eyes. She rarely went to the gym, unable to comprehend that culture. "Just walking? You must be starving yourself." The other wives and girlfriends would stare at her open-mouthed when she told them her secret. They persistently attended whatever class was deemed the next big fitness craze, spending countless hours in Brookfield Gym with personal trainers doing boxing, bounce class and Pilates, all followed by endless coffees. "Maybe skip the cappuccinos and scones!" Ann had said, almost choking on her Chablis from laughing. How people so educated could be so . . . thick!

"That was rude," Dom scolded her in the taxi home. "It wouldn't kill you to join them for a class and a coffee sometime, you know. Remember, you don't have the accent to be quite so aloof."

Ann had been hurt. There was nothing wrong with her accent. What did an accent matter?

"I'm sorry," he apologised the next day. "I just want you to fit in," he said, handing her an unlimited Brookfield membership. It was everything that someone else might have wanted.

"Ann! So sorry I'm late." Sophie kissed her on the cheek and looked her up and down approvingly. "Stuart Weitzman, nice. Statement cashmere sweater, tick. Nonchalant cream coat slung over shoulders, Chanel 2.55 handbag, tick, tick. My my, it appears you *are* a trophy wife, and I approve!"

"Shut up, Sophie. I'm no such thing," Ann laughed.

"Eh, yes, I think you might be. Listen, I'm not judging you. I'll be right there with you as soon as you introduce me to a few of Dom's single friends next Saturday night at the big 3-0 bash."

God, she loved Sophie. Sophie had grown up in Dublin like all of Dom's friends but was a little on the outside of the core set. "Cool but not cool enough," Sophie used to laugh. They'd shared an apartment in Grand Canal Dock, Dublin after Ann got her accountancy exams and could finally afford to move; though she still missed her cosy room in Mrs Crowley's house. She owed her so much for the kindness she'd shown her when she first arrived in Dublin, but it was Sophie she relied on more than anyone and they'd quickly formed a solid friendship, with Sophie knowing all the details of Ann's life that Dom always brushed over.

"Talking of Dom, how is Lord Farquaad?"

"Stop!" Ann swiped at her with her handbag as the two buckled over in laughter.

"Come on, let's get you something that'll wipe the smile off the WAGs' faces. Rose of Tralee contestant coming through," Sophie called as they swept through the doors of Brown Thomas department store and made their way to the second floor. "Now, promise not to be annoying. You are *not* to turn your nose up and instead, you are to trust me and diligently try on everything I show you, understand?"

"Yes, sir, I promise," Ann said, saluting her, knowing that her friend was far more fashion-forward than she could ever be and that resistance was futile.

It didn't take long to find the perfect dress. Everything looked great on her, but she was more suited to classic clothes than the impossibly edgy outfits that Sophie always managed to pull off so well. They settled on a black dress – super simple, super backless and super stunning.

"I hate you," Sophie said. "Look at your figure. If you go and eat a burger now for lunch, I'll never speak to you again. I'd have to jog home to be able to eat what you do. Where do you put it?"

"Would you speak to me if I promised to wear those great big ridiculous clown pom-pom earrings you picked out?" Ann winked at her.

"I might . . . would you also consider buying the ridiculously high shoes to go with the dress – that might appease me somewhat?"

"Deal."

"Easy-peasy," Sophie said and then rolled her eyes. "Much as I hate to use Dom's little nickname for you, but you'll be the *Bella* of the ball." Sophie still couldn't bring herself to call her friend anything but Ann, much as everyone connected to Dom had followed his lead and now called her Bella.

"Let's hope so."

Ann didn't get the same kick out of clothes that Sophie

or Dom's friends' wives did, but she knew the dress would go down well at the big party and Dom would appreciate the effort. She must remember to look at the label, so she could tell all the darting eyes what designer she was wearing and they could quickly calculate the total in their heads, as she'd so often seen them do. Ann did like looking nice, of course she did. It was just somewhat wasted on her. She'd survived for many years rooting through the sale items in the cheaper stores of Dublin's Grafton Street and no one would ever have guessed that her entire outfit had cost less than forty euros.

"What's up? You're a hundred miles away?" Sophie looked at her through narrowed eyes. "Oh, sweet Jesus. You're pregnant. Are you pregnant?"

They were sitting in the lounge of their favourite hotel, in prime position so Sophie could count all the designer bags that drifted past their table.

Ann burst out laughing. "No! For Christ's sake, Sophie. I'm not pregnant – just tired. Tired from doing nothing."

"Thank God. I'm not ready to be an aunty. Two glasses of Prosecco, please. Quick!" She gestured at the waiter. "I need a drink after that," she gasped before turning serious. "Why don't you go back to work if you're bored? You don't need to ask permission, you know. You worked so hard to get where you were and are you really ready to board the baby train?"

"No. I'm really not," Ann admitted, taking a sip of Prosecco and sighing. "Is that bad? Should I be ready? You know, I had to have a medical last week for this new life assurance policy thing and I couldn't fill in the bits about my medical history. What if there's some big thing I don't know about, some genetic disorder lurking in my chromosomes?" Ann screwed up her face as she spoke. "It just got me thinking."

"Oh, Ann, I'm sure there isn't, but maybe you should try to find out a little more, like we discussed. Maybe it's time. It's been twelve years and of course it's okay not to be ready for kids. Jesus, we *are* kids!"

"I know." Ann looked down, afraid her eyes would give her away. "Dom's so keen on them," she continued. "But he seems different lately. Maybe it's work. I always seem to be on my own, always waiting for him to come home, like some antiquated housewife from the dark ages. It's just not what I imagined it to be. You know?"

"Look, get this party out of the way and then reassess. Nothing is set in stone and you knew when you married him how hard he works. I mean, look at your life! Loads of people would kill for it. Remember, Sabrina nearly *did* try to kill you to get to Dom." Sophie held up the butter knife and pretended to jab it into Ann's heart.

"Don't remind me!" Ann laughed at the memory of Dom's ex, Sabrina, dropping her steak knife at a luncheon and accidentally slicing Ann's leg with it.

"Morto for her! Listen, Dom's mad about you and you him. Sometimes marriage takes a little getting used to. That's what my mum told my sister when she tried to come home two months after marrying Rob the Knob. It's just teething problems. Try to have fun. You deserve a nice life," she reassured.

Ann hoped she was right. There would undoubtedly be more than teething problems if she didn't stop taking the pill soon.

"Are you sure there's nothing else going on?" Sophie asked, concerned.

"Maybe I just feel like I'm at a bit of a crossroads and I'm not sure which way to go."

"Deep, man," Sophie said, attempting to lighten the mood. "Now listen, don't go making any hasty decisions, especially not in those heels you promised to wear. They're not designed for crossroads. In fact, you might need to get Dom a pair of Cuban heels for under his trousers to give him a little lift that night, otherwise you'll be looking down on him."

"Sophie, you are terrible," Ann scolded, wiping the tears from her eyes.

"Gosh, if you do have kids, they'll probably be taller than Dom," Sophie continued. Once she started, she couldn't stop. "Seriously, though, were they both tall, your parents? Where do you get it from?" she asked, catching Ann by surprise.

"Yep, they were both tall. Dad was taller than Mam, but only just," Ann smiled sadly.

Sometimes when she was least expecting it – there they were. It still shocked her after all this time, how fast the feelings could creep up on her, twisting her insides, making her feel instantly empty, disconnected, untethered. She wondered what her mam would make of Ann's life now, so different from the way she grew up. Lately, she found herself thinking about it a lot, at the most obscure times, even when she was enjoying herself, or surrounded by people at a charity lunch, or round at the Fitzgeralds'. What would Mam make of all this? She wished she could ask her.

All she wanted was for one more day, or even an hour maybe, to be with her own family and to feel what it was like just to be herself again instead of always feeling so lost.

She wondered, had her mam ever felt this way, this alone? There was so much Ann wished she'd asked her, taken notes so she could refer to her answers as each new life event unfolded. Her mam had lost her own mother when she was young too, had she felt like this? Although they hadn't got along, Ann knew that much. But why? Suddenly, it seemed more important than ever to know more about where she'd come from, who she really was. But maybe this was how it was when you were all alone in the world, with no links to your past.

Maybe she'd never know.

"Ann? Are you still with me?"

"Sorry," she smiled at her friend, the moment broken. "I'm still here. Now, tell me more about these shoes."

Felicity Montgomery

Then – 1985

Felicity grabbed her sensible brown leather attaché case and pulled the heavy front door behind her with a thud. She paused at the top of the three granite steps and tugged the handle of the bag over her shoulder before commencing her journey up the immaculate gravel driveway and through the iron gates that separated Knockmore House from the rest of the world. Felicity counted her footsteps as she went, reaching St Patrick's High, the Protestant boarding school, in a record twenty-seven. She stopped to take in the hordes of Catholic girls, noisily making their way towards the busier St Brigid's, just a mile outside Knockmore.

"Charli Pink Illusions, I think it's called," she heard one girl say, noticing her lips covered in the pale sticky gloss. It made her teeth appear yellow as she babbled away confidently to her friend.

"Did you see yer man at the disco on Saturday night? State of him, more gel in his hair than in the bottle," another giggled, her eyes darkened with the remnants of the weekend's clumpy mascara.

Felicity would have done anything to be among them instead of standing there spectating from the outside. She took in their canvas backpacks, emblazoned in biro with love hearts and the names of their favourite bands, strewn open, revealing dog-eared books and crumpled notes. Their hair stuck out in curious manners, as if they'd plunged their hand into a live socket, but to her they were exotic, outspoken, and they appeared far beyond their years as they strode assuredly up the road, their skirts rolled up in a way that made them shorter at the front than the back.

Felicity looked down at her own long skirt, trailing the ground with propriety. She smoothed her blonde hair, neatly brushed, not a hair out of place, her face scrubbed clean – no make-up for her.

"Common," her mother would say and the Montgomerys were anything but common. "Besides, why anyone would want to cover their faces in that muck is beyond me; soap and water, the old-fashioned way. If it was good enough for our Lord – well, maybe with a lick of face cream. That's all a young girl should need. You have good, clear skin – you get that from my side of the family," Mother finished, handing her the small jar of face cream as if handing over a pot of gold.

Felicity took it, terrified that by using the cream the veins would break open on her face, like the red spiders' legs permanently scribbled over Mother's flushed cheeks. Felicity hated the smell of that face cream. It smelled of nothing. Not like the spritz of Dewberry oil that Lucie had once sprayed on her wrist after a trip to The Body Shop in Dublin. She hadn't washed her hand for the entire day, sporadically savouring the sweet aroma of the coveted perfume, willing it not to fade. She'd never experienced anything like it; like happiness in a bottle.

She saw Lucie Maguire now, waving enthusiastically as

she passed. Felicity glanced over her shoulder quickly before lifting her hand in rigid acknowledgment and unsurely returning the smile. What she really wanted was to run across the road and throw her arms around Lucie. They'd been so close at one time – opposites in every way, of course, but it had never mattered. Lucie was small and wiry, with bright red frizzy hair and a smattering of freckles on her delicate face, in contrast to Felicity, who was tall and elegant, with creamy skin that turned golden in the sun and hair so straight it looked as though it were ironed.

They'd shared many years of laughter, hidden in the gardens of Knockmore House, out of sight of Mother. It had been so long since Felicity had been able to talk to Lucie, whisper the secrets they'd once shared. But she'd been warned to cease all contact after Felicity's mother accused Lucie's sweet, honest mother, Tess, of pinching the mink scarf.

"Irreplaceable," Mother had said. "A family heirloom left to me by my dear mother-in-law. You are *not* even to look in the direction of those people. Understand?"

Tess Maguire was just like her daughter, with the same red hair as Lucie only she'd learned to tame hers over the years, managing to stop it from breaking into the same fiery unruly mass that shrouded Lucie's tiny face. Tess exuded warmth from every pore and was always so full of life. She'd dutifully cleaned the Montgomerys' home for the last seven years and would never have taken anything from them – Felicity was sure of that. Besides, she couldn't understand why anyone would want to steal that dreaded scarf that still had both claws and head attached, and smelled as though it were silently decomposing every time Mother wore it.

"Perhaps the dog took it and buried it," Felicity bravely suggested.

"It was that Maguire one. Who knows what else she's stolen over the years? I witnessed her admiring it many times. I'd say she's wearing it to Mass now on a Sunday, like a trophy," Margot insisted.

Felicity felt sure that Tess had been staring not with admiration, but with curiosity as to why Margot was wearing a dead rat thrust around her neck. Before it was taken, Mother used to wear it herself to service on Sunday, teamed with one of her harsh woollen skirt suits from the drab palette of her closet and always accompanied by the same beige hat, much the same colour as her hair, which made it impossible to decipher where the hat began and the hair ended. It all blended miserably into one.

Felicity was sure she'd witnessed the scarf winking at her once or twice during Scriptures and wouldn't have been at all surprised if The Mink had escaped by itself.

"I'm not sure Tess would wear a mink scarf," Felicity attempted.

Though Tess and Mother were much the same age, Tess looked like a teenager beside her, with her brightly coloured mohair sweaters and jeans, a far cry from Margot's matronly belted jackets and skirts cut to the shin, which would have appeared out of place in the 1950s, let alone bang in the middle of the 1980s. But Mother wouldn't be swayed.

The exit of Tess from her position took away Felicity's only contact with the outside world in the form of Lucie, who'd accompanied her mam most weekdays to clean dusty old Knockmore House. Lucie had been her only salvation up until Mother's spiteful accusation and the dismissal removed the single shred of normality from her life.

"Oh, she's always been jealous of me. Jealous of how I came up in the world, leaving her behind, right where she was supposed to be, below me," Mother would say.

Felicity could almost repeat this statement verbatim as it spitefully exited her mother's tight little mouth, she'd heard it so many times over the years. It made her wonder if there was anyone in the entire universe positioned above Mother.

"We are different, Felicity. Your father's role in the community places him at the pinnacle of society, and as his wife and support, I should be treated with the utmost respect," she'd say.

Felicity was certain if it came down to it that Mother would even attempt to clamber her way past God. But Felicity did feel different and yearned for the way of life that Tess and Lucie often spoke of in their colourful descriptions of the goings-on in the Estates. A life of playing on the road, families, parties, running through the water sprinkler in the garden in summer, colourful clothes drying on washing lines, grazed knees and laughter. She longed to listen to pop music and go to discos, or watch *Top of the Pops* on a Saturday, all while eating a greasy fry-up for dinner, washed down with a litre of milky tea from a mug, in place of Mother's delicate china cups, which made Felicity's hand shake for fear of dropping one.

Felicity wanted to ride her bike through the town, stopping at the corner shop to buy a quarter of raspberry fizzers, which sat calling to her in one of those great big plastic jars in the window, then wait for her tongue to turn blue before sticking it out at the lads passing after football training. She wished she could go to the cinema or take a day trip to Dublin on the bus. Or eat one of those tiny boxes of cereals, "just enough for one bowl", which Tess bought for Lucie at the weekend as a treat. The only treat she'd ever known was a helping of both custard and cream on her apple pie on a Sunday.

Felicity would have done anything to live there, instead of being holed up in a big dreary house that she was sure was an exact replica of that from *Jane Eyre*, one of the few books deemed suitable by Mother. "Knockmore House is the finest dwelling in Knockmore," Mother would tell her. "Terribly sought-after, soaked in history." Soaked in damp, more like it. Of course, it must have been beautiful at one time, but it was now neglected, cold and dark. Suspended in a different era – just like they were, always dining in the formal dining room, the sound of the cutlery on the china bringing about the only break in the unending silence.

It was as though the 1980s had taken one look at their house and bypassed it, instead heading straight for the tightly packed-together houses in the Estates, filling them with big dollops of colour and a sprinkling of rhinestones for good measure on its way past. Felicity often imagined that an Iron Curtain separated Knockmore House from the rest of the world, just like the one she'd learned about in history class. If only she could find the opening, she might have slipped through it and never returned. Felicity wanted to read a magazine, or a teenage romance novel, to crimp her hair and wear clothes so bright they made you squint – all topped off with the palest lip gloss she could find, regardless of whether or not it made her white teeth appear yellow. Felicity wouldn't have cared. At least it would have made her fit in.

Instead, the highlight of her week was attending Sunday service, wearing one of the juvenile dresses Mother selected for her that made her look like a giant infant. She was fifteen years old, still wearing the clothes her mother laid out for her on the banisters each evening, still eating what she was told, seeing who she was told, doing everything she was told, but she didn't argue – there was no point.

Felicity didn't feel she belonged in her own life and she certainly didn't belong in Knockmore House with her externally pious mother. Of course, Mother was reverence personified inside the walls of the church and Knockmore House when the flock came to visit, with them almost genuflecting to her. But Felicity had long witnessed her tirades, her screams, her tantrums and a tongue so sharp it could take your eye out once the door closed behind those who came to seek advice from her father, only to be scrutinised by his formidable wife.

Felicity hadn't heard a kind word pass between her parents for years, maybe ever. Her father was a good man, who carried out his duties in the community diligently. He was well liked and admired, but Mother was quite the opposite. She remembered once hearing Mrs Walsh, the previous housekeeper, talking to the gardener.

"Oh, she put on a good show in the early days all right – sold her soul."

Felicity had pressed herself against the wall, holding her breath to become invisible as she'd listened.

"She wasn't a bad-looking girl in her day, either," Mrs Walsh continued. "Nothing like her sisters, mind. They were the real beauties of the family. Apple of their father's eye, God rest him. But she'll always be the bitter, envious girl she was, out to better herself. Never happy with her lot."

Felicity hadn't understood what it meant then, but she understood enough now as the years ticked by, revealing more and more. She'd slowly managed to close off her heart to Mother, knowing she'd never break her. Nor would she ever forget that dreadful night, much as she tried. It was permanently etched into her memory, tattooed onto her soul. She could still picture it when she closed her eyes – Mother stalking down the garden while Felicity watched on from her window, aghast. A little piece of Felicity's heart had splintered away that night and flown out of the window.

After that, everything changed. No amount of glue could ever mend it, nor fix the coldness she'd been subjected to from the day she was born. Her father too, once so interested in Felicity, had drifted away and gradually an awkward silence had developed between them. Perhaps a piece of his heart had splintered apart, too. At least she hoped that was it; it was too painful to imagine the alternative. Sometimes Felicity caught him watching her, a strange look on his face, as though he couldn't see her. Like those moments when you stare so intently that you end up seeing nothing at all – especially not the thing that's right in front of you.

But he always looked away.

She carried on up the driveway of St Patrick's. As the only day student, she was persistently excluded at school by the boarders, never privy to their inside jokes. She was an intruder at home, an outsider at school. Even her name set her apart, instantly isolating her among the Sharons and Collettes and Janes. She hated it: Felicity Margaret Montgomery, a mouthful of meaninglessness.

She sometimes wondered, did she even exist? Perhaps she was a figment of someone else's imagination, or trapped inside the chapter of a book and the disinterested reader had forgotten to turn the page. She'd often pinch herself so hard that the tears would prick her eyes, just to prove she was still there. She pinched her arm hard now, squeezing the flesh between her fingers, relishing the sting. It shocked her, but it felt good. It felt real. "Pain is real, Felicity," Mother would shout at her after one of her unprovoked attacks. "Pain is real."

She'd known nothing but pain for the past fifteen years. She longed for anyone to heed her, to talk to her and show interest in her. She wanted noise; so much noise she couldn't hear herself think. Felicity wanted to feel . . . anything. But most of all, she wanted to be free.

Margot Montgomery

Then – 1985

"Mornin', Maggie," Frankie O'Shea, her one-time suitor, shouted after her as she propelled her way towards St Patrick's Church for her extensive daily inspection. "Still working hard for the other side, I see. How are you managing with no housekeeper? Heard you let Tess go. Hard times, I suppose," he called after her.

"Yes, morning, Frankie." She didn't look up.

It was better to be polite, knowing if she ignored him now, he'd keep talking, or worse still, follow her, and she wasn't in the humour for him today. He'd grown braver over the years, after a long spell of putting his head down every time he saw her approach. She'd preferred that – it had seemed more appropriate somehow, respectful, rather than having to endure him shouting after her. But she supposed time makes you forget – some things, anyway.

"You're looking well. Fine and healthy. Must be well fed up there, Maggie," he winked.

"Prick," she muttered under her breath, continuing up the steps and avoiding his glare as best she could.

She stopped as she reached the door, pulling the belt of her tweed coat tighter as though the rough, staunch material would protect her from his taunts. Perhaps she should tell him to go away, but what was the point? They'd always be there watching her, waiting for her to trip up and slide back down to their miserable level. She'd heard on the grapevine he was out of work. Not that she was connected to the grapevine much any more, but she still heard things.

There were plenty more like him in Knockmore nowadays, hanging around all day with nothing better to do with their time than stare. "Tough times must be endured, better times will come," her husband, Michael, would say, trying to reassure those who were left jobless. Many had boarded the boat, forced to leave Ireland altogether to find work, but there were those who'd stayed behind, listlessly expecting the world to owe them a living. Well, she didn't have that problem. It was no wonder they couldn't bear to look at her, knowing she'd bettered herself like she always said she would. How were they to know that it hadn't all quite turned out the way she'd planned? That the perception hadn't quite reached her expectations – not at all, in fact. But then they saw what they chose to see.

She'd left them all behind without a backwards glance, why couldn't they do the same for her? She hadn't asked them for anything, except that – for them to leave her be. But she'd felt their stares then, as she still did now, when she first started climbing the hill towards St Patrick's Church to attend Sunday service with the *others*. "It's my business, I can do as I please," she'd shouted at her sisters, hell-bent on ignoring their pleas, determination burning in her mind. She'd seen them elbowing each other as she'd passed, keeping her head in the air to avoid their stares. They'd made sure she could hear them, though. "Where are you off to, Maggie?" "Not good enough for you here any more?" "Make sure you don't burst into flames up there. They don't want the likes of us."

She'd tried over the years to avoid them, keep herself to herself, but they seemed to know everything, be everywhere. Still, what could she expect in a town like Knockmore? It wasn't exactly small, but it wasn't big enough to hide in either, especially since she'd only escaped to the right side of the tracks, not to the other side of the world. Back then it had seemed greater somehow, as if moving to the far side of town would give her the anonymity she craved and the freedom to start over, but instead, it had slowly closed in on top of her, suffocating her. That's why she'd got rid of that Maguire one. You couldn't trust anyone in this town. They just couldn't leave things be.

It hadn't been an easy journey. At times she felt she was clawing her way up a mountain of ice. But she'd managed, did what she had to do, made her choices. But the past was the past; there was nothing she could do about it now. She'd learned that the hard way. She remembered her own mother's words, when she was small and after being caught out fibbing, saying to her, "Lies, like the past, have a way of catching up with you, Maggie."

Well, she'd been able to outrun them until now, keeping face after everything, every little disappointment. She just needed to focus – but it was becoming harder and harder lately. Even repeating it to herself daily, "The past is the past," didn't seem to stop her mind from wandering backwards. So much had happened. Of course, there were some things she wished she could change. She wondered sometimes should she have done things differently? Perhaps made amends with her mother, with her sisters. Maybe she should have boarded that ferry to England, disappeared in

31

the night. It hadn't even seemed like an option. She'd barely set foot out of Knockmore in those days. Back then she was naïve, alone, trapped. What was wrong with her? She must be going soft.

She pushed open the heavy door of St Patrick's Church, just as she had done almost every day for the past twenty years, letting the cold air wash over her, bring her back to her senses. Had it really been that long – twenty long years? She felt old and tired. She caught a glimpse of herself in the reflection of the brass plaque on the door and almost jumped. Was that her? The eyes were the same. She was in there somewhere, behind the sensible mousey hair and ruddy face.

She put her hand to the excess skin that now spilled out from under her collar, hoping the reflection belied the truth. She hadn't always looked like that, hadn't always felt like this. But still, she had everything she ever wanted, didn't she? A husband, notoriety, the big house, a child.

Had it been worth it? She thought of her daughter, Felicity, fifteen years old now, so perfect in every way and yet . . . it seemed she'd waited a lifetime for her. She closed her eyes, exhaling slowly, and suddenly shuddered as her mind catapulted back once more. *Stop!*

The anger began to twist its way through her veins, wind around her senses, take hold of her as it had done all of her life. Why couldn't it have been easier? Why couldn't it just have been easy? She put her hand to her head, recognising the dull pain that would soon turn to pounding. Stop now. Enough. You've made your bed – now, you must lie in it.

If only the bed weren't so hard, so damn hard.

Maggie Treacy

Then – 1965

Maggie was sick of living a life of poverty in a house in which you couldn't swing a cat. "Practically tenements," she'd heard *them* laugh, talking about the rows upon rows of houses, bunched together on the furthest outskirts of town. She walked home from work that evening, slowly descending the hill, looking down at the Estates from the main street. They stood out like a sore thumb in contrast to the houses on the other side of town; hidden away like an afterthought.

She was tired of sharing a room with her younger sisters, listening to their rambling squeals about "yer man and his fine boat race" or how "I wouldn't kick *him* out of bed for a few crumbs". She no longer wanted to trudge outside to the yard to use the outdoor toilet, looking at other people's stained underpants flapping in the wind on the shared washing line that ran the length of the terrace.

She detested her job in Kidney's, the butcher's, watching heaving parcels of meat being passed over the counter – enough to feed an army, while she was lucky to go home with a half-pound of grizzly mince on a Friday afternoon. Mr Kidney would hand it over with the same ridiculous aplomb every darn week: "Good girl, Maggie. That'll make a great big stew to last you the week. Every little helps! Isn't that right, Mrs Kidney?" He'd smile down at her, patting his own pork belly as he spoke.

Mr Kidney referred to everything he could in terms of meat cuts, often asking her to shift her rump or shake her shanks, and she despised it. Maggie knew what they thought of the likes of her, and she felt it more and more as she watched *them* take home their big bags of meat, day in, day out.

"Make sure to give Mrs Lawson a nice cut of beef now, good girl, Maggie."

"Slip an extra sausage in for Mrs Bowers, won't you?"

"Oh now, Maggie, Mrs Dixon likes a nice bit of fat on her pork chops, you know that!"

Maggie would have loved nothing more than to tell Mr Kidney to shove his job between his spare ribs, but her sisters barely brought in enough to put food on the table as it was and her mother's fragility grew worse with each passing year.

Maggie was twenty-eight, trapped in the wrong life, feeling as if she were standing on a ticking time bomb and unless something happened soon, she'd spend the rest of her life wrapping sausages and stuck looking after her mother's nerves. Her sisters encouraged her to settle for what was on offer.

"I see Frankie's been asking after you again, looking to show you his sausage. Maybe it's as big as his eyes!" Florrie jeered.

Her sisters giggled to each other as she stared on, gritting her teeth, wanting to explode.

"Why don't you give him a chance, go to the dance with

him on Friday? I'll lend you my micro-mini," Rosie laughed, knowing there was no way Maggie could pull off a short skirt with ankles that looked as though her socks had bunched around them and she'd forgotten to pull them back up again.

Maggie wasn't exactly what you'd have described as big, but she was short and not altogether perfectly proportioned. Not like they were. The twins, Florrie and Rosie, made her feel like a giant, with their slight frames, legs like twigs and shiny brown hair, like a pair of conkers.

"The image of your father, Maggie," Mam used to say. "The girls are cut straight out of me, but you're like him – the same hair he had, mousey."

Maggie started bleaching her hair after that, cleaning out the dirty dishwater colour she shared with him, washing him away.

"Go on, Frankie will keep his eye on you, or maybe two," Florrie erupted again.

"Feck off, the pair of you."

She never again wanted to endure bloody Frankie O'Shea and his great big bulging eyes calling every Friday to ask her out. No sooner was she in the door, still smelling of meat, than there he was. Maggie barely had time to wash her *hocks* before he was at the doorstep, rubbing the little brown envelope filled with his measly pay packet from the bin run up and down his leg.

"Jeez, Maggie, you smell good enough to eat . . . come on, one drink. I'll take you places," he'd wink in a never-ending attempt to entice her into an equally miserable existence. "Marry me now. We can move into the spare room in my ma's and one day the main room will be ours."

There was no way she was going to sit around waiting

for Mrs O'Shea to crank it, all for the main bedroom, with its perfect view of the life she hated. Even if his brown envelope were filled with gold, she wouldn't spend the rest of her days married to a man who smelled of potato peel, dutifully washing the stains out of his underpants to fly them on the communal washing line of failure.

"You'd be like meat and veg," Rosie spluttered.

No, she had different plans. Maggie believed in destiny, knew she was meant for something more, but fortune hadn't yet favoured her and she was growing increasingly impatient.

"Are you still with us, Maggie? Tut-tut, you're away with the fairies lately. Pull your head out of the clouds, girl," she heard Mrs Kidney say. "It's your break. See you in twenty minutes. Hurry along; we have the Friday orders to prep as soon as you get back."

Marvellous, Maggie thought. There was genuinely nothing she detested more than stuffing sausage meat into its skin-like casing, ready to be shoved down *their* wobbling throats for the Saturday morning fry-up. She removed her bloodied apron, carefully took the hairnet off her slightly deflated beehive and rushed out of the door, turning left.

Maggie always turned left. Left was her favourite place, where she could stroll up the town, watching the houses grow bigger as she went. She sat down on the wooden bench, perfectly positioned on a little green area at the top of the hill just opposite her favourite house of all – what she would have done to live there and sit in that big window, watching the world go by, looking out instead of in, being one of *them*.

She'd observed *them* her whole life, spied them climbing into their Morris Minors and pruning their immaculate rose bushes with their shin-length skirts flapping in the breeze. She'd watched their sensible shoes walking the path to the Big House, clutching their checked tea cloths concealing steaming apple pies. She'd served them in the butcher's; listened as they spoke of how "Alistair" was studying law or "Beatrice" was reading English. She'd craned her neck over the stone wall, watching the church fete – neatly dressed children running about, their parents sitting on their perfect picnic blankets, stuffing their faces with pie. Well, she deserved a piece of the pie, too. Didn't she?

Maybe she should accept Frankie's offer – at least it would get her away from her sisters. He wasn't a bad-looking fella either, if you could ignore the eyes, and he did have lovely tanned skin. "Spanish," she'd heard the other girls say. And good strong shoulders that could take some of the burden off hers – that same burden that constantly seemed to press down on her, even in her sleep.

Maggie thought of her mam, feeling instantly irritated. Mam was never the same after Da died. "His heart," she used to say. But Maggie knew what had taken him. Her father had spent more time in the pub than at home, guzzling pint after pint, and she hated him for it.

"Come on, Maggie, dance with me," he'd slur after returning from another all-day session.

"Were you not at work, Da?" She could feel her empty stomach begin to rumble, knowing they'd spend another night going hungry.

"Ah, life is for living, girl, lighten up. It's like an aul' one, you are! Come here, girls, dance with your old da."

She'd watch Florrie and Rosie flying into his arms, squealing with delight as he twisted and turned them, losing his balance as he went.

"A bricklayer needs to lay bricks to put food on the table," Mam used to shout after they were left hungry for the third day in a row.

The arguments, the shouting, the taunts – Maggie used to shut the door of their bedroom and sing as loud as she could, pulling the blanket up over her sisters' heads as if they were inside a tent, trying to block it out. She was only three years older than them, but they remembered nothing of it now. It was all forgotten, just like that. One day he was gone, never came home. He'd laid his head down on the counter of Murphy's pub and never woken.

"You'll have to leave school, love," Mam told her. "I can't raise the girls on my own. You're the strong one in this family. Your father always said that: Maggie's the one you can depend on, Maggie has the sense."

So she'd left – fifteen years old and with all the promise of a bright future. "The brightest girl in the class," the nuns said the day she was leaving. At least she'd had that over her sisters, smarter than they'd ever been, but what use was that now? The Kidneys had offered the position and she'd had no choice. The girls stayed on in school and she listened to them as the years went by, prattling on about the lads in the Estates – watching while her mother gradually lost her nerves, spending her days remembering her useless husband. "What a great man he was – taken too soon and me left to shoulder the burden alone." Her mother shouldered no burden. It was up to Maggie after that and she was tired of it.

She glanced over at the big houses once more. That's the life she'd been born for but somehow, she'd woken up in this one.

"Maggie, where on earth were you?" Mrs Kidney

rushed over to her, putting the apron around her before Maggie had time to remove her coat. "We've just received a big order from Mabel Lawson."

"Who?" Maggie asked, feeling as deflated as her hair and trying to remember which one Mabel was – eventually, all the Mabels and Mauds blended into one.

"You know, Mabel. She looks after the catering for the church. The new reverend has arrived and there's to be quite a welcome celebration!" Mrs Kidney could barely contain herself, her great big hams quivering with excitement.

"New reverend? I didn't know the old one was gone," Maggie said, pulling on the plastic gloves.

"Well, you wouldn't now, would you, dear? But yes, he retired and now there's a new one. Lovely young man, unmarried! I'd say there'll be a rush of young ladies lining the driveway."

Mrs Kidney switched on the sausage-stuffing machine. Maggie listened as it whirred to life.

"I doubt that," Maggie muttered as an image of Frankie and his lovely Spanish skin flashed into her mind. Perhaps she could ask him to wear sunglasses.

"Too big a house for one, mind," Mrs Kidney continued. "Will need loads of little piggies to fill it. Knockmore House is a splendid home, just splendid. I'm sure it'll take quite the girl to turn his head."

"A fine cut of a man," Mr Kidney offered, failing to establish an appropriate meat cut to compare the new reverend to.

"Knockmore House?" Maggie asked as much to delay the sausage-stuffing exercise.

"Yes, Knockmore House. You know the one, right at the brow of the hill. Opposite that little bench."

Maggie looked up suddenly. "Yes, I think I know the one."

It hit her like the tonne of bricks her father never laid. She was done waiting for her life to happen. Destiny wasn't a matter of chance – it was a matter of choice. She stood in front of the mottled mirror in her bedroom and carefully unravelled her beloved beehive. Maggie loved her hair, spending more of her hard-earned money on it than anything else, scrimping and saving to keep her next appointment at the local salon. Unlike her sisters, who put everything they had spare into the latest fashions, filling their closets with cheap miniskirts, statically charged polo-necked sweaters and ankle boots they couldn't walk in. But she'd have preferred to go without than sacrifice the one thing that set her apart.

She combed it through, relishing the soft white hair in her fingers before taking the scissors in her hand and lobbing it off, cutting it as best she could into a nice sensible bob – like the pictures she'd seen of the first lady Jackie Kennedy's hair but minus the volume. She looked at the hair on the ground, gathered around her feet, and then stared at her new reflection.

"Perfect," she whispered before swapping her favourite lime-green shift for an ankle-length skirt found in the depths of her mother's wardrobe, much kinder to her legs, and teaming it with the plainest cardigan she could find. As she slipped her feet into a pair of comfortable flat shoes, left over from her days at St Brigid's school, a frisson of excitement ran through her body.

"Jaysus, Maggie, what have you done?" Florrie's eyes were wide as Maggie walked into the kitchen. "You're like a bleedin' nun! Is it a fancy dress you're going to?" Florrie nudged Rosie.

"Shut up, you two. I fancied a change."

"Christ, Maggie, a change is a new lipstick, not a crewcut. All that money you wasted on the bleach! Are you going back to mousey brown?" Rosie said, gawking at her older sister.

"I'm trying to think who you look like . . . Got it, you're like Big Tom." Florrie erupted into laughter at her reference to the Irish showbands singer, who also sported a rather questionable "man bob".

Maggie ignored them, well used to being mocked by her sisters, always labelled the stick-in-the-mud. Let them think what they want. She had greater plans and despite it being her crowning glory, her future was worth more to her than the silvery white hair that now lay at the bottom of the straw wastepaper basket.

Maggie Treacy

Then – 1965

It didn't take long for Reverend Michael Montgomery to notice the quiet young lady who seemed somewhat unsure of herself among them. He watched her take her cues from those around her in the pew at Sunday service, gradually becoming aware that she followed his every move, gazing up at him with such reverence that he was somewhat taken aback by her unfaltering and obvious admiration. He, too, observed her quietly, taking in her plain attire, neat hair and outward serenity.

"Who's the young lady with the short brown hair?" he asked Mabel Lawson following a particularly satisfying service, during which he'd delivered his sermon seamlessly without once stuttering.

"Which one?" She squinted into the crowd assembled by the door.

"Ah . . . oh dear . . . she seems to have run off on me," he said, looking disappointed.

Mabel glanced at the reverend, who appeared rather hot under the collar.

"Leave it to me. I'll find out, Rev," she said, rushing down the aisle, knocking into parishioners as she went.

Anything to help the cause – the sooner he married, the better. She'd managed to get landed with the job as the last reverend's right-hand woman but she wasn't about to let it happen again and was only too willing to pass the baton to someone else, preferably a wife.

Michael agreed. He was thirty years old and indeed finding the responsibility of his first posting most overwhelming. There was no doubt that he felt very much at home within the walls of St Patrick's, but outside the church he found the social element of being the local reverend exhausting – that and the house, of course. Running a household, especially one the size of the vicarage, was no mean feat. He appreciated the help of Mrs Walsh, the housekeeper, but found her unfaltering watchful presence stifling. He'd been advised as soon as he settled to select a suitable wife and partner for the job. His brother, David, the artistic playboy element of the family, had suggested what to aim for as he slapped him on the back before Michael departed for his new life.

"Best go plain, sturdy and thirty."

"The name's Maggie Treacy, Reverend," Mabel said, returning moments later, totally out of breath from the exertion. "She works for the Kidneys. You remember them, at the butcher's?" she spluttered, holding on to the back of the pew.

"Ah yes, indeed," he said, trying to determine which ones they were.

"It appears, though, she's not part of . . . well, of this flock, so to speak," Mabel said, raising her thinly pencilled eyebrows.

"Oh . . . I see . . . interesting," he said, looking over the parishioners' heads as he shook their hands.

"Comes from Farmleigh," Mabel continued, speaking out of the side of her mouth so as not to be overheard. "They call it the Estates, mind. How should I put it? The wrong side of the tracks, Reverend." She turned up her nose.

"Oh, well now, Mrs Lawson. We are all God's children and everyone, *everyone*, is welcome inside St Patrick's," he told her, surprising even himself with his authority.

"Quite, Reverend, of course," she nodded in agreement.

Goodness, he did seem taken with her. But what did she care? There was no other woman for miles who'd take on the role of reverend's wife – you'd have to be out of your mind, regardless of the size of his house – and a reverend did indeed need a wife.

When Maggie finally plucked up the courage to approach him, several weeks after his arrival in Knockmore, Michael could hardly believe his luck. This young woman was neither plain, nor sturdy, nor thirty.

"Reverend Michael. I wonder if I might have a word," she asked quietly after service.

"Certainly . . . uh . . . um . . . " he stuttered, his face instantly colouring.

"It's Maggie. Maggie Treacy. Miss." She extended her hand.

He took it, relishing the softness. "Delighted to meet you, Miss Treacy."

He'd had been delighted, of course, and even happier when Maggie explained that for some time she'd felt lost in the Roman Catholic faith and wished to be schooled in the beliefs of the Church of Ireland.

"I'd be honoured to assist, honoured," he said, the colour in his face heightening gradually to beetroot red.

Michael, who didn't bear the boyish charm of his brother, nor his looks, had instead been gifted with weak shoulders and his father's nose. He was painfully shy and had never received any amount of attention from the fairer sex, but Maggie's sheer presence ignited something in him that he feared might not even exist.

Maggie was surprised when she finally laid eyes on the reverend. Mr Kidney's description of a "fine cut" couldn't have been more inaccurate, except for Michael's pallor, which was so pale it bore a striking resemblance to the skin of an uncooked shoulder of pork.

"It's for reasons of faith alone," she insisted when he quizzed her about her change of heart.

Reverend Michael gave some amount of thought to the fact that a "conversion" would indeed be a feather in his cap with the archdeacon and took on the task with the same enthusiasm as one might perform an exorcism.

"We shall start immediately."

And they had, meeting every Wednesday afternoon to decipher the Scriptures together carefully.

"You write beautifully," he observed as she posed studiously by his weak shoulder, watching his nose cast a long shadow over the Bible.

"Tanks. I mean, thanks," Maggie checked herself, at least grateful that her time at school with the Catholic nuns had unknowingly laid a solid foundation for "the other side" to work with.

"What's your opinion on this?" he'd ask.

"Well, I believe what's meant here is . . . "

She enjoyed being asked for her opinion and liked giving it. The more time she spent talking, the better. She gradually learned to condition herself not to take a breath while the reverend was speaking, since his breath carried a sharpness that was impossible to ignore. Michael listened attentively to her questions, spoken slowly to ensure she correctly pronounced her words, and it seemed to be having the desired effect.

"Beautifully put, Maggie. Excellent, Maggie. You have a marvellous way with words."

Her sisters were disgusted when they heard she'd been making the journey to Sunday service at St Patrick's and bypassing St Brigid's on the way.

"There isn't a fella in town who'll take out one of the Treacy Traitor Sisters, now what are you playing at, Maggie?" Rosie shouted at her, trying to make sense of Maggie's actions.

"It's not like you ever listened in Mass on a Sunday. You're hardly religious. Are you? What's the big interest now in the Prods?" Florrie asked. "Frankie O'Shea said he saw you coming out of St Patrick's, talking with the reverend . . . again. Said you've been up there all the time," she huffed.

"Who the hell is Frankie O'Shea to be keeping tabs on me? Only the local shit-stirrer! He has no claim on me. He's like an 'aul one, spying and gossiping. Besides, I'm a grown woman, I can do what I like," Maggie shouted.

"First the hair and the dumpy clothes, and now cavorting with *them*. Jaysus, did you get the calling or something?" Rosie was holding her stomach from laughing.

"Did God reverse the charges and call you personally to ask you to join Him?" Florrie added, sniggering.

"Your poor father would turn in his grave," Mam attempted.

But nothing would deter her; not the taunts, nor the

sneers, and certainly not the thought of her father turning in his grave. Let him turn. The exercise will do the lazy old sod good! And so what if they isolated her in the Estates – that's exactly what she wanted.

In contrast, the Kidneys were thrilled that Maggie had seen sense.

"Always been the superior faith," Mrs Kidney encouraged. "Isn't the new reverend a handsome young man? Do you talk about the Scriptures?" she quizzed.

"Yes, just the Scriptures. Quite fascinating," Maggie replied.

"I think we may need you for an extra few shifts here in the shop," Mrs Kidney announced.

She was as quick as she was fat, recognising that the reverend's interest in Maggie may be more than just spiritual. The thought of the Kidneys pandering to her was so satisfying that Maggie took her extra money and wistfully bought herself a sensible brown pleated skirt, to swing in celebration.

Reverend Michael Montgomery baptised and confirmed Maggie Treacy on a beautiful August morning, just six months after his arrival in the parish, with his entire flock bearing witness to the monumental event. The Kidneys stood as her godparents.

"We're terribly proud of you, Maggie. What an achievement!" Mrs Kidney cooed.

Maggie, too, felt proud. It was the first thing she'd done for herself, without first thinking of her mother shaking in the chair at home, or her sisters giggling at her.

Her family wasn't there with her to celebrate; she'd kept the final transformation secret from them, slowly detaching herself over the months, carefully backing away. No whisper of her big day had travelled down the hill, snaking its way into the Estates. The two faiths co-existed happily but rarely intermingled, which enabled Maggie to enjoy her day without distraction. She felt accepted, part of something greater.

The *others*, of course, knew where Maggie was from and they didn't necessarily approve, but the reverend seemed so mesmerised by his new follower that none of them dare suggest that it was an unsuitable match. Indeed, the young reverend looked so happy that it almost seemed like destiny.

The welcome party took place outside the church, with rows of trestle tables piled high with steaming apple pies. Maggie could hardly conceal her smile as she took her first bite.

Later that evening, high on achievement, Michael sat nervously beside her on the wooden bench next to the graveyard.

"I . . . um . . . well . . . I find myself most taken with you, Maggie, and I . . . well . . . might you consider perhaps becoming the . . . um . . . reverend's wife?" he asked, nervously twisting his hands as he spoke.

The bench they sat on was dedicated to the memory of Cyril and Margot Prendergast and their steadfast dedication both to each other and to their faith. Maggie ran her fingers over the elegant names etched into the small brass plate, shining with prosperity, and before accepting issued but one simple request.

"Call me Margot."

Maggie Treacy

Then – 1965

"Gosh, dearest, it does seem fast, but ready if you are," Reverend Michael said when Maggie suggested they should strike while the iron is hot.

"Yes, I think so, Michael. Best to get it over and done with it, not have it hanging over us," she smiled sweetly at him. "No time like the present."

"Indeed, let's get to it so."

Michael took her hand and guided her into Knockmore House. Maggie looked around smugly at the ground floor of the once stately home, so full of possibilities. Granted, it needed a little love, but she was confident she could slowly return it to its former glory. She was pleasantly surprised that it seemed even bigger inside than it looked from the outside and she could hardly wait to call it home. She'd finally swept up the long driveway, accompanied by her husband-to-be, thrilled to get inside the house that had for so long filled her dreams, never imagining a few months ago that this moment would finally arrive.

"Take an extra twenty minutes, Maggie, good girl," Mrs Kidney had said when the reverend arrived to meet his bride-to-be for lunch that day. "Good afternoon, Reverend.

I'll pack a few sausages for you on your return," she said, whipping the apron off Maggie and shoving her at full force towards Michael, who caught her awkwardly.

Maggie was dying to see the upstairs of the house, but it hardly seemed appropriate and there'd be time enough for that. Besides, she had no real desire to traipse through the bedroom with Michael, who might have passed out on the spot had she suggested it.

"Four weeks will be plenty of time to get everything sorted, Michael," she assured him, eyeing the staircase and the landing above, lit by a terribly grand but slightly neglected chandelier.

Michael followed her eyes. "Yes, that – bit of an eyesore, left over from previous days of grandeur, I suppose. Perhaps we should donate it."

"I adore it." Maggie's eyes lit up as she glimpsed her glistening future.

"Really? It doesn't seem like it would be your cup of tea. A bit fussy for you, so to speak."

"Yes, I suppose so, but let's leave it and focus on the wedding," Maggie replied, imagining herself sweeping down the staircase wrapped in pearls like Audrey Hepburn in *Breakfast at Tiffany's*.

The house was indeed grand, but it carried an air of shabbiness that she'd soon set right. The furniture was all donated, the rugs threadbare and the paint peeling, but she could picture her future in the dusty hallway and she liked what she saw.

It was a quick turnaround all right, but she was sure Mabel Lawson and her band of trusty tea makers could handle the wedding lunch. Maggie had already cleared it with her and Mabel had been thrilled with the idea of accelerating the wedding to early September, the baton now burning into her hand and her rose bushes suffering terribly.

Just four weeks after the proposal, on the morning of her wedding Maggie packed her meagre belongings into the old duffel bag, which permanently resided on top of the wardrobe on the landing should an occasion ever arise to travel. As yet, no such opportunity had ever presented itself to the Treacy sisters, so she could rest assured that the bag wouldn't be missed, at least until she was well gone.

"You're very quiet these days, Maggie," Rosie observed.

Her sisters had been eyeing her suspiciously for several weeks now.

"Yeah, what's up with you?" Florrie asked. "Are you after getting yourself in trouble? Should we expect the pitter-patter of holy feet? Are you the next Virgin Maggie?"

But she was so close now to the finish line that she allowed them to giggle away to each other, not bothered for once to rock the imaginary cradle.

There was very little she needed to make her journey – nothing that would be suitable for what lay ahead – and in the end, the large duffel bag was swimming with space, almost as empty as her heart.

"Mam, can you hear me?" Maggie held her mother's hand as she dozed in the threadbare armchair next to the Superser gas heater. "I have to go away, Mam. It's for the best. I've made a better life, but I'll be grand. Better than grand. But I can't come back. Don't look back, isn't that what you used to say before?"

Maggie kissed her mam's forehead, wondering what she'd say if she could – if she weren't trapped inside her own mind. Would she have approved? Would she be proud? What did it matter? There was no going back now.

Michael was kind if nothing else, but Maggie didn't really know him. Up until now, they'd spoken of nothing more than Scriptures and the last month had been a whirlwind of wedding plans. She couldn't deny that a certain awkwardness existed between them. Michael had only kissed her that one time on the steps of Knockmore House. Afterwards, she'd had to turn away to wipe away the excess saliva that lingered on her lips, but she was sure she'd felt something; some tingle of excitement as she'd looked up at the massive front door, flanked by the Roman columns. Perhaps she was just nervous. But she had that same fluttery feeling now in her stomach, which she'd felt the day she met his family, during a stilted high tea at Knockmore House.

"Are you sure you know what you're letting yourself in for?" his brother, David warned her having smacked her backside just moments after being introduced.

Maggie had been shocked how different he was from his brother, realising that under normal circumstances she'd have quite liked him. But his constant jovial demeanour proved too much for Maggie to take as she played the sensible, austere wife-to-be. Roger and Eunice Montgomery were very elderly and she was relieved that they apparently couldn't hear anything at all.

"What's that, dear? Speak up – all this mumbling. Can you understand her, Eunice?"

Maggie had never seen anything like them. It was as if someone had taken two of the oldest people they could find, plucked them from a nursing home, dressed them up as royalty and propped them upright in a chair. Roger smoked a thick cigar, sporadically tipping the ash directly onto the carpet and rubbing persistently at his long familial nose. While Eunice sat so silently – tight-lipped and motionless, save for the odd adjustment of a terrifying mink scarf, holding fast to her neck with its spiky little claws – that more than once Maggie feared she'd passed away. She wasn't sure who she should attempt to resuscitate first: the mink or Eunice.

The only saving grace was that they thankfully asked her very little about her background and Maggie was only too happy to close the front door behind them after two excruciatingly long hours. Much to Maggie's relief, they wouldn't be attending the wedding, knowing there was no way they could manage to stay alive for the duration of the wedding day. Not even the Mighty Mabel could manage the catering of a wedding and two funerals on the one day. David wouldn't be there either, which was lucky, as Maggie wasn't sure she could trust herself around him.

"Not my thing, Mags, you understand?" he told her, tracing his finger down her cheek while she blushed uncontrollably. "Besides, I'm working on a new manuscript," he said, referring to his fifth unpublished work. "But I hope to see you soon. Fancy my brother getting the flirty little Catholic girl."

Maggie had been mortified and elated all at the same time. But she was satisfied that she'd probably never see them again and sure that when she did, the only difference would be that Roger's cigar would be extinguished and Eunice would be unable to adjust her scarf.

There'd be no afternoon tea with the Treacy family, nor apprehensive introductions to be made.

"But shouldn't I pop by to introduce myself?" Michael had asked.

"The thing is, Michael, they haven't exactly taken well

to the news of my marriage, nor my conversion, and to be honest, they'd prefer not to be part of it," she'd sniffed. "Mother's too unwell and I'm afraid I'm quite alone in this world."

"There, there, dearest, perhaps in time they'll come round. Besides, you'll have an entire community to keep you company soon. Fear not."

On the morning of the wedding though, she felt quite alone. She'd decided weeks before what she'd write in the note, which she now placed on the kitchen table before walking through the front door of 37 Farmleigh Terrace for the last time. Afterwards, she'd swung her duffel bag over her shoulder, stuck her nose in the air, squared her shoulders and walked through the Estates as Margot.

She took one last look around at the place that had stolen her dreams and broken her down. She almost wished she could be there to see her sisters' faces. She could picture them, swinging in through the front door upon returning from their job in the laundrette, hair knotted up in colourful scarves, ready to plan their outfits for the local dance, only to discover they were no longer carefree and the burden would now rest with them.

Reverend Michael Montgomery of Knockmore House has requested my hand in marriage and I have accepted. By the time you read this, I will be married and henceforth will be known as Mrs Margot Montgomery. It is my wish that I leave behind my life here and commence a more significant existence of a duty to my husband and St Patrick's Church. Look after Mother, as I have done. I wish you no harm, but as opposites, there is no longer any reason

to stay in contact. It will not be acceptable in my
new community. Please do not contact me.
Sincerely,
Mrs Margot Montgomery

Yes, that would do it.

It had been Mrs Kidney's idea for her to wear the dress that she wore when she herself wed Mr Kidney twenty-five years earlier, in the same church where Maggie would take her vows today.

"Like history repeating itself." Mrs Kidney smiled wistfully at Mr Kidney, who was wiping his axe on his striped apron. "After all, it would be wasteful to spend hard-earned parish money on a gown, money that could be wisely dedicated to the Church. And nobody likes waste, dear – it's terribly wasteful – and don't let the big house deceive you, my dear," she'd continued. "A life dedicated to our Lord is one of frugality, but I'm sure the rewards are far greater. You'll soon learn to make do."

Maggie could hardly take in her words. Surely she was wrong. Jealous perhaps. Indeed, a man with such a high position, a huge house and a housekeeper couldn't live as frugally as Mrs Kidney was suggesting. She was about to say as much but was momentarily distracted as Mrs Kidney produced the dust bag containing the gown.

"I'm sure it'll be beautiful on you, dear. And remember, I was quite the slip of a thing in my day. A bag of bones, Mr Kidney used to say!" she snorted with laughter.

Maggie almost burst out laughing at the description, often likening the older lady's form instead to one of Mr Kidney's prize-winning sausages, but she stopped herself as Mrs Kidney ceremoniously unzipped the bag to reveal the dress. It was, just as she'd feared, a discoloured lace mess from 1940. Her hopes were further dashed when the dress was thrown over her head and she stood in front of the mahogany mirror in the Kidneys' bedroom staring down at what looked like two empty shopping bags dangling from the front of it, where Mrs Kidney's excited breasts had once nervously wobbled in anticipation. Not even two freshly plucked chickens could have filled the gaping material. It was a high-necked, long-sleeved disaster that confirmed Mr Kidney must suffer from profoundly impaired vision if he'd ever considered the contents of the dress to resemble a bag of bones.

"Stunning, absolutely stunning." Mrs Kidney clapped her hands together. "Look at the cut, the fabric, and it needs very little adjustment. I knew we were the same size and hasn't the lace maintained its colour so well! I was so careful to pack it away safely, in the hope that we'd one day have a daughter to wear it, but alas, my son Godfrey's wife, Daphne, wore her own mother's gown. It was an inferior vessel, but none the less I understood the sentiment."

Poor Daphne must have run a mile when she saw the vividly yellowing dress emerging from the bag. But Maggie had no choice, forced to make do with what was on offer. The Kidneys had undertaken their role as godparents beautifully, even offering to pay for the *minor* adjustments to the wedding gown, which in the end involved an entire remodelling of the lace.

"Totally unnecessary to remove so much! What poor workmanship," Mrs Kidney tutted when the dress arrived back and she pulled reams of excess fabric from the dust bag. "Don't worry, dear. I'm sure it won't be too tight." She patted Maggie's hand.

On the morning of her wedding, Maggie felt numb.

"It's perfectly natural to feel nervous, dear," Mrs Kidney assured her as she slipped the dress carefully over her head.

Her words about *making do* rang in Maggie's ears.

"There, you look beautiful."

Maggie looked at herself in the mirror, finally seeing Margot Montgomery staring back at her.

Maggie felt paralysed as they drove the short distance to the church with Mr Kidney proudly linking her arm. She was frozen with fear as they inched up the aisle towards Michael, whose shoulders were pumped up to a somewhat manly level, his wide smile revealing teeth so yellow that even the dress appeared whiter next to them.

Michael looked longingly at her as she approached and a simpler life unfolded before him. Maggie watched him glance excitedly at the archdeacon, his nostrils flaring in anticipation. She felt her skin begin to crawl as Mr Kidney handed her over, the antique lace suddenly smothering her, and Michael coughed nervously down at her, presenting her with a breath so sour that not even her veil could protect her. She wanted to turn and run, to shout *stop*, but she stood her ground. This was the prize. This was the goal.

The parishioners looked on fondly as the archdeacon led the ceremony and despite a few muffled chortles from the congregation as Michael's voice rose to the level of a soprano from nerves, he managed to issue his vows. In return, the bride's vows were uttered so softly that it was practically impossible to hear her.

"Nerves," Mrs Kidney told the other ladies afterwards. "The poor dear's terrified as to what lies ahead tonight. I did want to warn her, but Mr Kidney scolded me. 'These are the challenges all young brides must face,' he said." She shook her head sympathetically as the other women agreed embarrassedly.

One too many sherries had often been known to loosen Mrs Kidney's tongue and not one of them could stomach the vivid description of the first time she'd witnessed Mr Kidney's sausage.

The wedding party enjoyed a cold buffet under a pristine white marquee in the beautiful gardens of Knockmore House. Michael intermittently led them in prayer prior to the meal, during the meal, after the meal and, once more for good measure, when the enormous apple tarts, served with both custard *and* cream to mark the celebration, were brought out.

Mabel Lawson smiled proudly at her ultimate catering extravaganza. "Congratulations, Mrs Montgomery. I hand the baton to you," she issued haughtily to the rather pale-looking bride as the festivities ended.

All too soon, Mrs Kidney was wobbling down the driveway on the arm of Mr Kidney. She winked unashamedly at the new Mrs Montgomery as she went and Michael nervously led his new bride to the master bedroom of Knockmore House, which the bride had anticipated with high hopes. But it was as dreary as he was, save for the wonderfully large windows overlooking the gardens. She could see the carefully tended rose bushes and the trees whispering to each other in the orchard, which under any other circumstances and with any other man, beneath the evening's setting sun, would have been enough to ignite a passion in a newlywed couple.

"Lovely chair, don't you think?" Michael babbled. "And you can keep your things here . . . " He gestured towards various items of furniture.

"Should I undress?" she asked, her hands shaking as she spoke.

"Oh . . . um . . . well . . . yes . . . I'll give you a moment, shall I?"

She nodded as he left her alone and she sat on the bed, putting her face in her hands. What *had* she done?

She got up and walked towards the mirror, unsure if it was Maggie or Margot staring back at her. She'd been so sure of herself up until now, but she suddenly felt very out of her depth. She barely knew this man, wasn't yet convinced that she even liked him. But she was his now and this was her life, in among these people, who were to become her only contacts within this new peculiar existence but a stone's throw from her old one.

"You are Margot Montgomery. You are Margot Montgomery. You are Margot Montgomery," she repeated through a narrowed gaze until she saw Maggie fade away.

She pulled the heavy brown drapes together, blocking the trees in case they might tell what they were about to see, and removed the yellowing gown. She wondered should she remain naked but instead pulled on the white long-sleeved cotton nightdress Mrs Kidney had packed into her duffel bag before slipping between the icy sheets, draped with a heavy candlewick bedspread.

"Come in," she shouted when the watery knock on the door arrived.

Michael opened it, coughing uncontrollably with panic, unrelieved by the quick mouthful of brandy he'd taken downstairs to steady himself. He, too, had stopped in a mirror at the end of the staircase before making his way to his prize. He'd taken in his face, his long nose – reddened from the afternoon glare – and his cheeks flushed with both anticipation and the swift brandy anaesthetic. He'd never been with a woman before, never even kissed a girl before Margot.

"Mrs Margot Montgomery," he whispered proudly.

He knew that this sacred union was precisely what was needed to complete his duties as reverend. Yes, he hardly knew her, and perhaps marrying the converted Catholic girl would be frowned on by some, but she was beautiful and serene, and he'd do anything to fulfil his calling.

"You looked stunning today," he whispered to her now as she clutched the sheets tightly to her neck.

He crept under the covers in his striped pyjamas, freshly purchased for the main event of the evening, and gingerly took her hand.

"Will you join me in prayer before we consummate our union?" he asked, holding out his other hand.

She took it, wondering if he did anything without praying first, and couldn't help but think of Frankie O'Shea, whose dreaded attempts at flirting seemed far worldlier than this feeble come-on. Make it quick, she silently begged as he turned out the light and with no warning, rolled on top of her, like a walrus flopping into the sea.

He awkwardly removed his pyjama bottoms, simultaneously kneeing her in the stomach, and she felt his moist hands fumble at her undergarments and then something warm pressing into the inside of her leg. It stabbed at her, attempting and failing to find its position several times before reaching its destination. She gasped at the sudden intrusion and then lay still as he flapped about on top of her, like a goldfish having escaped its bowl, holding her breath to avoid his fervent exhalations before he collapsed on top of her with a sharp shudder. She wondered for a moment if he was dead until he duly gathered himself, fluttered his eyelids and inhaled deeply. He smiled at her, revealing his jutting teeth, before reaching once more for her hand.

"Let us pray."

Felicity Montgomery

Then – 1977

"Feliciteee, come at once!" The voice drifted up the stairs to find her, growing higher in pitch towards the end of the name.

Felicity folded the tiny clothes and carefully placed both them and her doll back into the little bag Mrs Walsh, the housekeeper, had given her to conceal them from prying eyes. Standing on tiptoe, she tucked it towards the back of the shelf in her wardrobe, where it would remain until she had the opportunity to take it out again and lovingly dress the treasured gift.

"She's just like you, Fliss," Mrs Walsh told her when she gave it to her for her seventh birthday a few weeks before.

"Feliciteee."

She closed the wardrobe door and ran as fast as she could, stopping at the end of the stairs to follow the direction of the high-pitched note towards the garden, where more than likely she'd be immediately swatted away, like an irritating fly, or issued with a string of orders.

"Straighten up, Felicity."

"Fix yourself, Felicity."

"Where have you been? What are you doing?"

"Children, like animals, should be seen and not heard."

She'd learned to be invisible from an early age, to avoid agitating Mother. The house was huge – "grand", Mother called it – but cold. It always felt cold. Not even the custard-coloured walls and ceilings seemed able to warm it. Felicity would lie on the landing on her back, her mouth open, imagining she was catching delicious custard-flavoured drops dribbling from the flaking ceiling. It was one of many imaginary games she played to pass the time until six o'clock undoubtedly rolled around and she was confined to the eerie silence of her bedroom once more. At least now she had her doll to keep her company.

She was rarely allowed to be seen around the house when the many callers came to visit the reverend or his formidable wife. But on the rare occasion that she'd crept down the stairs in the past, curiosity getting the better of her, she always heard the same.

"What a beautiful little girl."

"What a delicate little thing."

"Such lovely hair. Where does she get the blonde from?"

"Now, now," Mother would scold. "Beauty comes from within and we all know it's a sin to address physical beauty."

To Mother, everything was a sin. Indeed, everything that Felicity seemed to do was always deemed to be sinful.

"Greed is a sin, Felicity."

"Neediness is a sin, Felicity."

"Stop crying. Do you want to go to hell?" she'd tell her repeatedly until all Felicity could think about was going to hell, whatever and wherever that was.

Eventually, people stopped commenting on Felicity,

hardly speaking to her at all, since the exchange was always met with contempt and no one would purposely set out to incense the great Margot.

It didn't stop them, however, wondering behind closed doors how a union between Margot Montgomery and *Poor Michael* had resulted in such beauty. But they always concluded the same thing: that it could be nothing less than the mighty hand of God. Indeed, Michael was no looker and though Margot wasn't an unfortunate-looking woman, the years had gifted her a blocky form and a hardness to her features that not even motherhood had softened. Poor Michael, his shoulders weren't built for such a weight. Poor Michael – Felicity had heard it uttered so often on the steps of St Patrick's Church that for a long time she believed it was her father's full name.

"Will Poor Michael be home soon?" she'd innocently asked one day.

"What did you say, Felicity? Repeat yourself!"

"Poor Michael?" she whispered, instantly worried by her mother's tone.

"How dare you! What on earth do you mean? Where did you hear that?"

But she hadn't waited for an answer before sending Felicity straight to her room. It wasn't the first time Felicity had felt the back of her mother's hand, but it was the most painful yet, the indent on her leg remaining for days as a silent reminder to watch her words. Felicity had spent the entire day in her room, where not even the custard walls delivered a drop of sustenance. But she was used to being alone. Father was rarely at home, always so busy.

Felicity's family was different, Mother always told her. The other children had grandparents, brothers, sisters, cousins, uncles, aunties and she had no one, except for Mrs Walsh and later, Tess. Felicity used to stare at the bustling commotion as the other children ran off home to their busy lives after school while she walked across the road to silence. She tried many times to broach the subject with her mother as to the noticeable differences between the Montgomerys and the other families on the hill of Knockmore, but she was always told the same.

"Curiosity is a sin. Run along, Felicity."

Until today.

Mother was sitting in the garden eating a slice of apple tart with her afternoon tea. It was May, so the weather had warmed a little, making it somewhat warmer outside than it was inside.

"Sit down, child, and stop gawking at me," Mother said as soon as Felicity appeared.

Felicity sat on the grass, nervously watching her mother as she sat pensively, speaking slowly in between delicious-looking forkfuls of oozing silvery apple that today had injected a looseness into her acidic tongue.

"You do know how lucky you are, Felicity, to live such a privileged life, sitting here on the lawn, taking tea?" Mother started. "It's a far cry from where I was reared and I'm not sure how grateful you are to lead such an entitled life."

Felicity glanced up inquisitively at Mother, who was dramatically sucking the remnants of the pastry from her teeth.

"If you think for one moment that this is a normal life, you're sorely mistaken, child. Your father chose to serve God with me at his side, bringing hope to this small-minded community. Things are very different on the far side of town, you know. Very different, indeed."

Felicity, wide-eyed with fascination, seized the sudden pause in the conversation, brought about by the intense pastry dissection from Mother's back teeth, to pose a question.

"Where did you live, Mother, before here?" she asked.

Margot smacked her tongue loudly against her front teeth before answering.

"As close to hell as is humanly possible, Felicity. A place to which I choose never to return."

"And did you have a mother and a father and brothers and sisters?"

"Oh yes, I had a father who died when I was a teenager and a mother who refused to shoulder the burden. Oh, and two wasteful sisters – twins, in fact. One as lazy as the next." Mother stared ahead.

Felicity tried very hard to picture three Margots sitting round the table with dull short hair, giant itchy cardigans and the flesh of their necks spilling over their three-row pearl necklaces.

"And where are they now?" Felicity continued, hoping that two additional Margots weren't about to appear from round the corner.

"Right where I left them. In the past!" she quipped. "Now, enough questions, Felicity. Remember what I always say? Curiosity is . . . "

"A sin. Yes, Mother."

"Good. Run along now – I have so much to do."

Felicity glanced over her shoulder as she left, to where Mother was still sitting, staring ahead vacantly at the orchard, and wondered what it all meant. It was the most information she'd ever been gifted and yet she felt more confused than ever. Where was "the past"? Where was this other family?

Felicity's imagination whirled, filling with the idea of a grandmother and aunties, imagining great big family dinners and games with cousins who looked just like her. But she didn't have long to wait to find out more, when her thoughts were disturbed, just a few days later, by an unscheduled knock on the door. A disturbance without prior notice was a regular occurrence at the vicarage and yet it was always met with the same disapproval.

Felicity crept from her room to peer over the railings and could hardly believe what she saw. They stood before Mother, in a splodge of brightly coloured clothes and big hair, like a rainbow shining in through the dark hallway of Knockmore House. She'd never seen anything like it and instantly drawn towards the colours, she inched slowly down the stairs, huddling tight to the banister, stopping abruptly at the bottom step as the two women turned to meet her surprised gaze.

Their eyelids were washed with shades of blue with black wings that crept out at the sides, making their eyes look as if they were smiling. One wore an orange blouse and jeans, and the other was wearing a short bright blue dress. Felicity had never seen her mother in anything other than brown or navy; it was mesmerising.

"Upstairs, *now*!" Mother shouted at her as she turned to see what had captured their attention.

"You must be Felicity," the blue one said, kneeling in front of her.

Felicity looked uncertainly at Mother and then back at the woman, hypnotised by the blue colour on her eyelids.

"I'm your auntie Florrie and this is your auntie Rosie." She gestured towards the second woman. "Aren't you a little poppet?" she said, taking Felicity's hands in hers so that Felicity felt a sudden warmth run up her arm and through her body, settling in her stomach like a glow.

"Stop that at once! Go, Felicity, now!" Mother shouted.

Startled, Felicity jumped and turned to scamper back up the stairs, but Florrie caught hold of her hand and protectively put her arm around her shoulder.

"Oh, give over, Maggie, let us meet her. You've hidden away long enough up here." She looked down at Felicity. "Sorry, little one," she whispered before turning back towards Mother and lowering her voice. "We've come here today to tell you that Mam is gone. Died yesterday."

Mother stood up straight, suddenly lost for words as she looked from one to the other.

"Did you hear her, Maggie?" Rosie stepped forwards. "Mam is gone," she said, wiping at her eyes where tears had started to smudge the colour around them.

Mother stood frozen, staring ahead, and then all of a sudden, she put her arm out to steady herself on the door frame as if she might fall over.

"She asked for you every day, Maggie. Called your name. She hadn't spoken in months, years even, and it was you she called for, Maggie," Florrie continued.

Mother took a deep breath and closed her eyes for a moment before opening them and fixing them on Florrie.

"Well, I'm sorry for your loss, but it's in the past."

"It's your loss too, Maggie, for Christ's sake. It's your loss, too," Florrie spat.

"Why couldn't you just make amends? Why didn't you come?" Rosie added.

And for a moment Mother looked as though she might cry before she spoke again.

"It's in the past, like I said. What was the point? She

wouldn't have known me. There was no point." She shook her head. "No point."

"No point? Really?" Florrie threw her arms in the air. "She was your mam, that was the point, can't you see that? All those letters we wrote to you, all the times you slammed the door in our faces, hiding up here as if you were too good for us. It could have been different, Maggie. We're family, for God's sake, does that count for nothing?"

"It's in the past," Mother repeated calmly. "I left it behind."

"You should have come," Rosie piped in. "You could have sat on one of your shiny trays and skidded down the hill, or even taken your precious car out again," she sniggered. "Even your husband thought we were some form of muck, but we set him right about you. Even he's terrified of you, by the sounds of it, and by the looks of it, your daughter is too, Maggie."

Mother began to shake, blotches of red suddenly appearing on her chest, flowering on her face. Felicity had seen it before and knowing what was about to come, she started to edge back towards the stairs.

"*My name is Margot Montgomery*!" she screamed, her stern voice all at once saturated with an unfamiliar lilt that Felicity had never heard before. And then her hands flew to her head, clawing wildly at her hair.

The other two women looked at each other.

"Ha, there she is. There's our Maggie. You can take the girl out of the Estates, but you can't take the Estates out of the girl. Same old Maggie Treacy, trying to be something you're not," Florrie smirked.

Felicity watched as her mother grew a foot in height before bellowing at them.

"How dare you bring your sinful language and behaviour into my home! Get out. Get out now before I call the Guards."

"A fat lot of good that will do you," Florrie said, nonplussed. "Have you forgotten who I married, Maggie? You're nothing but a fake. We know it and everyone else does, too," she said, shaking her head in disgust but softening again as she turned to Felicity, reaching down to embrace her so hard that the air puffed out suddenly from her little lungs. "You're one of us, poppet, don't you forget that. You're one of us."

Felicity fled up the stairs and moments later heard the front door slam. She paused at the top of the stairs and briefly glanced back to look at Mother, who stood very still, with her fists clenched and her mouth downturned like a fish awaiting seasoning.

"Those fucking bitches!" she heard Mother murmur through gritted teeth before Felicity slipped back into her room to bask in the warmth of that hug and bury its heat in her heart.

"You're one of us, poppet. You're one of us."

Felicity Montgomery

Then – 1978

"There's my little pride and joy," Mrs Walsh said, looking up from where she was expertly rolling the pastry for yet another tart and smiling.

Felicity crept up beside her and nuzzled into her, savouring the familiar smell of talc mixed with baking. Mrs Walsh put down the rolling pin and turned towards her.

"What is it, little one?" she asked, noticing the red-rimmed eyes. "What's happened?" she asked again.

"Nothing. It's nothing," Felicity answered, looking away, trying not to meet her gaze.

"Come now, Fliss. You can tell old Nelly anything, you know that."

She kneeled as far as her knees would allow and took the two little hands in hers, covering them in flour. Felicity flinched. Mrs Walsh turned her hands over, noticing the fresh pink mark across the palm of each. She closed her eyes for a moment before silently going to fetch a tea cloth and running it under the tap, returning to wrap it gently around the raw skin.

"That should help." Mrs Walsh tried to muster a smile.

Felicity smiled back. She didn't want to have to tell

Nelly that she'd got all of her sums wrong again, certain that it would upset Nelly as much as it had upset Mother. All she seemed to do was upset everyone and she couldn't bear for Nelly to be cross with her, too. Mrs Walsh took a glass from the shelf, filled it with milk and put a freshly made scone in front of her.

"Eat up, little one. There's nothing a little sugar can't fix."

"Thank you, Nelly." Felicity took a drink followed by a big bite from the scone and immediately felt better.

"Where's Mrs Montgomery?" Nelly continued to roll out the pastry.

"Someone called to see her. They're in the parlour. We were doing some extra homework. Mother said she shouldn't be too long," Felicity told her between mouthfuls, trying to finish the treat before she was summoned again.

"Isn't it study enough you do at school? Why on earth does she have you holed up day after day? That woman!" Nelly raised her voice.

Felicity's eyes grew wide.

"Sorry, love. It's not you."

Nelly stopped to hug her and lovingly smooth her hair, knowing that if she could, she'd have packed the little girl into her old cart bag and wheeled her down the hill home with her. Nelly loved her like one of her own, practically reared her from the time she was a baby, but she was seventy-three years old now and her patience was beginning to wear thin. If it weren't for Felicity, Nelly would have packed in being treated like dirt long ago. But she'd made a promise to Florrie.

"Please keep an eye on her, Nelly. I don't know what I saw that day, but something wasn't right. I felt it," Florrie had begged her.

Nelly had known for a long time that something wasn't right. Of course, Margot had been only too happy for her to act as unpaid "nanny" to her daughter when she was a baby, but recognising the growing mutual affection between them, Margot had put a stop to it, and Nelly's duties had gradually reverted to cleaning and cooking. None the less, Nelly stayed devoted to the poor unloved scrap, the favourite part of her job being when Felicity burst into the kitchen after school to tell her about her day quickly before being beckoned to the dining room to be scrutinised for the afternoon by *her*. Nelly would have liked nothing more than to take that wooden ruler and smack Margot's hands with it, hard – give her a taste of her own medicine.

"Feliciteee."

They both jumped.

"I'd better get back, Nelly." Felicity hugged her.

"Take care, little one, and remember – how others treat you says more about them than you."

"I know, Nelly. I remember."

"You are brave and someday you'll fly like a bird, Felicity," Nelly called after her.

Felicity ran towards the voice, imagining great big wings sprouting from her back: wings that could take her far away, straight to where her mother had come from before here – to her aunts. That day, they'd made Felicity feel as though she were perched under a rainbow, with the warmth of the sunshine on her back.

"Where were you?" Mother asked as Felicity shot through the door.

"I went to get a drink, Mother, I'm sorry."

"Were you bothering Mrs Walsh, were you telling tales?" she asked suspiciously.

73

"No, Mother. I just got a drink and came straight back." Felicity sat back down at the table.

"Because I warned you before, Felicity. Staff are to be treated as such. There are differences between us that we cannot overcome."

"Yes, Mother. I understand," Felicity assured her, not understanding what she meant.

"Furthermore, as a Catholic, Mrs Walsh is privileged to hold such a high position within this household. You wouldn't want to ruin it for her by making her believe she's the same as us, now would you?"

"Oh no, Mother." Felicity would never ruin anything for Nelly.

"Now, let's start again with the eight times tables. You are eight, after all, so you should know them perfectly well."

"Yes, Mother."

"And please, no more mistakes – I don't want to have to reprimand you again and I have a lot to do. Tomorrow is a big day here at Knockmore. Remember, when you return from school tomorrow, make yourself scarce. I'll call you when I want to introduce you to the other women briefly."

Felicity was excited for tomorrow. She'd be able to spend the afternoon playing with no interruption and she hoped that Mother would be so busy with the other ladies that she'd forget to call her.

"Everything needs to be perfect," she heard Mother say the next morning as she prepared to leave for school.

Father had already disappeared and Mrs Walsh was dashing about in preparation for the five other reverends' wives, who'd descend on Knockmore later that day for their annual meeting.

"I've been selected to host the Reverends' Wives Club luncheon," Mother had revealed months before at dinner, referring to the RWC.

"A marvellous support system," Father encouraged.

"Irritating, intensely irritating," she'd responded. "Why you put me forward for it in the first place, I'll never know. Half of them were educated abroad and the other half are know-it-alls. I'm the youngest by far. Lillian Middleton must be at least seventy." Mother rolled her eyes at the thought of the elderly chairwoman.

"As for the others, well, I'm not sure I can decipher one from the other. Let me see . . . There's Julia Evans, who follows Lillian about like a lost puppy. Eleanor Budd – quite the budding gossip. Ursula Grimes – what a name! Need I say more? And . . . ah, yes, Honor Newenham, who speaks of nothing but books. Apparently, she attempted to write a novel. Can you imagine! Her house must be filthy, neglected from all that time spent with her nose in a book, which is probably the reason I'm hosting this year. Chosen at random, indeed."

"Come now, dearest. It's an honour to have them here at Knockmore."

"Snobs, the lot of them, Michael. Constant questions as to my background. It's like an inquisition – and don't think they won't be looking at the flaking paint in the dining room."

"I'm sure they're not interested in the ceiling, dearest."

"You know, I'm sure Lillian attached my name to her hand the last time she reached into the hat, reciting her silly little rhyme."

Mother had told the story of how each year they put all of their names in a hat and Lillian, as the most senior of the club, would reach her liver-spotted hand in, while uttering her tiresome poem, to select the following year's host: Who will it be? Who will it be? The RWC host shall be chosen by me.

"Of course, I pretended to be thrilled. But it was like being congratulated for contracting the plague!" Mother quipped, throwing down her knife and fork.

In the end, before leaving the room, Father had agreed to have the dining room painted. But the paint had given Mother a *violent* headache, which lingered for months afterwards and was still gnawing at her head on the morning in question as Felicity heard her shout orders at Nelly.

"My head is throbbing, Mrs Walsh. Come at once. What's the update?" Mother clicked her fingers with one hand, rubbing at the back of her neck with the other. "This dreadful headache, when will it pass?"

"Must be the stress, Mrs Montgomery," Nelly replied.

"Hah. When would I have time for stress? Stress is for the weak, Mrs Walsh. Besides, you know full well my back hasn't been right since . . . well, for years now, and the pain comes straight from there. Now, where were we?"

"Well, Mrs Montgomery," Nelly started. They'd been neighbours in the Estates years before and she still found it difficult to take orders from the poker-faced girl. "The tarts are made, ready to go in the oven, and the ham is baked. I have a few salads yet to make, but I'll whip them up in no time and then quickly bake the bread. I was here at six this morning, dressing the table in the dining room, as you can see, and then I'll give the place a quick one, two and Bob's your uncle," Nelly smiled.

"The salads are unmade?" Mother turned quickly, nearly knocking Felicity off her feet.

"Yes, Mrs Montgomery, but I'll have them done in a flash."

"And another thing, do you see that?" Mother asked, pointing up to the chandelier in the hallway.

All three looked up at the imposing light fitting.

"It's a disgrace. Please make sure you clean it."

Mrs Walsh looked at Felicity, making a face, and then back up at the chandelier, which sat bang in the middle of the ceiling and would be impossible to reach unless she had arms the length of a giraffe's neck. Felicity giggled back.

"Get to school, Felicity," Mother snapped.

Felicity ran to the door, catching Mrs Walsh winking at her as she went, and Felicity stretched her arms out like wings, pretending to fly through it.

"Get to it, Mrs Walsh!" Margot clapped her hands together. "I want that gleaming by noon. I have several correspondences to take care of in my room. Call me at 1 p.m., no later."

"The great big lazy cow," Mrs Walsh muttered to herself.

Margot had got as fat as her hair was short over the years, hiding in her room with yet another *headache*. It made Mrs Walsh sick. But there were greater things to pick a fight over than that dusty old chandelier. If there were any fight to be picked it would be about Felicity. She'd just about had enough of Margot's treatment of that child – abuse, in fact – and it was high time she spoke to the reverend about it. It was time for him to stop burying his head in the sand. Clean the chandelier indeed, she thought as she went to fetch the broom.

Felicity spent the day at school watching the clock, ready to run across the road and up the stairs to start her game. At

1 p.m. sharp she tugged her bag from the back of her chair and set off, counting her steps as she went. She reached the front door in a record number and pushed it open.

"Nelly!" she shrieked. "Nelly."

No, indeed Mrs Walsh didn't have arms the length of a giraffe's neck, nor the balance of a tightrope walker. When she dragged the chair onto the landing near the railing and reached the duster, tied to end of the broom, towards the old chandelier, she should have known it wouldn't end well. When the tremendous thud sounded out around the house, Margot should have rushed to her assistance, holding her hand as she gasped for a few moments before her heart stopped beating, her curved back broken in two with the impact.

But instead Margot was snoring away loudly in her room, when at precisely 1.30 p.m. the five members of the RWC knocked several times loudly. They pushed open the heavy front door to discover a broken 73-year-old lying dead on the floor, two apple tarts blazing in the oven and eight-year-old Felicity sobbing over the body of her only friend.

"Good grief!" Lillian Middleton shouted. "Call an ambulance. Quickly, Julia! And the reverend. Rouse the reverend!"

Lillian bent down, placing two fingers at the side of Mrs Walsh's neck, and then shook her head slowly at the four other sensible haircuts.

"She's so cold," Felicity whimpered. "She's so cold."

"Oh, you poor thing. Come here." Ursula Grimes bent down to pick her up and comfort her. "What happened, dear? Can you try to tell us?"

"I went to school. I heard Mother tell Nelly to clean the chandelier and then I came back and . . . " Felicity sobbed.

"Come, dear." Ursula pulled her onto her knee, holding her tight.

Eleanor Budd glanced at the others. By now, they'd all seen the broom on the floor and Honor Newenham, who adored a good mystery novel and prided herself on always being able to pre-empt the ending, had just spotted the overturned chair on the landing.

"You don't suppose?" Eleanor asked.

"Eleanor!" Lillian gestured at Felicity. "I'm sure there's a perfectly reasonable explanation."

"Yes, look . . . " Honor pointed up. "It looks like she was using the broom to reach the chandelier in the hallway," she concluded in an effort to solve the mystery, harking back to Colonel Mustard in the drawing room with the infamous lead piping.

"Ambulance is on its way," Julia Evans said, returning and looking down at the blood that had now settled in a murky pool by Mrs Walsh's head. "Sorry, Lillian, I'm not great with blood." She fanned her face frantically.

"Where's your mother, dear?" Lillian turned to Felicity.

"Her room. She must be in her room," Felicity said, not taking her eyes off Nelly.

"Let's find her, shall we? What a shock for you. What a terrible shock."

Lillian started for the stairs, followed closely by the others. Felicity pointed towards the bedroom door and Lillian pushed it open slowly to reveal Margot fast asleep, mouth wide open, releasing thunderous snores.

"Another missing piece of the puzzle." Ursula raised her eyebrows to the women.

"Margot. Margot," Lillian called softly.

"What the . . . ? Goodness, I must have nodded off."

Margot was woken with a sharp shove in the ribs by Julia where Lillian's dulcet tones had failed to rouse her.

Lillian closed the door, leaving Ursula and Felicity on the landing outside. From there, they heard a shout and then witnessed Margot explode through the door, coming face to face with the dreadful scene below, a smell of singed apples lingering in the air.

"Oh, Lord. Dear Nelly, so dutiful. Such a perfectionist," Mother said, bursting into frenzied tears, forcefully seizing Felicity and holding her so close to her heaving chest that she almost squeezed her to death.

Eleanor bent down to fix the toppled chair, but Honor grabbed her arm.

"Leave it," she said. "For the investigation."

"Investigation?" Margot looked up sharply. "Investigation?"

"Well, there's always an investigation." Honor started to blink uncontrollably.

"Come, sit down, Margot." Lillian led her back into the bedroom, shooting Honor *the look*. "Just an accident, dear. Just a dreadful accident. Did you ask the elderly housekeeper to clean the chandelier?" she asked cautiously.

"I did *not*!" Margot was shaking. "She was always doing things like that, always. Isn't that right, Felicity?" Margot called to Felicity.

"Yes, Mother," Felicity lied, watching the colour rise in her mother's face and wondering would she burst open.

They were interrupted by the arrival of the ambulance then watched from the landing as Reverend Michael sprinted through the front door and immediately back out again to empty the contents of his stomach onto the lawn. Once he gathered himself, they were all ushered to the parlour. Sergeant Hughes was next to arrive, briefly questioning each lady in turn before Margot was led into the room.

"Almost exciting," Felicity heard Eleanor say to the other women as they went off to the kitchen to make tea.

It was Father who came to her next, awkwardly putting his arm around her shoulders.

"I'm so sorry. I know you were fond of her. Are you all right?" he asked.

Felicity shook her head. "I loved Nelly."

He patted her back. "I know," he replied, unable to meet her eyes.

"I think I'll go to my room, Father."

"Yes, dear. I'll pray for Nelly, Felicity. I'll pray," he promised.

Felicity sat on the landing, out of sight, observing the comings and goings below. She watched as they covered Nelly with a sheet and lifted her onto the stretcher. She wanted to run after her as they slid the shape that used to be Nelly into the ambulance.

Next, Mother emerged from the parlour, followed by Sergeant Hughes, who shook Father's hand and patted him on the back. She saw the five women gathering their bags and coats, staring at the place where the housekeeper had fallen, now vacant save for the blackened blood on the wooden floor.

"All is not as it seems," Honor said to the other women in a whisper before closing the door behind them.

Felicity saw them at the funeral in the great big Catholic church. She'd never been inside it before, but there they were, smiling at her. Felicity's face immediately lit up, but Margot grabbed her by the arm, sucking in her cheeks with disgust as she walked past her sisters.

The house was silent again after the callers stopped coming to pay their respects. Each time the doorbell rang, Felicity would bound down the stairs in the hope it was them, but they never came – and then Mother went to bed.

"A nervous breakdown," she heard Dr Gallagher whisper to Father. "Total rest. I've asked Margot to consider some time in hospital."

"Oh no, Doctor. Margot doesn't like hospitals. We'll manage here. I'll make sure she rests," Father promised.

"Maybe consider getting some help. I might know someone looking for a position. I could give you their phone number," the doctor said, handing Father a piece of paper.

In years to come, Felicity would ponder if life were a series of predisposed episodes that unknowingly walked you along the path to which you were destined. And she always secretly wondered if Nelly had given her one last treasured gift in her departure.

Felicity Montgomery

Then – 1978

Felicity sat on the steps of the big house, lining up the stones and feathers she'd gathered from the driveway, arranging them in little patterns. She pulled a pink flower from the trellis around the door, leading to the eternal silence inside, and laid it at the top of her design.

It was five weeks now since that day and she couldn't believe Nelly was gone. She still rushed in from school, expecting to see her there in the kitchen, only to remember she was never coming back. Felicity hadn't been able to wake her. She could still picture her lying there, Nelly's eyes staring ahead blankly, blood pouring from her head, seeping out onto the shiny floor. She couldn't remember much after that – it was all a blur of women rushing from room to room, her mother screaming, the sergeant arriving, the sound of the ambulance, the smell of burned apples and her father telling her everything would be okay. But it wasn't okay. Nelly was gone.

All evidence of the tragedy had been removed, all traces of Nelly gone, except for the stain on the floor in the hall. The floor had been scrubbed so hard that it had removed the varnish with it, leaving one lighter patch, a pale reminder of what had happened there. Felicity didn't know if *they* could see it, but she could, always careful not to stand on it might she somehow fall in and disappear as Nelly had. It reminded her of the map of America, where Nelly's daughter lived. Maybe Nelly had fallen into America and was with her daughter. She always used to say she'd like to visit someday.

Mother wasn't well and had disappeared too, locked away in her room for weeks, leaving her and Father by themselves. She liked it being just the two of them and while she missed Nelly every single day, she was happy that Mother had gone away upstairs. Father never told her to go to her room and instead they took little walks in the evenings together. Felicity liked praying with him too, especially since he always included Nelly at the end of their prayers. They ate dinner together in the kitchen and she didn't have to watch her fork or knife or where her elbows were as they chatted happily over one of the many meals that the parishioners had dropped round to them.

"When will Mother be well again?" she asked him one evening.

"Ah . . . well . . . um . . . she's had a terrible shock. The doctor says she needs lots of time to recover," he explained.

Felicity couldn't quite understand why Mother was so upset. She was forever saying that she'd love to get rid of nosy old Nelly and now she had.

"Is it because she'll have to cook and clean now?" she asked innocently.

"Not quite, Felicity," he almost laughed. "But talking of which, I do need to get back to work, so I've found a nice lady to take over from dear old Nelly and help look after you. She'll be here tomorrow."

84

Felicity was upset. "I don't want anyone else. Can't it just be us?"

"No, my love. We're not replacing Nelly, don't worry, and perhaps you'll like this new arrangement," he winked.

Felicity sat back now to admire her floral design before picking it apart and starting the calming ritual again. She was so ensconced that she barely noticed them approach.

"Hello, Felicity," Tess Maguire said, sitting down on the steps beside her.

Felicity looked up suddenly at the lady and the little girl, the latter of whom had her hands tucked into the pockets of her brown corduroy dress, concealing her wiry form. She had fuzzy red hair, tamed into two plaits hanging down her back. The woman had the same hair, albeit shorter, and the same wiry form as if neither of them sat down for very long. Tess was smiling warmly at Felicity, who couldn't help but smile back.

"I'm Tess. I'm going to be the new housekeeper here and help take care of you in the afternoons while your mam isn't well," she explained.

Felicity looked inquisitively at Tess and then at the little girl.

"Hello," Felicity whispered shyly.

"I knew Nelly, you know. She lived near us in Farmleigh. She told me all about you. Am I right that you're very good at drawing?" Tess asked her gently.

"Yes, I love to draw. Nelly keeps . . . I mean, kept all of my pictures in the pantry on the door," Felicity said, looking down sadly at the step as she spoke, realising she'd never again see Nelly take out the little box of colourful pins to attach her best pictures to the wooden door.

"Well, I'd love to see your pictures. Old Nelly spoke of

you all the time, little one. She told me lovely stories all about you as a baby and how proud she was of you. You know, I bet Nelly's now your very own guardian angel. Look," Tess said, reaching over and picking up a tiny white feather from the second step. She handed it to Felicity. "You know, they say feathers appear when loved ones are near."

Felicity took it, turning it over in her hand. She liked that. It made her feel better. She smiled and tucked the feather into her pocket for safekeeping.

"Now, this little monkey here is none other than Lucie Maguire. She's my little angel. You two are both eight years old and she's going to be with me in the afternoons during school time and then in the mornings over the summer holidays, so you'll have plenty of time to play and get to know each other."

Lucie waved enthusiastically at Felicity, who started to giggle.

"Come on," Lucie said, reaching down and grabbing Felicity's hand. "Let's do cartwheels."

Felicity allowed Lucie to lead her to the grass, where she demonstrated the move.

As Lucie's eyes swept past Felicity's feet in an expert tumble, Lucie shouted, "I like your shoes."

Tess watched on laughing as four little words cemented a lifelong friendship.

Margot Montgomery

Then – 1965

Most objects made of glass contain something beautiful: a jar filled with sticky strawberry jam or runny golden honey; a hand-tied bunch of wildflowers, presented to the recipient hidden behind the back of a child looking to please. Most glass objects are merely the vessel to the wonders that lie within. At first, some glass is hard to crack. And some glass isn't entirely translucent – some glass shatters.

"It'll be like a stay-at-home honeymoon – far more sensible," Michael told Margot enthusiastically the morning after the wedding over his habitual two hard-boiled eggs, a slice of toast cut into four even squares and cup of tea – no milk with a slice of lemon.

"Yes, indeed," Margot answered unenthusiastically, staring blankly ahead.

Michael had set out an activity for each day for his new bride: riding bicycles, a picnic in the countryside, a walk on the beach. It was as if he'd read a manual on blossoming romance and how to woo a young lady and included all the elements to ensure success.

"Marvellous fun," he said, cracking the top of the second egg.

Margot was still in a mild state of shock following the "fish out of water" lovemaking encounter the night before. She hadn't been sure what to expect – not having thought beyond the goal of reaching new heights in becoming the reverend's wife – and though she hadn't necessarily expected to reach new heights in the bedroom, she couldn't help but feel perplexed.

"All will fall into place, dearest," Michael told her as the white of the egg jumped off the spoon and he stuck his lower jaw out to catch it triumphantly. "We have the rest of our lives to carry out God's duty and it's been a huge change for you," he said, sensing her sudden reluctance.

"Yes, of course, Michael," she agreed, pushing away the plate untouched.

Perhaps she was just tired. Her mind flitted briefly to her mam, probably still in the same position she'd left her the day before, and a sudden regret swept over her. No, don't look back, she told herself and then smiled, imagining her sisters reading her note. Would they try to contact her? She hoped not. She'd been clear enough about her wishes.

Margot looked at Michael, sipping his tea, oblivious. This could be just the fresh start she needed if she kept looking forwards.

"Yes, let's try to have a nice time, Michael. Perhaps the sea air will settle me," she said, trying to remain optimistic.

But by the third day, Margot was anything but settled and her doubts were quickly confirmed – Michael was a bore.

"It's a huge responsibility, but I have many plans. Many plans for the parish. With you by my side, we shall conquer the world," he told her, barely drawing breath. "I'm particularly interested in the elderly and ensuring they're at the forefront of the community . . . "

Of course you are, Margot thought, confident that Michael had more in common with the elderly than the elderly themselves. She tried her best to listen, to feel somewhat aroused by his enthusiasm, but try as she might, she couldn't seem to muster the right emotion.

There was only one respite. After the initial consummation, he seemed wholly disinterested in continuing the journey of discovery into the female anatomy and would climb into bed beside Margot at night, lead her in prayer and then lie on his back, his mouth open, releasing thunderous snores. Margot watched him in his slumberous state, imagining stale green smoke puffing out into the air with each exhalation. It made sense, of course, that such a large nose should induce such a triumphant snore, bringing with it sleep deprivation for her, leaving plenty of time to ponder the future.

Margot pictured herself as a first lady of sorts, attending various luncheons, wearing a chic pillbox hat. She imagined being wined and dined by the more affluent members of the community, hosting a garden party on the lawn, and finally, she dreamed of the many children he promised her, which might one day fill the gaping hole in her heart. Michael wanted four. But she'd settle for two: a boy and a girl.

She'd heard whispers in the Estates of ways to prevent multiple pregnancies and she certainly wouldn't be afraid to use them. She didn't want to be left running around after multiple Michaels. She liked children. Well, not the snotty-nosed ones from the Estates, who continually wiped their noses on the sleeve of their threadbare sweaters, leaving a transparent slime on the wool, but the type who'd sit quietly. Yes, perhaps all was not lost. Time would sort it all out.

"Might I have a word?" Michael called her into the parlour on the Monday morning after their week of respite, ready to set out a list of duties for his new wife as Margot stared on, horrified. "First and foremost, your main role is to act as a support to me," he began nervously. "Keep the vicarage clean and tidy and ready for visitors at a moment's notice. There's always plenty of them. Never a dull moment!" he laughed. "You'll also need to visit many members of the community."

Pillbox hat at the ready, she thought, finally seeing some light at the end of the narrowing tunnel.

"Mostly the elderly, the sick and infirmed."

Oh, Christ.

"There are various events that you'll be expected to host and of course, *tea and sympathy* are what we live by, as well as frugality," he chuckled to himself, forcing enormous snorts to escape his nostrils.

"Frugality?" She almost dropped her teacup. There it was again, that word.

"Well, waste not, want not. How can I put it?" He struggled to find the words. "The house doesn't entirely match the post, if you understand. A bit grand for a reverend, really."

Mrs Kidney had been right. Her imaginary pillbox hat drifted into the air as he continued.

"Inside the home, I've arranged for Mrs Walsh to instruct you in the running of the house and as an accomplished cook, she'll be teaching you how to prepare the cold buffets and stews that always go down so very well. Any questions?" he asked, finally relieved to have divulged the intricacies of her new role.

"Certainly, Michael. That all seems satisfactory. And no, no questions."

She hardly flinched. What on earth? Frugality, sick and infirmed, and Nelly bloody Walsh? She'd rather take instruction from Satan than that nosy old cow. Nelly would be only too delighted to put Margot back in her box and would surely take pleasure in gossiping behind her back in the Estates, whispering that the "lady of the house" didn't know a pot from a pan.

"Will Mrs Walsh be here all the time?" Margot asked. "It's just, I'm afraid she'll find me quite ridiculous in my culinary skills and it is a small town – you know, people gossip."

"Dearest!" he chuckled. "Mrs Walsh is a kind old soul and she's here to help, when and where you need it, or at least until you've found your feet." Michael placed his moist hands over hers. "Well, it's all settled. Together, we shall conquer the world," he repeated. "Now, I must dash. People to see, places to go. I shall see you at lunch hour, when I'm sure there'll be a wonderful meal."

Margot went to her room to gather herself before the morning's "lessons" commenced, stopping briefly at the mirror. She looked at her drab, functional hair, so different from the highlighted mass that she'd hacked off just a few months ago. Her mouth was set into a thin straight line and even if she tried, she couldn't seem to make the muscles in her cheeks move to force a smile. Her eyes, once alight with determination, looked flat as they stared back at her. It was as if she'd snapped her fingers and aged twenty years overnight. Even her clothes were dreary, but frugality surely wouldn't push to a trip to His 'n' Hers, the local fashion emporium.

"*You* are Mrs Montgomery!" She repeated her mantra firmly to her reflection before setting off to find Mrs Walsh.

Nelly Walsh was ready for her, with everything neatly laid out in preparation for the morning's tuition. You could have knocked her over with a feather when the news had travelled to the Estates that Maggie Treacy had only gone and crossed to the other side. Everyone was all talk about it now, of course, continually asking Nelly to fill them in on the gossip. But Nelly knew her place and she was fond of the new reverend.

But Maggie Treacy! She always was a little snob, thinking she was better than them all. "Too good even for herself," her own mother used to say about her until she lost her marbles. Well, Maggie must have found them and shoved them all into her gob, the way she was talking now. Nelly didn't mind folks wanting a better life, but not like this. But it was none of her business. She'd treat Mrs Montgomery like she would any other lady of the house: with respect.

"Right, let's begin, Mrs Walsh. Although, why I must learn when you're here is beyond me. I never cared much for menial tasks."

Nelly rolled her eyes and began what would turn into weeks spent differentiating between boiling, baking, roasting, braising and frying, all the while Margot shouting at her with frustration. Margot spent more time with ingredients laced through her hair than in the bowl.

"Um . . . ah . . . goodness, dearest, you *are* a wonder, quite the cook. Yum yum," Michael would say each day when he returned to sample their delights, thrilled that his wife was making such headway.

"I've given Mrs Walsh the weekend off," Michael announced after lunch one day.

"Is she ill?" Margot questioned.

Much as she hated having her around, Margot was terrified of being alone in the kitchen and was happy to keep up the pretence for a little longer.

"No," he said, putting his arm around her proudly. "I thought it was time to show off your culinary creations to some friends."

The colour slowly drained from Margot's face. "Really, who?"

"I've asked Paul Delaney, my old friend from Trinity, and his lovely wife, Cynthia, to come down from Dublin for Sunday lunch right after service."

Margot could hardly breathe. "Oh! goodness. Wouldn't you prefer Mrs Walsh to prepare the lunch? I'm still learning."

"Nonsense. I've tasted your food. Delicious! They'll stay the night and leave on Monday. Now, must dash. Mrs Sullivan's cat has had kittens and the poor woman is in a terrible state. Said I'd pop by." He dropped a kiss on her head and fled from the room.

Margot exhaled in frustration at the thought of the old woman and her constant demands of Michael, which always seemed to come at a time when she needed him herself. Well, Mrs Sullivan's cat wouldn't be the only one having kittens if she didn't pull this one out of the bag. She needed to prepare, but there was no way she'd give Mrs Walsh the satisfaction of asking for her help, especially after her comment last week when Margot had burned her fifth pastry in a row.

The old biddy had looked at her smugly and said, "There, there, Mrs Montgomery. There's only one thing worse than a wife who can cook and won't. It's a wife who can't cook and does."

Margot had to stop herself from picking up the rolling pin and throwing it at the back of Nelly's head. But it was true. She couldn't cook. Her white sauce was thicker than porridge and her mash firmer than cement. She burned everything, even vegetables, and her ham could make you thirstier than a stint in the desert.

That Sunday morning at service, Margot sat alone in the front pew, reciting the recipes and timings in her head as the rest of the congregation sang from their hymnals. As the last note of "All Things Bright and Beautiful" rang through the church, she was out of the door and running past all the ladies waiting to chat with the reverend's new wife. Back in the kitchen, she feverishly chopped, trying to recreate Mrs Walsh's offerings. "You can do this," she repeated, downing her second sherry to settle her nerves.

By the time the guests arrived, the chicken was in the oven, the potatoes were roasting, the apple pie was ready and Michael was thrilled that his wife was in such high spirits.

"A little offering from France," Paul Delaney said, presenting her with a bottle of wine and looking his friend's new bride up and down.

"We honeymooned there," Cynthia added with a tinkly laugh.

Cynthia was all mouth and struggling to keep her lips shut over her immense teeth.

"How lovely. Thank you," Margot said. "We didn't get abroad for our honeymoon. The reverend has such an important role here in Knockmore and the house, as you can see, needs constant supervision."

"Of course," Cynthia said. "It's a beautiful home. You're fortunate. We live in an annex in my parents' house in Ballsbridge in Dublin. Terribly central but quite pokey."

"Poor you," Margot offered. "What a shame. Once you get used to such a huge home, it would seem a terrible trial to be in an annex. Please, make yourselves at home while I check on lunch," she quipped. That would show her.

"Hurry back, dearest, and we can tell you all about our time at Trinity College Dublin," Michael called after her.

Margot managed to get the meal onto the plates, refusing any offer of help from Cynthia, whose authentic marble-mouthed accent was beginning to grate on her nerves. She dashed between cooker, hob and worktop, covering the meal with a slightly thicker than usual gravy to disguise the crudely cut carrots and roughly carved chicken. Michael poured a thimbleful of wine into each glass and the meal commenced.

"Delicious, dearest. Lovely and moist," he assured her.

"Frightfully well done. I can hardly boil an egg," Cynthia revealed.

"Really? How rustic!" Margot laughed, beginning to relax.

They were full of it, prattling on about Dublin and university, but she was enjoying seeing the more youthful side of Michael, who for once wasn't entirely focused on the Church.

"Do you remember John? Up and moved to America. What a joker he was!" Paul told them as Michael laughed along. "And Victor? He has four kids now. Did you ever think you'd see the day!"

"Let's take a walk in the garden," Margot suggested,

eager to show it off and sensing that Paul would continue his stories all evening. She was struggling to make small talk with Cynthia, whose teeth were making it impossible to concentrate.

"You know, the house was previously owned by the Prendergasts and in its day saw many influential people sweep up and down its steps," Margot told them confidently, guiding them through the grounds. "Original sash windows! The orchard is my favourite part."

"And how did a lowly reverend come to live here?" Paul joked.

"I'll have you know that the reverend is the pinnacle of society and would need more than an annex in which to conduct his duties," Margot told him curtly, disgusted with his insult.

"I think Paul's jesting, dearest," Michael said, slapping Paul on the back before going on to explain that the Prendergasts had left the house to St Patrick's. "The antique rugs are long gone and the original furniture sold, I'm afraid. They *were* too much for a lowly reverend," he laughed.

"But the gardens remain beautiful," Margot piped in, taking the time to point out various plants and shrubs, delighted with the knowledge she'd gleaned in such a short time.

They sat chatting on the patio for some time, watching the sun slip down behind the apple trees.

"How about some coffee and pie?" Margot asked as the light began to fade.

"Just what the doctor ordered," Michael chuckled, placing his hand on Margot's lower back and guiding her back inside.

"Ready when you are," Margot called a short while later, wheeling her hostess trolley into the dining room, loaded with cream, custard and pie, to be greeted by three solemn faces. Cynthia was sitting in the armchair clutching her stomach, Paul was ashen-faced by the table and Michael was sweating far more profusely than normal.

"Goodness, dearest. We all feel a little off colour," Michael said, exhaling like a woman about to birth.

"Yes," Cynthia added. "I have terrible pain, coming and going in waves," she struggled before bolting upright and rushing to the bathroom under the stairs, hand over her mouth.

Margot heard a squelching sound escape from beneath Cynthia's skirt as she dashed past, nearly upending the hostess trolley and its wobbling contents. Paul was next to flee the scene. He, too, rushed past Margot, almost knocking her off her feet. He paused momentarily in the hallway and with no other escape option, hauled open the front door and hurdled down the salubrious granite steps before violently ejecting the contents of his stomach onto the pebbled drive.

"What the hell?" Margot stared at Michael, her last hope that the gut-wrenching sounds she could hear from outside and under the stairs had been brought in the form of a stomach virus from the annex and not from her roast dinner.

"Language, dearest," was all he could manage.

Michael was now the colour of the contents of the children's noses from the Estates as he stood clutching the back of the mahogany dining chair, gently swaying. The sweat from his brow and upper lip gathered speed as it travelled in slow motion down his neck onto his blue shirt. Margot watched as his shirt began to change colour, growing darker in great big patches. He closed his eyes and suddenly jerked forwards, projectile vomiting the contents of his stomach onto the dining table.

"Michael! Pull yourself together, for Christ's sake!"

He slowly met her eyes and she watched as some other warning issued inside his body and he ran past her, clutching his buttocks together, trying to retain what was about to exit.

"Upstairs, Michael. *Run*!" Margot shouted after him.

Margot stood in shock, staring at the dining table covered in red wine-tinged vomit, then bolted from the room towards the kitchen. She whipped the covering off the chicken and probed the remainder of the breast with a fork, stabbing the blush meat. The feathery whiteness at the outer parts of the carcass gave way to great big rosy spots of jellylike raw chicken.

"No. No," she said, putting her hand to her face in shame.

She felt fine, but then again, she'd hardly eaten anything, she'd been so focused on her guests. She quickly threw the evidence into the bin, placing a cloth over the top to further conceal it.

How had she got it so wrong? She'd put the chicken and the potatoes into the oven at the same time. The potatoes had crisped over beautifully and the chicken had appeared to follow suit. Then she suddenly remembered Mrs Walsh's little mantra: *after forty, put in the spud, for a chicken dinner that tastes good.*

Shit, shit, shit, she thought, inhaling and exhaling quickly, her face now as pink as the chicken and a mottled rash slowly creeping up her neck. No, she mustn't admit her mistake. She'd deny it.

Margot knocked on the downstairs toilet, where she could hear pained moans escaping from under the door.

"Cynthia, dear, open up."

"I can't," came the feeble reply.

"Come now, Cynthia, open up. Let's see if we can get you fixed up."

The handle turned slowly and Margot pushed open the door, to be greeted by a putrid smell.

"Good grief, Cynthia, what *have* you done?"

Margot took in the scene. Cynthia was sitting on the floor, one arm cradling the toilet. It appeared that Cynthia's meal had left via two emergency exits and she'd failed on both counts to reach the toilet. Margot's nose upturned with disgust as she glimpsed the stained carpet under Cynthia's skirt.

"I'll have to scrub the carpet on my hands and knees," Margot said, unable to hide her irritation.

"I'm so sorry, Margot. I think the chicken may have been a little undercooked."

"I don't think so, Cynthia. I'm perfectly well. You've obviously brought a vile dose of something from Dublin with you. Now, stand up," she snapped.

Cynthia struggled to stand, allowing Margot to hoist her by the arm and lead her upstairs to the bathroom, where she undressed her and ran her a bath.

"Undercooked chicken, indeed," Margot laughed. "Now, Cynthia, if it happens again, please run faster and aim at the toilet this time," she said, leaving her alone to go and clear up the mess downstairs.

Cynthia was too weak to argue. Michael had disappeared off to bed, clutching his stomach, and Paul was feebly splashing water at the gravel to remove his contribution.

What a mess. What an absolute mess! Margot stood in the hallway for a moment, wondering how she'd failed so miserably at the first hurdle. What else would she fail at? What else couldn't she do? She suddenly felt as though she were drowning, flailing out of her depth.

She opened the door to the downstairs toilet, sank to her knees and began to scrub.

Margot Montgomery

Then – 1966

Margot tore the envelope in two and threw it into the bin. What was the point in reading it, suffering through the same questions, listening to them begging her to come and see Mam? She knew what they wanted. They'd have her back taking care of everything, so they could continue to swan around, footloose and fancy-free. She'd read the first few letters all right, gradually noticing the change in tone – moving from angry to questioning – but never once did they admit their mistakes. She had a new life now and she didn't want to go back. She'd done her time. She wished they'd stop now, leave her be, leave her alone.

Alone. Something Margot was only too accustomed to feeling as the reverend's wife: alone in the house; avoiding the sniggers as she walked through the town; alone with her thoughts; alone on a Sunday in the front pew. She even woke up alone every morning, Michael's side of the bed smooth and untouched – six consecutive months of lying awake at night, watching his chest rise and fall, counting the seconds between his snores, had all too soon forced the conversation.

"Are you aware of your issue?" she'd asked after one particularly difficult night during which little irritating clicking noises replaced the snores. She'd tossed and turned all night waiting for each tormenting clockwork-like interruption.

"Um . . . ah, no, dearest. Am I dreadfully noisy?" Michael asked.

"Yes, Michael. That's one way of putting it. As a matter of fact, I'm not sure I've slept a full night since the wedding."

"Oh dear. I'm dreadfully sorry. Have you tried giving me a little kick?" he suggested.

"Yes, Michael," she said again impatiently. "I'm surprised you're not black and blue with the number of kicks I've been forced to administer. It seems the Lord blessed you with the gift of heavy sleep. But I, too, require sleep. How do you expect me to function?" she finished.

"Well . . . I . . . goodness," Michael said, folding the corners of the sheet and tucking them diligently under the mattress as he'd learned at boarding school.

"I think we'll have to come up with an alternative arrangement, don't you?"

She almost wished he'd put up a fight, but he was so eager to please and hopeful that her mood swings were attributed to sleep deprivation and not utter discontent that he'd agreed to sleep in the spare room almost immediately. So here she was now, alone and growing increasingly paranoid – their first year of marriage had failed to extinguish her feelings of inadequacy but instead nurtured them. No one wanted to speak to her except to ask after Michael.

"Could you ask the reverend . . . ?"

"Could you remind the reverend . . . ?"

"How is the reverend?"

The doorbell rang incessantly and she soon discovered there was *always* someone who needed Michael urgently, for anything from mending a broken heart to a broken bicycle. "All confidential, Margot," he'd tell her when she asked what they wanted. Michael would usher the callers into the parlour and close the door. Margot would diligently bring the tea, her interruption always causing an unwelcome pause in proceedings until she left the room and the counselling session would recommence. She gradually grew suspicious of those who crossed the threshold of his office and had taken to pressing her ear against the door trying to listen in until Mrs Walsh caught her.

"Mrs Walsh! Are you spying on me? I need you to change all the sheets on the beds. Idleness is a sin. Chop-chop."

Each new day became a day to get through, with little to occupy her mind. Even Mrs Walsh rarely looked up any more when she passed Margot in the house and it was clear that her services were no longer required in the kitchen. "I think it might be wise for Mrs Walsh to take over the cooking, dearest," Michael told her following the chicken incident. She'd stayed in her room after Paul and Cynthia had slunk out of the house the next morning, never to return to Knockmore, and remained there until a rather peaky-looking Michael had come to check on her, trying desperately to reassure her. "Accidents happen, dearest, nothing to be ashamed of," he'd said.

"It was *not* the chicken!" she'd screamed.

"Come now, Margot, it was undercooked. An innocent mistake," he'd said, taken aback by her outburst.

"If I never see them again it'll be too soon. And I

103

thought you were on my side," she'd said, still obviously mortified.

"Margot, you're being entirely unreasonable." Michael shook his head in disbelief.

She'd stared at his weak form in the doorway, not knowing she was going to pick up the glass jar until it was in her hand and then suddenly hurtling across the room in his direction. She'd missed. Instead, it hit the wall and splintered outwards, leaving little shards of glass surrounding his brown leather sandals.

"Margot!"

He'd looked at her then in the same way *they* did and she'd let him see – tired of hiding, bored of pretending.

"How could you, Margot?" He'd looked from her to the shattered jar on the floor.

"No, Michael, how could *you*?"

He'd left then. She'd looked at her reflection in the mirror, hoping to glimpse Maggie, waiting for her to appear and shout at her, tell her she was good enough, that she deserved the big house and the big life, but she was gone, too.

"What is it, dearest?" Michael asked her later that day, full of concern, his calmness restored, not even a glass jar aimed straight at his head enough to ignite him. "I'm very concerned, Margot. You're acting dreadfully out of character."

She'd wanted to stand on his desk and shout at him: I'm a big fat fake – common as muck. I always was. I married you to escape. I thought it would be different. I saw the big house, not you. I miss my hair and wearing skirts cut up to my arse. I miss The Beatles. And I don't give a shit about the Church. I never did. You're a bore. I'm not attracted to you. I don't belong here. I want to go back. I want to be Maggie.

She wanted to kick off her comfortable shoes, replace them with sky-high platforms and march back through the Estates, hips swinging. But she couldn't. She'd burned her bridges there, too.

"I'm sorry, Michael. I've found the last few months challenging," she said instead.

"Yes, indeed. It's a tough job being the reverend, but even tougher being the reverend's wife," Michael assured her, smiling down at her as if he were talking to one of his parishioners. "I think it's time we get you out in the community. It's not good to be locked up in here all day. It's lonely. Let's show them who the reverend's wife really is," he chuckled, hoping dearly that it wasn't the version he'd just seen.

But over a year into her community-based role, Margot felt no better. Every day she'd come downstairs to find the dreaded list, sitting on the console table in the hallway, of those who required a visit. Mrs Walsh would religiously leave a batch of freshly baked scones for her to tuck into her basket before she wobbled up the road on a rickety old bicycle. Her pillbox hat was prematurely retired, replaced with a simpler straw version that would see her through rain or shine. And her recipients usually comprised of recently bereaved or those who'd undergone some minor surgery; typically bunions, so that much of her days were spent inspecting feet, particularly Mrs Sheppard's.

Olive Sheppard lived ten miles outside Knockmore and Margot's visits always entailed a forced examination of chronically arthritic toes that reminded Margot of coiled slugs, primed to spring from Olive's sheepskin slippers and duly placed on Margot's lap, to allow a more detailed examination. Margot would try and fail every week not to recoil as the slugs were presented to her while Olive prattled on about whatever she pleased, her politically correct filter having malfunctioned with age.

"Why are you *not* pregnant? A reverend needs a family of his own, Margot. Do you deny a man of God?" she'd ask.

"No, Mrs Sheppard, I do not," Margot would say, trying to manoeuvre the slippers back over the splayed toes.

"You know, Mr Sheppard, God rest his soul, impregnated me on eight separate occasions no less. Only had to look at me and the deed was done," Mrs Sheppard told her proudly every time.

"Well, pity he isn't here to look at me now!" Margot mumbled under her breath.

"What was that, dear?" Mrs Sheppard lifted her head. "Speak up."

"How are your hands, Mrs Sheppard? Let me look," she shouted.

"Very bad, dear. Very bad."

"Terrible for you," Margot soothed, wondering how the same arthritic hands managed to grab the scones each week before Margot had even dismounted her bike.

But Mrs Sheppard was right. Why hadn't she fallen pregnant yet? Margot was beginning to think that Mr Sheppard had more chance of impregnating her from the grave than Michael did of fulfilling the task. His conjugal visits to her were few and far between, but she'd noticed a pattern: the watery knock on her door always arriving on the last Friday of the month. Margot would await the knock on the door and for Michael to enter the room before feebly entering her.

At first, she'd wondered as to the significance of the day, but soon realised it was to do with completing his list of duties by the end of the month, matrimonial commitment coming last. Spontaneity rarely featured in their lives and everything followed a strict pattern, even the visits themselves. She'd calculated that each episode lasted precisely sixty-three seconds before he collapsed on top of her and took her hand in prayer in conclusion. She'd almost considered playing dead to avoid it, but she wanted a baby so had no choice but to endure his sweating form. But each month she experienced the same feelings of failure upon realising that both the good Lord and Michael had yet again failed to deliver, and she'd need to endure Mrs Sheppard's inquisition, again.

Michael adored watching Margot cycle past the church each morning on her rounds, delighted with how she'd taken to her new role, providing comfort to the corns and bunions of the community. The last year had been tough on her, but she seemed to have found her niche and just as he always said, "The Lord works in mysterious ways."

"Morning, dearest," Michael shouted after her as she made her descent from Mrs Sheppard's, having had her reproductive organs prodded.

Margot smiled back thinly. She was always relieved when her visit to the old lady ended so she could freewheel her way down the hill to Mr Cooke's. Of course Margot couldn't abide him either, but her legs were always grateful for the rest. She sucked in as much fresh air as possible on the journey, in preparation for the pungent waft of ammonia that would instantly hit her nostrils upon crossing his threshold, always managing to shock her, even though she knew what to expect. She was sure Mr Cooke hadn't bothered to take a bath since Mrs Cooke had left the world three months previously and the house was filthy.

"Make sure he's eating," Michael shouted after her and she nodded in reply.

Mr Cooke was most definitely eating, judging by the amount of food permanently lodged between his teeth. Perhaps he was storing it there for later, like a hamster. She always made a concerted effort to breathe through her mouth during her visits, to protect her nose, until she imagined giant molecules of grime drifting into her mouth and resting on her tongue. After that, she'd tried holding her breath, which always left her feeling light-headed. She'd be sure to conduct her visit quickly today, to escape unscathed.

Feeling the first droplets of rain as she reached the bottom of the hill and silently cursing, she began to pedal faster. She saw them before they saw her. The bin truck approached with three men crammed into the front cabin like sardines and Frankie O'Shea dangling off the back, his arm extended, waving frantically at her.

"Whoop, whoop, there she is. There's Maggie Treacy. Look at you now!" Frankie shouted.

The lads in the cabin hung out of the window to catch a glimpse and the driver beeped the horn furiously.

"There she is, Holy Mary herself," she heard. "Not so flashy now, on the rusty old bike!"

As the truck drove past her, she saw Frankie throw his head back and laugh with all his might.

"Fuck off, you pricks!" Margot shouted, instantly filled with rage. "Fuck off, the lot of you," she screamed before turning back to the road, veering to the centre of it and losing her balance.

She wobbled precariously in slow motion for a moment and briefly caught the shocked faces of the passengers in the oncoming car before flying over the bonnet and rolling to the ground, where she landed on her back, skirt above her ears.

"Are you all right, Maggie? Maggie? I'm sorry. Maggie, can you hear me?" Frankie's face morphed like a kaleidoscope and then everything went black.

Margot saw a very bright light coming at her as she opened her eyes and squinted against it.

"Welcome back, Mrs Montgomery," Dr Gallagher said, lifting each eyelid and shining his torch at her. "You've had a little bump, but you're all right now."

Michael hovered nervously in the background as she slowly came to. She felt very out of it and could barely remember what had happened. She'd been unconscious when the crowd gathered to see the reverend's wife hoisted into the bin truck, her skirt flapping and her straw hat hanging on for dear life. Sergeant Hughes was immediately summoned and arrived in record time to take a statement from the elderly driver of the car. Sergeant Jim Hughes could hardly stop his shoulders from vibrating when the gentleman quietly whispered the string of profanities that had escaped the reverend's wife's mouth as she flew over his bonnet. The car was all but stopped when Margot cartwheeled past the windscreen.

"Well, Sergeant, it was a terrifying ordeal, absolutely awful. To think I could have died," Margot told him later that day, holding on to her head and nursing her bruised ego. "I remember well those ruffians abusing me, driving towards me at high speed. I have no doubt they were trying to hit me, run me off the road, no doubt at all." She stopped to dab at her eyes.

She was some actress, Jim thought, letting her continue, almost enjoying the performance. Like he always said, "There are people so addicted to exaggerating, they can't tell the truth without lying."

"I'd estimate the car was travelling at well over sixty miles per hour and the truck even faster. I'm sure I saw my life flash before my eyes."

He'd been waiting for that bit.

"Now, Magg . . . I mean, Mrs Montgomery. The car was all but stopped. Let me tell you if it had hit you at that speed, you wouldn't be standing here to tell the tale."

Jim Hughes had recently started courting Florrie Treacy and he felt a degree of loyalty to the sister of his new love interest. Even though from what Florrie had told him she didn't deserve it. None the less he listened, jotting down a few notes in his little leather-bound book as he went, happy to give the reverend's wife the benefit of the doubt until she proved she didn't merit it.

"I think what we have here, Mrs Montgomery, is an unfortunate accident," he said, snapping his book shut.

Margot sat up. "An accident? I don't think so. No, I'd like to press charges against the men in the truck. They may have been drunk – did you check, Sergeant?" she went on as he started to reverse out of the room.

"Okay, Mrs Montgomery, you rest up now. I'll have a word with your husband." Jim rolled his eyes. He should have listened to Florrie.

The reverend's face fell as the sergeant delivered a slightly censored sequence of events to *Poor Michael*.

"Oh . . . well, oh dear. Yes, well . . . I see," Michael

stuttered, flinching when the sergeant reached the part about Margot's screams. "Fear can bring out the worst in us, Sergeant," the reverend said at last.

It was far from what Jim had been thinking. It was on the tip of his tongue to say what his dear Father used to tell him. "A foul tongue reveals more about you than those you use it against." But now was evidently not the time to regurgitate one of his quotes.

"We won't be making a formal complaint and I thank you for your time. But please do ask the men not to jeer at her again. She is, after all, my wife."

"I surely will, Reverend. Leave it with me," the sergeant said, happy to wipe his hands of it.

Margot, of course, had other ideas. She replayed it repeatedly, talking of little else during the many weeks of her recuperation.

"Their faces, Michael, their language. I'm appalled. How is the enquiry going with the sergeant? Does he need to speak to me again?"

Margot wanted retribution, or indeed blood, it seemed. She'd gradually come to believe her own lies, using the term "attempted murder" several times as she rehashed the story, which had by now gathered more legs than a spider.

"And the couple in the vehicle?" she quizzed. "Surely they witnessed those men leering and trying to kill me? I won't rest until they're behind bars."

"Yes, dear."

It was all he could manage, his usual patience waning and at a total loss as to how to stop her. He knew precisely what the couple had witnessed: a mass of cursing floral who took her hand off the handlebars to stick her fingers up at the bin truck. He needed to put a stop to Margot's rhetoric, unable to risk the archdeacon getting wind of his wife attempting to press charges for every crime ever listed under the sun.

"Will you come with me to see Mr O'Shea, Reverend? See if we can quench the fire before it takes hold," Sergeant Hughes suggested after a trembling Michael visited him to ask his advice.

They were both peacekeepers by trade and Sergeant Hughes was fond of the reverend, felt sorry for him. He'd bitten off more than he could chew with that wife of his.

"Nothing is ever Maggie's fault," Florrie warned him when he told her about the accident. "No, she'd rather see *anyone* else take the blame."

"How are ya, Jim? Everything all right?"

Frankie answered on their second knock. If he was shocked to see the sergeant and the reverend on his doorstep, he never once dropped his guard. He ushered them into the front room.

"What can I do for you, lads?" he asked, hands in his pockets, casually swaying back and forth.

Michael stood back, a little behind Jim, forcing the sergeant to commence negotiations.

"Listen, Frankie. The reverend is here on behalf of Mrs Montgomery. She's mighty upset still about what happened and well, I'm sorry to tell you but she's looking to press charges for . . . well, for all sorts. But let's not get into that for now."

Frankie suddenly looked nervous.

"Now the reverend here, well, he's heard the reports from eyewitnesses and he's happy to leave this where it is, but it seems Magg . . . Mrs Montgomery has other ideas," the sergeant continued, looking to the reverend to jump in.

"Mr O'Shea, we're hoping that you might write a letter of apology to my wife and hopefully it'll satisfy her distress, then perhaps we can all move on," Michael finally squeaked.

Frankie looked from one to the other, smacked his thigh and burst out laughing.

"Ah, Reverend, you're after taking on a real live wire there," he laughed. "Maggie's all talk, always was. I woulda married her myself if she'd have had me. Promised her the stars, I did. But she wanted the moon – a real looker, too. You're a lucky man, Reverend. Hope you can handle her. A real handful. Ah, but she was always after better, our Maggie. Not good enough down here for the likes of her. But she got you, Reverend. I'd say she got you hook, line, and sinker!"

Michael nearly choked, commencing a violent coughing fit that quickly put a stop to Frankie's soapbox rant. The sergeant smacked Michael on the back and glared at Frankie.

"That's enough, Frankie. Show some respect and let me remind you that the reverend and . . . erm . . . his wife are well respected in several circles, which might go against you if this were to go further. Now, all we're asking is for a nice letter, saying you're sorry for any distress but admitting to nothing. Understand? That's the way to put the skids on this, would you agree with me, Frankie?"

Frankie's smile faded. "I did nothing. Laughed at her, maybe," he said, suddenly looking worried. "She's the one who flew off the handle," he added, resisting the urge to laugh at his unintended pun.

He was still miffed that she'd disappeared off one day with no explanation. Frankie had been sweet on her since he could walk – still was, maybe. Silly old Maggie. But she had a bit of pull now, married to that reverend of hers, and there was no way he was going to upset his ma with a possible court case.

"Yeah, all right," he agreed. "If that's what you want. But I'll tell you, I'm no good at writing, so if you'll write it, I'll send it," Frankie offered.

The reverend extended his hand and Frankie took it. You can have her, Frankie thought to himself. It was time for him to move on.

Michael prayed it would be enough when he delivered the letter to her a few days later, accompanied by tea and toast on a tray. He watched her read the rustic yet heartfelt note, apologising for causing her distress. She ripped it open, scanned it, read it, reread it. He watched as she opened her mouth in protest.

"Surprise," he said, pulling out the keys of the shiny Triumph 2000 that now sat in the driveway of Knockmore House. "I think a safer form of transport might be required, dearest," Michael smiled woodenly.

Margot dropped the letter, her eyes lighting up, and a little piece of Michael's heart broke – hook, line, and sinker.

Margot Montgomery

Then — 1967

Margot adored looking out of the parlour window at the shiny silver car in the driveway, carefully parked at precisely the correct angle to ensure it was visible from the road. She found it almost regal being driven through the town, headscarf knotted under her quickly developing double chin. The ostentatious gesture of the vehicle had indeed served to appease her following that dreadful business with those brutes, giving her a much-needed lift in spirits.

Her community visitations had become few and far between in the last six months. Dear Mrs Sheppard had passed away suddenly, now reunited with horny old Mr Sheppard, and Mr Cooke had gone to live with his son and daughter-in-law, may the Lord have mercy on their nasal passages. She'd steadfastly avoided learning to drive the Triumph, knowing that Michael would recommence issuing the dreaded list of foot casualties for her to call upon. Sitting in the passenger seat, Margot would sometimes glance at him fondly. Indeed, if she squinted for long enough, she could imagine she was being driven instead by a handsome young suitor and not a staid middle-aged reverend.

Margot swore she'd never get on a bicycle again after

the horrific incident, which she still found difficult to forget. Michael assured her that those involved were heavily reprimanded by the sergeant and would cause her no further distress. Even she had to admit that she was now treated with more respect and people looked down reverently as she passed them in the town. The story of Frankie O'Shea and her witch-hunt against him had travelled fast through the Estates. No one was now brave enough to risk giving Margot a sideways glance for fear of being prosecuted for visual assault – and she felt triumphant, like her car. Very few people from the Estates owned one and in her mind, it once again thrust her to the pinnacle of Knockmore society.

A pleasant little routine settled upon the vicarage. Margot rose later than Michael, eradicating the need to listen to his morning babble. She took her time in the mornings, enjoying breakfast in the dining room alone, opening the odd letter and pretending to read the paper. She'd then issue Mrs Walsh with her daily duties before walking through the garden, picking at a stray weed here, watering a plant there.

This was followed by her mid-morning break, consisting of coffee in the parlour, where she watched passers-by staring in enviously. Mrs Walsh delivered a small silver tray each day at precisely 11 a.m., accompanied by a scone with cream and jam. At precisely 11.02 each day, Mrs Walsh closed the door of the parlour behind her, threw her eyes up to heaven and blessed herself. The tedious afternoons were still filled with multiple callers for the reverend, when it was Margot's turn to deliver the tray before exiting the room and throwing her own eyes up to heaven.

"Marvellous news, dearest," Michael said as he blustered

into the parlour one morning just as she was smoothing a great big lump of cream onto her scone.

"Yes, Michael. I wonder what it could be . . . another funeral, perhaps," she quipped, frustrated by the interruption.

"Ah . . . um . . . not quite, Margot. You've been invited to join a club! What fun," he enthused.

"A club? For God's sake, Michael, haven't I enough on my plate?" she said, licking the cream off her fingers. "What sort of club?"

"Well, they call it the RWC, the Reverends' Wives Club," he chuckled. "All a bit of fun. The archdeacon tells me it's a great support system."

Margot knew Michael would have bent over backwards for the archdeacon if he'd asked him. He was a tedious old man, full of self-importance.

"And what do they do, pray tell, in this club?" she asked, bored already.

"Well, they host a luncheon in their various homes and sit about discussing the trials of being second in command to a man of God, I imagine," he guessed, nearly choking with laughter.

"Oh, sounds all right, actually," Margot said, sitting up.

She'd have plenty to say on the subject and perhaps it would be jolly to have a little circle of her own of like-minded, refined individuals. She'd enjoy seeing their houses, confident Knockmore was most likely the superior residence, despite the fact she'd been asking for months to have the house repainted at the very least.

"It's Saturday week, hosted by Lillian Middleton, at her home in Killashee. Perhaps you should buy yourself a new frock for the occasion," he offered.

Margot couldn't believe her ears. Michael must

genuinely want to impress if he was willing to part with money. The purchase of the car had brought about even further adjustments to the household outgoings, allowing no unnecessary purchases, and much of Margot's wardrobe already consisted of items donated by Mrs Kidney.

"Oh my, too many goodies for you, Margot," Mrs Kidney teased after the seamstress pointed out that the most recent plaid skirt offering needed minimal adjustment.

Margot looked at her settled form in the mirror. Either Mrs Kidney was shrinking, or she was gaining weight. Margot turned to the side and attempted to suck in her once flat stomach, now a rounded tartan mass. She rubbed her hand over it.

"Any news at all, dear?" Mrs Kidney asked, raising her eyebrow inquisitively.

No, no, Mrs Kidney. Still barren, she wanted to shout. She'd thought that Mrs Sheppard's passing would cease the inquisition on her maternal status, but almost three years of marriage and nothing to show for it was a constant concern for others. Lately, she thought about nothing else.

Mrs Kidney put her arm around her. "I suggest a trip to Dr Gallagher might be just what the doctor ordered," Mrs Kidney said, snorting at her joke. "It's been almost three years, Margot, and you're not getting any younger. In my time, Mr Kidney just had to look at me and I fell pregnant," she winked.

"Yes, perhaps I will," Margot said, promising to make an appointment, if only so she no longer had to listen to stories of everyone else's husband's fertile eyes.

But for now, Margot had more pressing items on her agenda. She needed to put her best foot forward for the RWC meeting and she knew exactly where to go. His 'n'

Hers, the boutique in the centre of town, was owned by Nancy Quinlan, who prided herself in stocking all the latest fashions for both men and women. Nancy, now in her late forties, had spent many years working in London in the fashion industry and had returned to Knockmore eight years ago to care for her ageing mother. No sooner had her mother popped her clogs than Nancy had sold the farm left to her as the only child and bought the shop on Main Street. She now lived above it in a flat that Nancy described as "bijoux", whatever the hell that meant, and used Knockmore Main Street as if it were a Paris catwalk. Margot had heard the ladies in the butcher's describe her as "an exotic flower among the daisies".

The "Her" section took up almost the entire premises, consisting of chic two-pieces, dresses and hats. The "His" section consisted of tweed jackets and linen trousers that no man in Knockmore would ever be seen dead in. None the less, Nancy had a handful of wealthier customers who kept her ticking along. Everyone else from Knockmore travelled to the larger town of Lismore that catered for the tighter purse strings of the Estates. Margot used to watch the window display change every Friday from the butcher's window and longed to sashay into the boutique to buy a jaunty hat. Well, she now had just the occasion.

On the Thursday before her luncheon with the reverends' wives, Margot put on her best skirt and jacket, courtesy of Mrs Kidney, and set off to town to be dressed by the infamous Nancy. Michael drove her in the Triumph and she made him circle the town twice to ensure he could pull up right outside the door, where she took her time gracefully exiting the vehicle.

"I'll walk home, thank you, Michael," she said, waving

119

him off, thrilled at the prospect of swinging her labelled bag through Knockmore.

Margot pushed the door of the boutique open, relishing the sound of the little bell above the door announcing her arrival over the threshold of the coveted boutique. Margot took in the plush carpet, the glistening light fittings and the high desk at which Nancy was sitting smoking a cigarette with an extended elegant filter.

"Good morning. Mrs Montgomery, isn't it?" Nancy teetered off the stool, hand extended to Margot.

"Yes, good morning, Miss Quinlan," she said, taking her delicate hand.

"How can I help you? And please, call me Nancy. I despise formality. In London, we rarely use the formal any more."

"Oh. Yes, certainly, Nancy," Margot stumbled, in awe of the confidence and worldliness of the exchange.

"Would you like to look around a little before we try on? Please . . . " Nancy gestured towards the rails.

A beautiful lemon-coloured dress and jacket immediately caught Margot's eye, followed by a pencil skirt and matching top with a boat neck in raw silk.

"Beautiful," Margot whispered, running her fingers over the soft material. "I have an important luncheon with several reverends' wives on Saturday and I was hoping you might have something appropriate."

"Certainly." Nancy led her towards the rear of the shop, where the colours faded from sherbet to earthy. "Perhaps some of these would be suitable," Nancy said, lifting a navy shin-length skirt and matronly jacket from the rail. "Or this?" she offered, holding up a beige-and-brown patterned dress in a stiff starched fabric.

"Well, I was hoping to try some of the lighter pieces at

the front." Margot waved towards the sherbet wonders.

"I'm not sure I'll have your size in the newer items, but I shall indeed look. What size are you, Margot?"

"A perfect 10," Margot answered confidently.

Nancy stepped back and slowly looked Margot up and down. "Of course," Nancy smiled knowingly. "And might I offer congratulations to you and the reverend? What wonderful news!"

Margot's eyebrows furrowed. "Ah, yes," she said unsurely before realising to what Nancy was referring. "Silly me, the car, of course," she laughed. "Yes, it was a huge surprise. Michael bought it for me and will be teaching me to drive."

This time it was Nancy's turn to look confused. "The car?" she laughed. "No, my dear. The baby!" she said, reaching over and patting Margot's belly.

Margot jumped back, immediately swatting her hand away.

"I beg your pardon?"

Nancy looked shocked. "I'm so sorry . . . I just assumed . . . please forgive me . . . " Nancy said, wishing the plush carpet would swallow her, all of her earlier confidence disappearing into the smoky air.

"How dare you! How dare you!" Margot snapped. "You can shove your cheap clothes." She picked up her bag. "I'd rather drive to Dublin than shop here and let this be a reminder to you to be *more formal* in future," Margot issued sourly, sweeping past her, knocking the mannequin wearing the sugary pink version of the lemon suit. She slammed the door behind her and rushed up the street.

* * *

121

Margot silently fumed as she sat waiting to be seen by the doctor. She'd certainly gained a little weight, but what an insult. It was true her diet had improved radically over the years, but Mrs Walsh's cooking was rather dull. Surely that couldn't be contributing to the unexplained weight gain. There must be more to it. Margot's absence in the kitchen did, of course, mean that she never bore witness to Mrs Walsh's secret addiction to butter. Dear old Nelly slathered everything in great big dollops of creamy butter – half to add flavour and half as a little joke as she covertly observed the reverend's wife's bottom enlarge with each passing month.

Revenge is a dish best served sweet, Nelly would chuckle to herself as she spooned a second serving of fat onto the carrot batons that Margot insisted were cut uniformly. The fact that Margot had been completely sedentary for months, ate copious amounts of cream and insisted on dessert every evening didn't help, all resulting in a bottom the size of the bin truck and at least an addition of 8 onto her supposed dress size.

Dr Gallagher was met by a rather flustered Margot that morning as he ushered her into his office for the consultation.

"Mrs Montgomery, how is the reverend?" he enquired.

"The reverend is very well, Doctor."

"And you, Margot?"

"Well . . . " she stumbled. "I am well, but I have a concern of a delicate nature, Doctor, one that's difficult to speak about."

"Margot, this is a confidential place, so please speak freely."

"Well, Doctor, it seems I've gained an amount of unexplained weight," she began.

The floodgates opened and she uncharacteristically

poured her heart out to him. She told him how *stupid bloody Nancy Quinlan* had mistaken her womanly form for the pregnancy that she longed for, how no one wanted to be in her company, how she was second fiddle to the reverend.

"And try as I might, they can't seem to accept me, nor respect me and, well, if I had a child of my own . . . " she trailed off. "But while I might look pregnant, I most certainly am not, Doctor," she cried.

Dr Gallagher watched with interest as the tears fell from her usually austere eyes and slowly rolled down her healthy rounded cheeks. Margot accepted the tissue he handed her and loudly blew her nose. Dr Gallagher felt sorry for the great Margot Montgomery, but it was clear to him that she did very little to help herself. She was aloof, snobbish, angry and always picking battles with the universe.

"There, there, Margot. Let's start at the beginning." He took a breath, wondering how he could tell her that the womanly form she referred to was, in fact, a vast weight gain for a young woman with no children. "For a start, if you feel you've gained a little weight, let's perhaps look at your diet. Has your size greatly altered?" he started, trying not to ignite her temper.

"Perhaps a little, I suppose, Doctor. But I'm thirty now and I'm getting on. Maybe I've just grown into myself."

"Um, yes, perhaps. Does your diet include much confectionery?" he probed.

"Well, we are privileged at the vicarage to have a full-time housekeeper," she explained. "She caters for the home, so perhaps a little more confectionery than usual."

Dr Gallagher tried not to laugh. My God, she was a tough nut to crack. The earlier tears had quickly evaporated and the exhausting façade was slowly creeping back.

"Okay. Let's refrain from all niceties and revert to three square meals a day. I'll give you some information before you leave. Ask the *catering staff* to remove butter and sugar from your diet with immediate effect," he advised. "Introduce daily exercise. Maybe you should get back in the saddle, Margot," he suggested.

"We have the Triumph now, Doctor, no need for the pushbike."

"Well, then I'm prescribing a brisk daily walk and you should notice a visible difference in no time. Now, I think you need to get back out into the community – a young mind needs a focus. And perhaps it's time to reconcile with your family, Margot. It may alleviate your stress," he said, leaning back in his chair, ready for the assault.

Margot looked at her feet.

"You know, your sister Rosie is expecting her first child and Florrie just last week accepted a marriage proposal from Sergeant Hughes, and . . . " The doctor was on a roll now.

"*What*?" Margot looked up. "Sergeant Hughes?" she shouted.

"Yes, they've have been courting for over a year now."

"She must be pregnant – the brazen hussy."

Dr Gallagher coughed. It was like watching two different people. The doctor was almost impressed with how quickly Margot could revert to Maggie and immediately back again.

"No, Margot. She's not with child. But these are happy events that you should be a part of. It's 1967. We should all be able to exist together and support each other, no?"

"Dr Gallagher, let me remind you, we're here to talk about me and my ailments," she snapped.

She'd heard Rosie had married a construction worker last year, moved to England, but how in God's name had Flo, with her stringy hair and buck teeth, managed to snag the sergeant? The Station House was a fine home, though not as grand as Knockmore, of course. And Rosie, pregnant? Before her! They'd been quick enough to shove their mother into a home as soon as Margot left and look at them now. It was too much.

"Dr Gallagher, I am going to speak plainly. I need to have a baby. Right now, as soon as possible. What can you do to help?" she asked, her eyes narrowing as she awaited her prescription.

Oh, Christ, he thought. There was very little he could do to "help" impregnate Margot, aside from doing it himself. So instead, he gently probed her about her menstrual cycle, listening as she revealed that she was quite regular in her *women's ways*.

"And copulation, Margot? Is it regular?"

"Very healthy, Doctor. The last Friday of the month," she said proudly.

Dr Gallagher nearly fell off his chair. He managed to stifle a giggle by coughing loudly and briefly turning to jot something in his notes. It wasn't unheard of for women to be innocent in the ways of conception, but this! The last Friday of the month? Good grief! Most of the young married couples around here fell pregnant in the first few months, but one shot a month doesn't a baby make.

"Mrs Montgomery, for the best chance of conception, copulation needs to take place at least four to five times a month. Now, for you, based on your individual cycle, that would mean towards the middle of each month." He watched her eyes widen. "That coupled with a good diet

125

and plenty of 'exercise' should increase your chances greatly," he finished.

"Thank you, Doctor. We'll make it six to seven times, just to be sure," she issued, determination shining in her eyes.

"Best of luck, Margot," he grinned.

It was the first time that he'd needed to explain the *unsafe* time. Nowadays, the women of Knockmore were more concerned with when the *safe* time was, trying not to add another mouth to feed to the four or five they already had. He shook his head, exhausted. He stood up to fetch his next patient from the waiting room and glanced at the calendar on the back of the door. Midmonth. The reverend best prepare himself.

"Next," he shouted.

Margot Montgomery

Then – 1968

At first, Michael had been thrilled with the midmonth extra-curricular activities and on a Thursday no less, which began the very evening of Margot's unplanned visit to Dr Gallagher. That first night, Michael had settled himself into bed, folding the sheets down neatly in the same manner he did every night, and had just finished his prayers, when he heard the gentle knock on the door.

"Oh . . . um . . . yes?" he called.

"Good evening, darling," Margot purred, slinking around the door.

She was wearing a robe, previously owned by Mrs Kidney, bought to lure Mr Kidney back into her arms following somewhat of a dry spell brought about after a little prostate trouble. The lemon satin gown, trimmed in alluring ivory lace, had either worked and was no longer required, or had miserably failed and been passed to Margot as a conception aid.

"Dearest?" he stammered. "Are you unwell?" Michael asked upon seeing his wife manoeuvring her ample form around the door like a giant shining jar of lemon curd. Michael sat bolt upright in bed, pulling the flat sheet around his neck.

"On the contrary, Michael. I'm very well – very well, indeed." Her lips curled into a mysterious smile.

"What on earth is it then, Margot?" he asked, staring at her undulating eyebrows.

"I was just feeling lonely, Reverend, all by myself in that great big room. I thought a little company might be just what the doctor ordered," she added with a wink.

"Ah . . . yes . . . all right . . . I see . . . sit for a while?" He patted the bed, miserably failing to read the signals.

Margot closed the door behind her, awestruck how someone who prided himself on being so in tune with the congregation could be so clueless when it came to his wife. Now or never, she thought. Time to take the bull by the horns. She inhaled, filling her lungs with enough oxygen to survive the next sixty-three seconds, then slowly untied her gown and let it drop to the floor in a puddle of lemony desire.

"Margot! You'll catch your death!" Michael's jaw fell with the gown as she revealed all that God had given her, helped along by Mrs Walsh's butter obsession.

"Michael," she whispered, launching herself at him, snatching her hand away as he tried to seize it for the aperitif prayer and kissing him to seal his saintly lips.

She tugged at the flat sheet with her free hand, pulling it back to reveal his striped pyjamas, straining in just the right place.

"*Margot* . . . dearest . . . wait . . . " he muffled from behind her pressing lips.

"Now, Michael!" Margot urged, hauling him on top of her with the strength of a mother lifting a burning vehicle off a child.

Swept up in the most erotic episode of his life, he

obliged. She closed her eyes and concentrated, counting to sixty and finishing with three, two, one as he exhaled and fell on top of her.

"Well done, Michael," she uttered, slipping out from under his limp form, collecting the gown from its resting place and dashing from the room, leaving him exhausted and speechless.

She closed the door to her room behind her, took out her diary and wrote DAY ONE in block letters under the date, suddenly filled with hope for the future and what lay ahead.

"Good morning, Reverend," she purred the next morning.

Michael had whistled his way into the dining room, stopping when he saw Margot sitting at the table.

"You must be ravenous," she smiled, pouring his coffee and placing the customary two boiled eggs in front of him.

"Ah, um, yes, indeed . . . thank you, Margot," he grinned, pleased by her unusually sunny demeanour. "Everything all right, dearest?" he questioned, not sure what had got into her.

"Marvellous," she smiled. "Actually, I thought I might pay a visit to Mr Cooke at his son's house. See how he's getting on there."

Michael almost spat out his tea. "Mr Cooke, really?" Good Lord! maybe she was possessed.

"Yes, poor old thing." Margot took a sip of her coffee, her eyes never leaving his.

"Would you like a lift?"

"Not at all. Lovely morning, I think I'll walk. See you tonight?" she winked, leaving Michael perplexed.

Margot fixed her straw hat to her head and smiled to herself. She gently ran her hand over her stomach, wondering if last night's efforts were already taking effect. Not, now, Margot, she thought. Success requires effort. She knew that. She picked up her brown leather bag and marched out of the front door at a pace that her body hadn't encountered in years, swinging the bag enthusiastically.

She walked up the main street, stuck her nose in the air as she passed His 'n' Hers and briefly waved at Mr Kidney placing the expensive cuts of meat at the front of the window, backed up by the grizzly bits that required extra chewing, and arrived at her destination. She had no intention of visiting Mr Cooke. She'd had enough of a sensory overload last night and instead strode through the gates of the library, whizzing straight past Miss Joyce, who was watering the window boxes either side of the heavy wooden door.

Harriet Joyce stopped, confused. She thought she'd imagined it for a moment until she peered through the window to see a straw hat bobbing up and down through the aisles. No rest for the wicked, Harriet thought, placing the watering can down and taking up her station behind her high wooden desk. Harriet watched as The Hat gathered speed before settling in Human Science and listened as books were pulled from their home and placed on a reading table, then The Hat disappeared. Creeping out from behind her station, she peered down the fiction aisle. Oh, dear God, give me strength.

Harriet knew the reverend's wife all right. She knew her when she was a teenager, when Maggie used to come to the library with her sisters to peer at the magazines. Harriet remembered seeing Maggie stuff a copy of *Woman's Way* down her school skirt. She also remembered Maggie telling her in no uncertain terms to "Go and shite," when she'd asked the plucky teen to return it. Harriet had called the sergeant to report it, but the next morning had found the copy of the magazine outside the library door. For some reason, Harriet still remembered the headline printed on the cover: "How to Marry the Ideal Man." She'd stopped displaying the magazines after that, having previously always been a firm believer in expanding the minds of the young women of Knockmore, not limiting them. But of course the removal of the magazines, and the need to ask to see them now, meant that Maggie hadn't set foot inside the library since – until today, of course.

Harriet grabbed her feather duster and headed down the poetry aisle for a closer look. Nowadays, it appeared, from what she could make out from between the rows of books and after having already married the ideal man, that the reverend's wife's preferred topic seemed to be Human Anatomy. Harriet peered over the books, watching Margot ensconced in her research, and sneezed unexpectedly from the recently disturbed dust. Margot looked up.

"Can I help you, Mrs Montgomery?" Harriet asked, materialising from behind Irish History.

Margot tried to cover the giant hard-back books, scooping her arms around them. "No, thank you," she responded as one of the books fell to the floor and opened on a page with a large diagram of the male reproductive organ. Margot flushed.

"Let me get that for you." Harriet bent to pick it up, replacing it on the desk under Margot's nose. "Quite the selection you have there. Are you sure I can't point you in the right direction?"

"Well . . . I . . . I'm not sure . . . I wanted to see . . . " Margot stammered.

She couldn't make head nor tail of the contents. What on earth was a cervix? She'd just been reading about a temperature method, but Margot wasn't sure if it was her temperature or Michael's, and the temperature of what exactly. And what in God's name was viscosity?

Immediately sensing her distress, Harriet pulled up a chair and sat beside her.

"Mrs Montgomery, when I trained as a librarian, many moons ago, I took an oath and within it, I'm bound by confidentiality. You can ask me anything and I cannot and *will not* discuss it further – unless there's a theft in the library, of course," Harriet said, raising her eyebrows for the last part. "Let me assist you."

Margot looked at her and then back at the disarray of books on the table. It was on the tip of her tongue to tell her to *go and shite* again, remembering the day the sergeant had pulled into the Estates demanding she return the copy of *Woman's Way*.

"Well, perhaps you could assist me," she agreed, knowing full well that there was no possible way she could stuff the hard-backed copy of *Human Anatomy* down her nylons. "The thing is," Margot began, taking a deep breath. "Well . . . I can't seem to get pregnant. I've been to see the doctor, who issued basic advice, but I thought one can always do more." She looked down.

"I see. Well, let's look and see what we can find. If there's information to be found, it can be found in a book," Harriet assured. "Let me just put the sign on the door. I think we may need some privacy for such a sensitive research topic."

There was a vulnerability to the reverend's wife that tugged at her conscience. Besides, Harriet loved a challenge.

The unlikely pair sat and rifled through the books, gradually making a conception plan for Margot. They eventually managed to decipher the temperature method.

"See here, Margot, you must chart your temperature daily and when it peaks, you . . . well . . . go for it, so to speak," she encouraged.

Harriet herself had never married nor had a relationship, so she found the research subject fascinating; although even she drew the line at the section covering cervical mucous.

"Now, with the healthy eating plan and a solid exercise regime, there should be little Margots along in no time," Harriet laughed, closing the books and resting her hand on Margot's.

"Harriet, I can't thank you enough. I'm delighted that seven consecutive conjugal visits may not be a requirement," Margot said, relieved.

"No, indeed. I can hardly imagine one." Harriet shook her head. "But keep the faith, Margot. It took my sister many years to conceive and let's not forget, there's always the option of adoption. There are plenty of babies who'd be fortunate to land themselves in the home of the reverend."

"No, not for us, I'm afraid." Margot shook her head. "Adoption would be unsuitable for such an upstanding family. Not suitable at all. If we can't have our own child, well then it's simply not meant to be."

"Well, let's take one step at a time." Harriet decided not to push the delicate subject. "Now, I must get back to work," she said, unlocking the door.

"I'll keep you posted," Margot called over her shoulder.

For the next two nights, Margot had again delivered the unexpected knock on the reverend's door. The second night was met with double the surprise of the first and the added enthusiasm of a record seventy-one seconds from Michael, leaving Margot a little light-headed from the lack of oxygen as a result of the additional eight seconds. The third night resulted in seventy-eight seconds and Margot practically hallucinating. By the grace of God, when Margot checked her temperature on the evening of the fourth night, it appeared incompatible with conception.

Margot was intensely disappointed by the arrival of her monthlies following the first month's efforts. She'd prayed every night for success and when she noticed the telltale sign of failure, she was momentarily deterred before setting about putting the next steps together for the second attempt.

Over the coming months, Michael witnessed several changes in both his wife and in their day-to-day life at the vicarage. First, it was the severe lack of flavour in their meals brought about by the reduction in butter. There was also no longer any dessert during the week and Mrs Walsh's apple tarts were now reserved for Sunday alone. Margot rose earlier each morning and at the time when she was usually taking her morning coffee and scone, she was now often seen marching up and down the road with purpose.

"How about a spin in the car, dearest?" Michael offered one evening following a rather bland boiled chicken and broccoli meal.

Margot was sitting by the window in the parlour ensconced in a book. She looked radiant. In a short space of time, she'd slimmed down and seemed far more settled.

"Yes, indeed, let me just finish this passage," she said.

The evening sun caught her face and he was momentarily mesmerised. The past few months and her renewed interest in him had sparked feelings that reminded him of the young lady he'd first spied staring up at him from the church pew. Had it only been three years? It seemed longer.

"How about we teach you to drive?" Michael asked, and she immediately dropped the book and looked up wide-eyed.

Perhaps it *was* time he gave her a new focus.

"Oh, Michael, I'd love that," she smiled. "I'll be right with you," she said, rushing up the stairs to retrieve her headscarf.

"Let's head to the beach outside Knockmore. Hopefully, the tide will be out and we can have a good run at it for your maiden voyage," Michael laughed as they drove through the town and out towards the coast.

It was indeed the safest place to learn, with nothing much to hit, and Michael always deemed the sea to be one of the more relaxing elements.

"Righto," he said, stopping the car on the flat sand, leaving the engine running. "Hop in."

As she scuttled round the front of the car, her headscarf caught the wind, fluttering like a kite. Margot reached up to grab it before it flew off into the evening sky, letting out a natural youthful laugh, and he felt as though he were seeing her for the first time. How had he missed it?

"Right, let's begin. This one is the accelerator," Michael pointed out. "The clutch is to the left and the most important one of all is the brake," he instructed. "You mustn't be afraid to use it!"

"Yes, okay, clutch, accelerator, brake," she repeated. "Got it."

Michael then detailed the gears, the mirrors and indicators before asking her to put her foot on the clutch and put the car into first gear.

"Now, Margot. When I tell you, you're going to

accelerate slowly while simultaneously releasing the clutch at a nice slow, steady pace."

"Yes, Michael, get on with it!" she said, ready to try.

Margot gently put her foot on the accelerator and felt the engine rev beneath her. She felt a ripple of excitement surge through her, far greater than any other ripple she'd ever felt before.

"Goodness, Michael, it's mighty," she said excitedly.

"Now gently does it, Margot," he tutored, demonstrating the action her feet should make on the pedals using his hands on his lap.

Margot slowly accelerated but quickly lifted her foot off the clutch, causing the vehicle to lurch forwards at high speed and promptly cut out.

"Good grief, Margot, slower," Michael said, gathering himself after the sudden thrust.

Undeterred, she fired the engine once more, forgetting to take the car out of gear, and the Triumph once again objected, leaping forwards.

"Ah . . . okay . . . let's go through it once more," Michael offered, his upper lip now emitting small apprehensive beads of sweat.

"I can do this, Michael!" Margot answered, staring ahead, her eyes ablaze with determination.

"Very well, Margot," Michael said, starting to shake with fear.

He once again explained the stages, removing the gathering moisture from his lip with his forefinger as he spoke. She lifted her foot from the clutch, with the same speed one would have run across burning coals, and the car lurched again.

"Goddammit!" she shouted.

"Language, Margot." Michael was now quite pale.

"I can do it!" she said through gritted teeth.

The pattern continued several more times, leaving Michael drenched in sweat as her resolution grew. The earlier softness left her face and her nostrils were now flaring like a bull as she crunched the gears impatiently.

On the tenth go, Margot raised her foot off the clutch as slowly as she could, her left leg shaking with adrenaline as she held the clutch in position. She removed it a little further and as she did so, the Triumph took off in a series of bunny hops down the beach.

"*Brake, Margot, brake!*" Michael shouted, clutching the side of his seat.

Margot ignored him. "I'm doing it, Michael. Look! I can do it," she shouted as the bunny hops merged and the car began to move smoothly.

She pressed the accelerator, testing the feel of the engine beneath her. She heard it race and pressed further. Flinging her arm out of the open window as she drove, Margot felt her hand whip back against the wind, the cool air injecting her with victory.

"Both hands on the wheel please, Margot," Michael shouted nervously, wishing he'd closed the driver's window before the momentous maiden voyage.

Margot didn't hear him. Drunk on achievement, she looked out towards the sea and saw *them* staring back at her. Her two sisters, watching her, Flo's stringy hair blowing in the breeze and Rosie's stomach strained with pregnancy. She watched their jealous faces as she waved, rotating her hand like royalty.

"You have the baby, but I have the Triumph!" she shouted.

"Watch out, Margot!" Michael screamed, grabbing the

wheel and pulling her back to reality as he swerved the car out of the path of an enormous rock. "Brake! Brake!"

Margot launched her foot at the brake, once again forgetting the clutch, and the car came to an abrupt stop just inches from the water's edge.

"Thank God, thank God." Michael threw the car door open and collapsed on the sandy surface on his hands and knees, puffing for air.

Margot pushed open her door and stepped out, allowing the sea to lap over her shoes as she looked back to where the imaginary sisters had been standing, watching her. She'd done it until she hadn't, always so close but never quite getting there. Good but not good enough, but she'd keep trying. She wouldn't give up. She put her hands on her hips, threw her head back and laughed.

"Margot, what's funny? Who were you shouting at? What's got into you? What baby?" Michael looked up, shocked.

The light had begun to fade and she looked different, almost menacing, as she turned to him.

"Oh, stand up, Michael, for God's sake. Just stand up."

He stood, the earlier blissful moments swallowed back from where they'd come.

"Let's go back," he whispered, climbing back into the car.

Back to where they'd been before the sunlight had caught Margot's face and clouded his brain. Back to Knockmore House, where unbeknown to Michael, the thermometer waited on the bedside table, ready to reveal a temperature ripe for conception.

Margot Montgomery

Then – 1969

"But it's been two years, Dr Gallagher." Margot sat impatiently opposite him looking for answers. "And things don't appear to be progressing in the manner I'd hoped for," she said.

It had been a gruelling time of healthy eating and religiously taking daily walks to increase her stamina. She'd already worn out two pairs of Mrs Kidney's brown leather lace-ups, not to mention the other business, and she'd had enough of that, too.

"There, there, Margot. I understand it's hard to keep the faith, but you look tremendously healthy – a far cry from the girl who sat before me on your first visit," he smiled encouragingly. "You've done everything in your power to increase your chances and unfortunately, now is the time for patience."

Indeed, she was losing the will to live, her initial enthusiasm diminishing by the second and now replaced with obsession. She took her temperature daily, making sure she was ready to spring at Michael as soon as she noticed the habitual spike. Her diary was a mass of scribbled notes and stars, marking the days she'd have to endure Michael bearing down on top of her, and she was now so in tune with her body that she could feel the signs of ovulation without even reading them.

Owing to her now slighter frame, towards the middle of each month she'd notice a fullness to her breasts, no longer the great big matronly chest of before. Margot would sense the familiar twinges in her abdomen as the egg was released and floated to its position to await intervention, which always failed to arrive. Then a few weeks later, she'd experience the dreaded pain of inadequacy.

"Is there any further way to help things along, Doctor? Am I missing something?" she persisted.

Margot was confident based on her extensive research sessions with the librarian that the problem must lie firmly in Michael's court. There was no doubt she was ovulating each month and ensuring regular sexual intercourse at the correct times, but the entire process had gone from being manageable at first to quite unbearable. If it were at all possible, she'd have asked him to collect a *sample* and done the deed herself in the privacy of her room.

"I'm afraid at this stage, Margot, we must let nature take its course," the doctor told her, trying to wrap up the visit. "Have you discussed how you're feeling with Michael?" he asked, at a loss as to what to suggest next.

"No, Dr Gallagher. The reverend is a very busy man."

Well, too busy for her, certainly. It had taken him several months to click as to what was going on and to realise that he was not, in fact, the object of his wife's affection but the victim of her goal. But he, too, felt an element of failure when month after month in place of tidings of joy, he'd await the knock at his door, which of late had changed to a pounding of impending doom. The enticing lemon gown that had at first tickled his imagination was over time replaced with a flannel nightdress, which in recent months was no longer removed during the attack.

"Come along, Michael, get on with it!" she'd shouted the last time and he was becoming quite terrified of the wild-eyed apparition stood at the foot his bed.

Michael prayed for an answer, begged that it would all end well, resolved to persevere through these hard times, but he was finding it difficult, especially with the pressures of his job, and lately he felt very under pressure. It was hard to concentrate on a new life when he'd been so intensely affected by the recent passing of a young parishioner.

Of course, it was part and parcel of his job. As a man of God, he had to accept that.

"We are only travelling through this world, on our way to a greater place," he'd so often say to lend support to those left behind. "God has a reason for everything. We may never understand it, but we must trust His will."

Michael tried to treat death as a celebration of life during his sermons, but even for him, with his unwavering faith, he always found the passing of a child a bitter pill to swallow.

The most recent was a boy who was just eight when he was first diagnosed with leukaemia, and Michael had watched him and his family battle for two long years before the child bravely took his leave, surrounded by his family. It had knocked Michael, causing him to wrestle with his faith ashamedly, and he'd had a tough week trying to console the grieving family while he was simultaneously struggling with the injustice of such a bright young boy being torn away too soon.

"I think I'll turn in, dearest," he told Margot shortly after dinner the day before the boy's funeral. "It's been a long week."

Margot barely looked up as he left the dining room, shoulders slumped. It was purely coincidental, of course, that young boy's passing coincided with Margot experiencing the familiar niggling in her abdomen and did not, as it should have, deter her plans for the evening.

"Ah, dearest, come in, of course," he smiled weakly, hearing the knock at his door but an hour later. Michael looked drawn as he sat there in his bed, the weight of the world weighing him down. "What can I do for you?" he asked, hoping it wasn't as he suspected.

"Are you unwell?" Margot asked, sitting on the edge of the bed.

"No, no, just a little down, perhaps . . . can't help but see his face. What a brave boy," he said, his mind drifting back to the child.

"Yes, indeed, terrible business," Margot agreed.

"It was his mother, really, which got me. I've never heard a sound like it. It was as if someone had severed a limb," he said, describing the final moments where he'd watched the boy's mother gripping on to the final flicker of life in her beloved son. "And his sisters . . . it was like they were frozen, they were so still at the end of his bed. I thought their father was going to break through the wall, he punched it so hard. The wall crumbled, Margot!"

He stopped then, closing his eyes, remembering how the boy's body had shuddered, relinquishing the last of the air from his lungs, his body finally beaten by the disease.

"I've never seen anything like it, Margot – devastation. And well, for the first time I can't seem to make sense of it for them. I can't seem to find the words."

Margot watched the tears smart his eyes. She reached out and put her arms around him and he gratefully accepted her embrace. Margot held him for a few minutes, lying beside him, holding his hand, and then reached up and gently kissed him. Michael pulled her closer, enjoying the physical comfort but misreading the signs, as she immediately tried to hoist him on top of her.

"Margot, please. I'm exhausted. Could we just . . . ?"

"Just what?" she spat.

"It's just I feel upset – lost, really," he attempted.

"Lost? And how do you think I feel, Michael?" she snapped. "I don't want to talk about someone else's child. What about *my* child? Where's my child?" She threw her hands in the air. "I've done everything to be the perfect reverend's wife. Am I not good enough for you? All I'm asking for is a child, but you can't even oblige," she screamed, frustrated by his slight. "It's always about someone else, isn't it? I'll always be second fiddle to everyone else. You're pathetic. A pathetic excuse for a man."

"Margot, please. I'm sorry . . . "

"Yes, me too, Reverend. Me too."

She didn't wait for an answer. She gathered herself and stormed out of the room, slamming the door behind her.

Margot sat on her bed fuming, grabbed the thermometer and hurled it into the bin. Taking out her diary, she opened it and scribbled violently on each page – months and months of persisting with a miserably failed plan . . . Mrs Walsh had told her all about Rosie and her daughter in England, and even Florrie now had a son. Bloody Florrie. They'd all managed to get what they wanted except her. She'd made the sacrifices and here she was, stuck. She *would* have a baby! She wouldn't let them all know how she'd failed. She'd *make* it work. She had to.

Margot woke early after a fitful sleep and not wanting

143

to see Michael, she left the house. She was still fuming as she walked briskly to the other side of town towards the Catholic church. She wanted to be somewhere that felt familiar, somewhere away from *them*, away from him.

She walked through the grounds of the church, memories of her youth flooding back as she went. Tired, she sat on the wall just behind the imposing sycamore tree. She closed her eyes, enjoying the early morning silence, but was suddenly disturbed by hurried footsteps and hushed voices. Her ears perked up as she tucked herself closer to the trunk of the tree under the overhanging branches.

"Annie's pregnant – three months gone. Her father will kill her. He'll kill her. She's fifteen years old and he'll murder her. My baby, my poor baby."

Margot listened.

"Come now, Deirdre, he'll come round. It's happened before around here. It won't be the first time and it won't be the last. You'll get through it. The Lord works in mysterious ways. Keep the faith," she heard.

"Please don't tell anyone. I don't want anyone to know, least of all Father Nugent, looking to make an example of her. I just need to figure it out."

"It'll work out, Deirdre, it'll work out."

Margot peered round the tree. She recognised them from the Estates – Deirdre Slaney sobbing as her friend comforted her. Margot was suddenly angry. Furious at the injustice of it all. Here she was, barren and longing for a child, and some young one from the Estates had gone and got herself pregnant, probably the first time, with an unwanted child. It was so bloody unfair! It wasn't right. Not right at all.

She waited for them to scuttle away before emerging

from behind the tree. What should she do? But she knew what she was going to do almost before she asked herself. It was the right thing to do. It was what should be done.

If anyone had seen the reverend's wife coming out of Father Nugent's house the following morning with her coat pulled up round her face, they probably wouldn't have questioned it. It wasn't unusual for the two churches to work together from time to time, especially this close to Christmas. They'd have assumed that they were making final plans towards the candlelit prayer service that took place in the centre of Knockmore every festive season. If they'd witnessed her scuttling up the road, they might have seen the smug little smile on her face. A smile that she could barely contain. She'd done the right thing and in doing so, she'd be rewarded. She was sure of it.

"There's no choice, Annie," Father Nugent explained.

Annie Slaney shook her head, her eyes pleading at her parents. Deirdre Slaney was shaking and her husband sat with his head in his hands as the parish priest spoke to them.

"But who told you, Father Nugent, how did you know?" Deirdre begged.

She wasn't sure what they were going to do, hadn't got that far yet, but she couldn't bear for Annie to be taken away.

"That's neither here nor there, Deirdre. The Lord saw fit that I should intervene. Now, it's the right thing to do. You know that. There's a sin been committed here and we must do what's right. This child will have every chance of a future now."

He went on to tell them about a wealthy family in Dublin – a doctor and his wife.

"They're willing to adopt Annie's baby and give it all

the chances Annie could never offer a child."

"Please, Mam . . . Da, I'm begging you. Don't send me away. Don't take my baby. Please. I'm so sorry. Please."

Annie kneeled in front of her father, who couldn't bring himself to meet her eyes. He was ashamed of her, all of her innocence gone. She'd let him down, let herself down.

"Who is he?" her father asked through gritted teeth. "I'll kill him! Who is he?" he screamed.

"Now, Mr Slaney. This is exactly why this is the right thing to do. One sin can lead to another and another. We must nip it in the bud."

Father Nugent told them about a woman, a midwife, just a few hours away by car, who was willing to take Annie in and deliver the baby safely. Annie would then be allowed to return home as if it had never happened and start her life again.

"It's all arranged."

"It's for the best, love." Deirdre hugged her only child. "You'll be back with me soon. I'll write to you. We'll say you're with your aunt for a while, helping her. Don't make this harder, Annie. Please, Lord, don't make it harder. I'm begging you."

"Please, Da," Annie tried again. "Please!"

But he couldn't look, his eyes as broken as his heart.

Annie walked to the priest's car as if walking to her grave. Deirdre would never forget it, never forget her daughter being taken from her, or the look on her face. It would stay with her until the day she died – her beautiful Annie.

But it was the right thing to do and in doing right, we're always rewarded. Aren't we?

PART TWO

Margot Montgomery

Then – 1970

"She's beautiful," Michael said. "Perfect."

He glanced from the baby to Margot, who was sitting up in bed, cradling the infant. He looked at the silvery halo of hair shimmering around her tiny head like an angel and felt tears prick his eyes as he watched her peacefully sleeping in her mother's arms, her tiny fingers balled into fists, ready to take on the world.

"And how do you feel, dearest?" he asked.

He'd been sure when the moment of arrival finally came that he'd know all about it. He'd been on edge for weeks now awaiting the occasion, praying for the safe arrival of their firstborn, convinced he'd hear the pains of labour, accompanied by possible cursing from the next room. But he'd slept so peacefully the night before, the nurse having assured him that it would more than likely be several more days.

But now here she was.

"Quite well, Michael. It was a long night. I'm tired and a little tender, perhaps," Margot answered, her eyes not leaving the baby.

Michael coughed nervously. "Yes, indeed. Yes, you must

be," he said, his eyes twitching with embarrassment. "I can't believe I slept through. Did you not think to call me?"

"No need. Mrs Montgomery was more than capable," Nurse Abbott quickly assured him.

"Thank you, Nurse. I can't thank you enough and for the last few months also," Michael praised.

"Just doing my job, Reverend," the elderly woman answered, not a smile breaking her sullen mouth.

"Well, we're very grateful, indeed," he assured her and she nodded curtly in response, preferring not to engage in idle chat.

But she'd been a fantastic support throughout such a difficult pregnancy. Margot had spent the last six months on bed rest, with very few visitors, and it had been necessary to employ the private nurse and midwife for the duration – a costly necessity, but looking at the scene before him, it had been worth it. He swept his hand over the baby's head lightly, savouring the velvet feel of her skin.

"I was thinking. I'd like to call her Felicity. It means joy. Don't you think we look alike, Michael?" Margot asked.

"My little joy, Felicity. It's perfect. Um . . . yes, a little alike, I suppose," he said, trying to see the resemblance.

"Well, it's settled," she smiled. "Margot and Felicity, quite the ring to it! Felicity Margaret Montgomery."

"Now, it's time for mother and baby to rest." Nurse Abbott hovered over them.

Michael bent to kiss Margot's forehead, wishing he could stay longer to appreciate this long-awaited gift. He'd be happy when the nurse left them. She somehow unnerved him and had all but kept him away from his wife for the entire pregnancy. But he supposed this was the usual course of events with such a high-risk case.

He bent once more to kiss Margot. "Rest now, my love. Hopefully, life can return to normal now that Felicity is here with us, by the grace of God."

Nurse Abbott scooped up the baby, instructing Margot to rest, leaving her alone with her thoughts.

Margot was exhausted. She'd hoped for a little girl and now here she was. Everything had finally aligned and she could hardly believe her luck. She felt the tension of the last six months melt away as she lay back against the pillows and closed her eyes. She could picture them all discussing the tidings of joy at the vicarage. Margot would have loved to see her sisters' faces when they heard the news. She had everything now – everything she'd always wanted. She'd *made* it happen.

Michael was thrilled and she was sure he was at this very moment hurtling himself at the altar to give praise. He'd told her time and again that the Lord would deliver when the time was right. Margot's eyes fluttered and then firmly shut as her jaw relaxed and her mouth fell open to release a little snore.

Yes, it had been a very tiring night.

Mrs Kidney was the first to burst into her room the next day once the news had filtered through town.

"Let me see the little piggy," she shrieked, lifting the slumbering baby, immediately waking her. "Oh, it's all coming back to me. They said I took to it like a duck to water when young Godfrey was born," she gushed, looking down at Felicity's little face, who'd once again settled with the bouncing motion of Mrs Kidney's breasts as she swung her precariously from side to side.

"Now, who is she like?" Mrs Kidney looked quizzically

into the baby's face, trying to decipher the features. "Is it Michael? Hmm . . . perhaps around the eyes. She certainly doesn't have his nose!" she laughed. "No, she's not Michael. Not at all. You know, they say babies start out looking like their father, so they don't eat them," she chuckled. "Dates back to when we were in the wild. A tasty little pork chop this one would make," she laughed some more, her shoulders bobbing up and down.

"Well, let's hope Michael doesn't eat Felicity," Margot said.

"Ha ha, of course not. Not a bit like you either, though. Not one bit."

"I can see it. Very like me as a child. I was once quite fair, you know," Margot said defensively, wondering why it was always so important to compare every feature of a child to the parent.

"Yes, maybe I can see it a little." Mrs Kidney's brow furrowed as she continued to stare at the baby.

"Give her here," Margot demanded a little more sharply than intended.

"Here you are. And how are you feeling?" Mrs Kidney enquired, passing the baby to her.

"Quite well. The doctor from the hospital was here this morning and confirmed that I'll be back on my feet again in no time," Margot said proudly.

"That's good. Not healthy for you being holed up in this room for so long, but you must rest now. The birth of a baby is traumatic on a woman's body." Mrs Kidney looked her up and down, her eyes flitting over Margot's belly.

"Yes, I do feel rather tired," Margot said, feigning sudden exhaustion and yawning loudly.

"Rest now. You'll need your energy," Mrs Kidney warned. "Babies don't wake up until day three or four!" she added, waving goodbye.

Margot was relieved to be alone again. She looked down at the baby. It was strange to have her here at last after such a long wait and yet it seemed so sudden. She thought she'd feel more prepared, having spent so long anticipating the arrival, but it almost felt like an anticlimax. What had she expected to feel? She felt irritated after Mrs Kidney's visit, that's what. She wasn't sure she was taking to it like a *duck to water*.

Felicity stirred in her arms, almost time to be fed. Who knew that administering a bottle could be so complicated? Watch the amount. Take a break. Wind the baby. Hold the baby upright. Hold them facing out. Hold them over your shoulder. Margot wasn't sure that even if she held the baby by her toes she'd be able to get her wind up.

"It takes time to get the hang of it," Nurse Abbott assured.

Margot glanced down at the baby again. It was all so alien and where was the burst of love she was supposed to feel? She hadn't experienced it yet. Would she ever? The trees waved at her from the garden, always there, always watching. Patience, she thought, isn't that what was always needed?

"Nurse Abbott," she called. "The baby needs a feed."

Margot Montgomery

Then – 1970

"I've some business to attend to in Dublin tomorrow, Mrs Montgomery, so you'll be alone with Felicity for the day," Nurse Abbott told Margot brusquely on her fourth day of motherhood.

"Oh, well, I'm not quite ready. So soon?" Margot asked nervously.

"Come now, you're doing very well and besides, I can't stay for ever. Best to get on with it."

It was true. While day two had been unsettling, Margot felt much more positive by day three and the nurse was right, the reverend's wife couldn't be seen to have a full-time nanny, as much as she would have liked.

"Now, I've laid everything out in preparation for you. That's the key, Mrs Montgomery. Always be prepared. All you must do is feed and change her and enjoy her. You need to spend time with her to bond."

Margot nodded in agreement. Surely it couldn't be too hard. Of course she could do it.

By mid-morning, everything was going swimmingly and she could hardly believe her luck. She fed her, winded her, changed her and settled her successfully.

154

"Not bad, Felicity. We're quite the team." Margot smiled at her sleeping daughter.

She tidied around and dressed, even managing to read a chapter of her book. As if by clockwork, four hours later, Felicity once again stirred in her crib. Satisfied that the appropriate amount of time had lapsed between feeds, Margot relaxed into her chair by the window then once again fed her, changed her and settled her.

Perhaps the winds have changed, Margot thought as she peered into the crib. She does look a little like me, she mused, feeling a small unfamiliar flicker pass through her heart. Margot sat back in her chair, closing her eyes, lulled asleep by the consistent shallow breathing beside her.

She was woken with a start some hours later as Felicity opened her little eyes and omitted a frantic cry, which try as she might Margot was unable to stop. She looked at the clock. It was five thirty. A little early for another feed, but she set about the procedure none the less.

Only this time, the baby fussed and spat the bottle out, twisting her body between screams, so that by the time Mrs Walsh found her the following morning, Margot was in a state.

"I've tried everything but she won't stop," Margot told her, looking wide-eyed and terrified.

Even Michael had tried to step in and soothe young Felicity, but Margot grew frustrated with him and sent him away, determined to solve the problem alone. Each time she thought she had Felicity quiet, she'd gently place her in the crib and reverse away slowly. But it was as if Felicity could sense her disappearance and she'd begin to twitch, bunching up her fists as the cycle started again.

"Give her here. You look done in." Mrs Walsh had heard the cries as soon as she arrived at the house.

Michael had slunk off early that morning, leaving Margot to fend for herself, but it was obvious that the reverend's wife was struggling.

"It's perfectly normal, Mrs Montgomery. Don't fret," Mrs Walsh assured her as she cradled the baby in her arms, gently shushing and rocking her.

Margot slumped onto the bed.

"You sleep. I'll take her for a bit," she said kindly.

Nelly was sure that the new mother was asleep before she even left the room and had all but settled the baby before reaching the bottom of the stairs.

"There, there, Felicity," Nelly cooed, habitually placing the baby over her shoulder as she'd done so many times before with her own.

Felicity omitted a gigantic burp and with no more fight left in her, Nelly listened as her breathing quickened. She sat down on the chair in the parlour with Felicity on her chest and relished the sound of the infant's snuffles as she settled into a deep sleep. Nelly had never sat in the parlour before, usually reserved for the reverend's visitors, but she was sure on this occasion that Margot would neither notice nor care. Margot – a mother! Wonders never ceased.

She snuggled the poor child closer to her, hoping that this baby would soften the lady of the house. She'd been surprised to learn that Margot was with child after such a long time – five years was a long time to wait for the arrival of a first baby – and what a way to discover she was pregnant!

Nelly remembered being in the kitchen the day she'd heard the door slam and the car engine revving to life. She'd assumed it was the reverend, hadn't even thought to question it until Michael had rushed into the kitchen ashen-faced not an hour later.

"There's been an accident. Margot, it's Margot . . ." he'd stammered.

What on earth she'd been thinking, Nelly would never know. Just taken a notion to head out in the car, in the rain no less and her barely able to start the engine, let alone drive. Margot had made it out of the driveway, heading towards town, and then crashed at full force into the wall of the library. Swerving to avoid a cat, the reverend told her. Silly woman. Damaged her back something terrible. Still, it wasn't all bad. The reverend had returned that evening with the news.

"Mrs Montgomery is with child," he'd announced proudly.

Margot had missed all the signs of her little stowaway, which didn't surprise Nelly. Margot was forever forgetting things lately and had seemed distracted for months.

"She'll be home in the coming days. The nurse has instructed total bed rest. Her pelvis is very weak. In fact, she's agreed to be her private nurse for the duration. Took a little convincing, but it's all set," Michael told her, flushed with excitement.

Nelly had breathed a sigh of relief. She didn't have the patience to assume the role of nurse to Margot. Instead, Nelly had enjoyed a wonderful break for the last six months, barely setting eyes on Margot the entire time. Nurse Abbott seemed better able to handle her than most and Margot had stayed in bed as instructed. And now look – a beautiful baby.

Nelly kissed the velvety cheek of the infant. Perhaps she should check on Margot, make sure she was all right; after all, new mothers need lots of care. Nelly was feeling particularly soft after the sad news she'd heard that morning. Which reminded her, she needed to ask for some time off to attend the funeral.

Margot was still asleep when Nelly crept into the room, expertly carrying Felicity, who was still in a deep slumber. She laid the infant in the crib and tidied the room a little as she waited for one or the other to wake. Realising both were utterly exhausted, Nelly scooped up the glass baby bottles and went to clean and prepare them in the kitchen. She enjoyed the task, reminding her of her times at home with her young babies, and she was just finishing, when she heard the familiar cries of a hungry baby wafting through the house. After gathering the bottles, she made her way back upstairs, to find Margot pale and disorientated, staring over the crib at the crying child.

"Good afternoon, Mrs Montgomery," Nelly smiled encouragingly. "You know, I remember when I had my first. The greatest gift was when someone offered to feed him. It was like a gift from heaven. Would you like me to feed Felicity?"

"Yes, please." Margot didn't hesitate and slumped back onto the bed, leaving the chair by the window free for Mrs Walsh.

"Nice and slow with the feeding until they find their feet," Nelly advised. "I think they sense it if you're stressed, so don't rush."

For once Margot watched and listened, happy to take the older lady's advice.

"I'll stay while you change and settle her. You'll get the swing of it, Mrs Montgomery, don't worry. Now, on another note, I must ask that I have some time off on Friday morning to attend a funeral, I'm afraid, but I'll be back before lunch. A tragic death," Mrs Walsh explained.

"Isn't that always the way, though. One life ends and another starts." She reached down to stroke Felicity's cheek.

"As long as you're back by lunch," Margot agreed.

"Tragic, just tragic," Mrs Walsh continued. "Poor little thing took her own life. Her mam found her. Said she'd never seen the likes of it. She'd been away for a while now, staying with a relative – only home a few days. Wasn't herself at all. The family is inconsolable."

"Oh dear – a sin, though? To take your own life," Margot asked.

"Yes, Mrs Montgomery." Nelly threw her eyes up to heaven, wondering couldn't she just once be understanding. "I suppose it is a sin. Awful all the same. Poor girl – had her whole life ahead of her. Beautiful too – not that that matters now, of course. Poor Annie, everything to live for – just a child, really."

Margot looked up suddenly. "What . . . what did you say . . . what was her name?"

"Annie. Annie Slaney. Did you know her?" Nelly looked puzzled.

"No. No, of course not," Margot snapped. "When did she die?"

"Yesterday evening they found her. Probably around five thirty, just after Deirdre got home from work," Nelly continued, absently stroking the baby's cheek.

"Please leave, Mrs Walsh. Can you watch Felicity for me? I feel most unwell all of a sudden, terribly light-headed."

"Would you like me to fetch the doctor, Mrs Montgomery?" Nelly asked, noticing the colour had drained from Margot's face.

"No, no. I'll be fine."

Nelly picked up Felicity and left, sensing this wouldn't be the last time she'd be left holding the baby.

Margot pushed back the covers, threw her legs over the side of the bed then stood for a moment before her legs gave way and she sank to the ground.

The girl was dead.

What had she done? She'd barely thought of her since that day. Everything that came after was so sudden that she'd hardly considered her since. What had she done?

She looked out at the trees. They'd witnessed it all, seen it all. She closed her eyes, feeling the pressure deepen behind them, and let her mind drift back.

She'd known immediately what to do – took it as a sign. Father Nugent hadn't needed much convincing.

"It's a disgrace. A young girl and an unwanted baby, you must intervene," Margot told him after he let her into the house.

"It's not my business, Mrs Montgomery, not unless they look for my help," he'd pleaded.

"Now now, Father. We all know what you were up to years ago – was that not our business, either?" she'd threatened. "Boy or girl, it didn't matter to you, did it? But it'll matter now, Father."

That Father Nugent had never laid a hand on any man, woman or child was neither here nor there. She knew he'd take the bait – too comfortable up in the parochial house, enjoying his last years before retirement, to risk losing it all. Besides, she'd heard it whispered in the Estates of fallen girls disappearing for months at a time before returning looking deflated and old. There were some who didn't return at all and Father Nugent wasn't the innocent he was playing.

"You have until the end of the week. Now, you do your part, Father."

A couple of days later, Margot had sat in the car and gripped the steering wheel tight. She took a deep breath and started the engine, bunny hopping out of the driveway before finding her flow. She'd driven up the main street, feeling every fibre of disappointment for this life. The energy had surged through her leg and she'd pressed the accelerator hard before suddenly swerving, crashing straight into the library wall.

Margot vaguely remembered Harriet Joyce rushing out of the door of the library to her aide before everything blurred and the next thing, she was waking up in the hospital with Nurse Abbott looking down at her. She'd heard her talking to Michael.

"Yes . . . a slipped disc . . . some back damage . . . pregnant . . . high risk."

Nurse Abbott took over everything after that. Margot would return home in a few days and would need total rest for the duration of the pregnancy. The nurse let Michael talk her into taking the position to care for his wife and she'd agreed immediately, marking the start of a lengthy, frustrating period for Margot, locked in her room alone with the surly nurse.

It didn't take long for Nurse Abbott to comprehend Margot's true nature, but it was too late by then and she knew as soon as the baby arrived, she'd depart quietly and never return. The handsome payment would be enough for her, along with the sale of her small house, so she could move to Dublin to be with her sister. She'd worked tirelessly for the last thirty-five years – this would be her last good deed before she retired and had some well-earned time for herself.

Margot fretted for the duration of the pregnancy, willing everything to work out, and when the baby was finally placed into her outstretched arms, Margot knew it had all been worth it. It hadn't been easy. It never was. But as she held the baby in her arms, it had felt right. Maybe if Margot had witnessed it all, she'd have felt differently. Perhaps if she'd seen all the steps that led to that moment . . .

Margot hadn't seen Annie Slaney screaming in pain, tears of dread spilling from her eyes, her beautiful blonde hair drenched with sweat as she'd delivered a baby girl, who was ripped from her arms moments later and placed into the those of Father Nugent. Nor had she seen Nurse Abbott slipping the crushed sleeping pills into Michael's drink that evening when the nurse received the call that the girl was in labour.

The nurse had waited at the window in the parlour for several hours before she saw the lights of the car approaching and slipped outside to take the bundle of life from Father Nugent's trembling hands. As the baby was placed in Margot's arms, Annie Slaney's own heart was wrenched open as she lay curled up, sobbing for the stolen child – destined for a life of privilege with the doctor and his wife in Dublin but instead delivered to the reverend's wife, just as they'd planned all along.

Nurse Abbott had barely wrestled with the moral dilemma of it all. She'd seen enough young lives ruined through sinful behaviour and Father Nugent had assured her it was for the best. The reverend knew nothing. The fewer people who knew, the better. All Margot had to do was fake an accident, which would lead to the discovery of her fake pregnancy.

Nurse Abbott almost admired the woman for having the strength to drive into a wall – surely anyone who'd go that far must desperately want a child of their own. Nurse Abbott had been waiting in the hospital for them, ready to deliver the news of the pregnancy to the reverend, and it had gone seamlessly. She always took great pride in her work, whatever it was.

The nurse wouldn't be returning the next day as she'd promised Margot – she was already ensconced in Dublin, having washed her hands of the past. She wouldn't hear the news that the girl, Annie, had taken her own life. She wasn't there the day before to see Margot witness Felicity's tiny eyes fly open, accompanied with blood-curdling screams, at the exact moment that Felicity's real mother cut the life from herself.

Annie Slaney, after returning home bereft and broken, had sat in the bath, watching the water lap over her now empty stomach. She'd picked up the knife, taken from the kitchen, as her mother left for work and sliced into her wrists. Annie had then watched her life seep from the open wounds, twirling through the reddening water, until her eyes turned to glass and she could see no more. Her head sank backwards slowly as she thought of her father, still unable to meet her eyes, and of her baby, her beautiful baby.

No, Margot hadn't seen the pain she'd inflicted on Annie Slaney, but she felt it now. She hadn't thought of the girl after she'd made her plan with Father Nugent. She'd somehow blocked her out; had almost believed she herself was pregnant as Nurse Abbott padded her stomach out further over the months. What had she done?

Margot thought of Felicity, her bundle of joy, ripped from the life for which she was destined. She thought of the secret she was now doomed to carry for the rest of her life. She imagined Annie Slaney reaching over and seizing all of Margot's ambitions with her bloodied hands. She looked down at her own shaking hands, for ever stained with that same blood.

Margot swallowed her sobs and stared at her mottled face in the mirror – even more broken and twisted than before. Felicity wasn't hers. She never would be. What had she done? Her own life would never now be as she hoped it would. It was over. They must never find out – she'd make sure of it. What had she done?

Margot closed her eyes and let her heart finally harden in her chest – towards everything and everyone, and towards the baby who'd ruined it all.

Felicity Montgomery

Then – 1987

She closed her eyes and moved to the beat of the music. Felicity let the crowd gently sway her from side to side and she gave in, allowing the movement to lull her and dull the usual tension that resided between her shoulder blades. She felt the bass pump through her body and concentrated on the sound echoing inside her, making her feel alive.

"*What*?" She turned towards Lucie, who was shouting at her over the music. But she couldn't hear her and continued to sway, relishing her first taste of freedom.

"Come on, follow me," Lucie said as the song ended and she motioned towards the door.

Felicity followed, leaving the crowd behind, watching them move as she went, not wanting to miss a second.

"It's roasting in there." Lucie fanned at her face and smoothed down her hair that had started to frizz.

They stood in the small lobby of the pub and let the cool air from the door wash over them.

"Well, what do you think?" Lucie asked, smiling.

It had taken ages to plan it, with lots of secret exchanges and whispered conversations.

"I love it. I love it! Let's go back," Felicity squealed in response.

Lucie laughed and pointed towards the back of the stage, where she could see her brother peering out at the boisterous crowd, waiting to see his band perform.

"You ain't seen nothing yet. Wait until you hear them."

Lucie had been telling her for months about her older brother's A-ha tribute band.

"They're called Ha-yeah and I swear, Felicity, you wouldn't know the difference between them and the real thing, much as I hate to admit it. Mind you, Sammy says he hates the word 'tribute band'. They only do two A-ha songs, you see – said he doesn't want to be pigeon-holed by it – but the other lads in the band think it's the way to go. Mainly because everyone says he's the living image of Morten Harket, the lead singer. I can't see it though, not one bit. Sammy plays guitar, too. He's good, but for this act he's lead singer."

Felicity looked over at where they were waiting to go on, catching a brief glimpse of stonewash denim disappearing behind the partition.

"Is that him?" she asked. She'd never seen Lucie's brother before and she craned her neck to get a better look.

"Yeah." Lucie threw her eyes up to heaven. "That's him all right. He's ruined A-ha for me now."

"I love A-ha." Felicity was still trying to get a look at the band.

"I think they start with 'Take on Me' and then the one about the TV, then they play them again at the end. They do other stuff, too," she told her. "Serious music, Sammy says." She rolled her eyes again. "It's only their second gig, but everyone's saying they're good enough to make it. Imagine someone famous coming out of Knockmore!" Lucie laughed.

Felicity couldn't believe she was actually here. She'd never even heard of A-ha until Lucie had started slipping copies of *Smash Hits* magazine over the back wall to her, later followed by her most prized possession: a small silver cassette player with a handle across the top and the word Panasonic written under the tape drawer. It was small enough to hide inside her attaché case but just big enough to open Felicity's mind to a whole new world. Lucie had given it to her a few weeks after her seventeenth birthday, following their reunion at the Brownie meeting after over a year apart.

"I nicked it from Sammy," Lucie said, giggling. "He'll never notice. He's after getting himself a Sony yoke with a double tape deck. Mam says she's never seen so many buttons in her life. She's terrified to dust near it in case it takes off!"

Felicity loved hearing the lively stories of the Maguires, a far cry from the vicarage and Margot's mood swings. She'd like to have seen the giant hi-fi with all the buttons, but she loved her little cassette player, even though it sometimes chewed up and spat out the shiny black film of her borrowed tapes. It never ceased to amaze her that the music was all there, ingrained into the shimmering paper, ready to go as soon as she pressed Play. Felicity used to imagine miniature musicians queuing up inside it, waiting to perform just for her. She was always careful to ensure that Mother was snoring away before she settled the little player under her sheets and put on the thin silver headphones with the slightly chewed orange ear covers.

"Pop music is for ruffians and drug addicts," Mother told her all the time. "It'll rot your mind."

Felicity was sure that if it wasn't for the music and the miniature members of Duran Duran, Madonna, The Bangles and Bananarama that resided inside her precious tapes, her mind would have exploded by now. Ever since Tess Maguire was ejected as housekeeper, Margot, with little else to occupy her mind, had taken to staring unnervingly at Felicity. She'd often catch Mother sitting stock-still, just staring as if she'd seen a ghost. Though lately, her headaches had worsened, often preventing her from getting out of bed at all, giving Felicity some welcome respite.

It had been Father's idea for Felicity to sign up with the Brownies.

"I've arranged for you to become a leader," Father told her proudly on the evening of her seventeenth birthday.

"Really? I'd love that."

She was delighted at the thought of having just a little freedom. She'd never been allowed to join the Brownies before. "Why on earth would I allow you to mix with all those common children?" Mother had said, pursing her lips when she'd asked years before. But Michael as the reverend had a certain amount of pull and had fixed it with the Brown Owl for her to become a helper.

"But what about Mother?" Felicity had asked.

"Leave that to me. You're almost an adult. It's time you got out into the community," he said, repeating the words he'd once issued to his wife.

"Thank you, Daddy." She'd hugged him then and he'd flushed red, stepping back and nearly falling over the chair.

Felicity adored it from the moment she stepped foot into the dusty church hall filled with exuberant little girls in yellow sweatshirts. The mix of them from frizzy-haired to prim and proper was like someone had shaken up the contents of Knockmore and spilled it out onto the waxy wooden floor. Felicity had been watchful at first but soon found her flow as the little girls flocked around their new helper. She'd ended up sitting on the floor among them, telling stories, so caught up that she didn't even notice her standing there.

"Fliss? What are you doing here?" Lucie's eyes were wide.

Felicity jumped to her feet, stumbling over the sea of Fruit of the Loom sweatshirts. "Lucie! Oh my God." Felicity launched at her, hugging her so tightly that they ended up falling to the floor laughing as the little Brownies stood over them in awe.

"How come you're here?" Lucie asked.

They lay on their backs staring up at the long plastic light fittings, filled with flies and creatures that had flown towards the light but failed to escape.

"Father arranged it. I'm a helper now. How come you're here?"

"Go, Reverend." Lucie pumped the air. "I'm the Tawny Owl! I've been a leader for the last year."

It was the greatest gift Felicity had ever received. The Brownies met every Thursday evening and on a Saturday morning for activities, meaning they'd have plenty of time to spend together and rekindle their friendship.

"I've missed you so much," Felicity repeated.

It had felt as though she were drowning for the last year. There had been no warning to the dismissal. Felicity had just returned from school one day and they were gone.

"No contact, none whatsoever, do you hear me? I won't have you mixing with common thieves," Mother had warned.

169

Losing Tess was like losing Nelly all over again, but worse because she was losing Lucie as well, and she'd grieved for them as if they'd fallen into the wooden floor, too.

"I like the hair," Felicity said, reaching over and running her fingers up and down the uniform bumps.

"I got a crimper," Lucie said.

"And some bleach," Felicity mused, looking at the white stripes at the front of her hair, making her look like a tiger that had run through an electric field.

"Yes, a little," Lucie laughed. "Yours is as lovely as always," she said, taking in Felicity's thick hair, perfectly straight and naturally blonde. "And I see you finally got them!" Lucie giggled, gesturing towards Felicity's breasts, which were full-looking in contrast to her tiny waist and shapely hips.

"Yes! I kept doing the exercises!"

The pair collapsed into giggles as they remembered the afternoons spent behind the apple trees thrusting their arms in and out at high speed shouting, "I must, I must, I must increase my bust."

"How's Margot?" Lucie asked, suddenly serious.

"Still looking for the mink!"

They both burst out laughing. Lucie hugged her again and the lost year slid away. Lucie was so far the greatest love of her life, her soul mate, her person, and she vowed never to let her leave her life again. Perhaps her seventeenth year was going to the best one yet.

Felicity was catapulted back to the present day with a sharp nudge in the ribs.

"Wake up, will you! It's about to start. Wait until you see the drummer! What I wouldn't do to 'Get into the Groove'

170

with him," Lucie laughed, referring to their favourite Madonna song. She grabbed Felicity's hand and clambered her way to the front of the crowd. "Coming through, coming through," Lucie shouted as they reached the front.

"Hey! watch it," someone shouted from the group of girls who were hogging the area at the front of the stage, where they were waiting with bated breath to see Knockmore's answer to Morten Harket stride out in all his glory.

"We're family members. This area is reserved," Lucie said curtly, winking at Felicity.

The other girls looked them up and down but let them pass. Felicity could hardly take it all in. She stared at the exotic outfits on the girls. Aside from the pictures in *Smash Hits*, she'd never seen style like it and couldn't help but admire the sea of black lace tops, shocking pink tube skirts, bangles in every colour under the sun and thick velvet hairbands that moved through the dark pub like a textured rainbow. She suddenly felt very out of place.

"Do I look okay?"

"Gorgeous. Don't mind them, *jealous cows*," Lucie said just loud enough for the girls to hear.

Lucie had given her a plain black tube dress to wear and Felicity had tried to object. It was tighter than a pair of swimming togs. As Felicity had wriggled it over her head, Lucie had flown at her with a red patent belt and a pair of kitten-heeled shoes, complete with a diamante velvet bow.

"I can't go out like this," she'd protested as they'd quickly changed behind the church hall earlier that evening.

"Oh yes you can! Look at your body! What I wouldn't do for your curves . . . Now, take out your ponytail and I'll backcomb your hair."

Before Felicity could stop her, Lucie had whipped out a

can of mousse from her backpack and squirted a great big fluffy dollop into Felicity's fringe, lifting the front part of her hair into a rock-solid arc that not even a truck could have knocked over. She'd then produced a tube of pale lip gloss and smoothed it onto Felicity's full lips before standing back to admire her handiwork.

"You're like one of the girls from the Robert Palmer video now, only better. Not the one with the massive boobs where you can see her white bra through her black dress, though. I feel quite proud!"

Lucie smiled approvingly, delighted to see her friend, at last, in something other than the usual frumpy beige outfits Margot provided. Felicity had no idea who Robert Palmer was, but Lucie looked so pleased with her styling that she'd said nothing and instead took a few sips of the sweet cider from the cans that Lucie had taken from the house.

"You look incredible," Lucie assured her now. "Relax, everything will be fine."

Felicity nodded, praying she was right. She'd been terrified at first when Lucie revealed The Plan to her. It had started innocently, when Felicity told her that her father would be away at a seminar in Dublin for the weekend. Lucie nearly exploded when she discovered it was the same weekend that Ha-yeah would be playing their second gig in Lennon's, known for its younger clientele. Not only that, but Sammy's friend was also the doorman and often let Lucie sneak in if she promised not to drink.

"I have an idea," Lucie told her and Felicity had listened, wondering if they'd be able to pull it off.

Margot had been particularly quiet of late, spending much of her time in her room, so it seemed a possibility for Felicity to be able to sneak out after dark.

"It's too risky, Lucie. What if she wakes up? I'd never be allowed to leave the house again and I don't want to stop seeing you after all this time."

"Okay, okay, let me think . . . Oh my God, I've got it. We'll invent a Brownie sleepover night – it happens all the time. One that will surely require your wonderful leadership qualities!"

Lucie went as far as typing a permission slip for Michael to sign, which he duly had. He'd barely looked at it before agreeing to let her go. Mother put up a weak fight at first but had given in, heading to her room in a huff. Felicity suspected that her mother would use the opportunity of being alone to sink a bottle of sherry, which seemed to be happening more and more lately. Well, at least Mother had given up hiding it so much. Which just left Tess.

"That's a done deal. Mam's still furious with your mother over the scarf. Mam said of course you can stay the night at ours. She's dying to see you."

It was almost foolproof.

"Okay, I'm in," Felicity agreed.

It was now or never. It was time for her to live, time she had a piece of the pie. She needed to breathe – she needed to feel alive and hold on to the light she'd found again with Lucie. There was so much she still hadn't told Lucie, so many dark moments that her friend didn't know about. Felicity wanted to tell her about the past year, confess that her mind had at times drifted into the darkest of places and she'd almost succumbed to it, thinking it would be easier not to exist than to exist like this, but she couldn't find the words.

"Here they come!" Lucie said as the lights suddenly went out and the four figures made their way onto the stage shrouded in darkness.

173

A hush descended over the room, led mainly by Lucie, who turned towards the crowd, giving a dirty look, commencing a wave of people shushing each other, which gradually reached the back of the room. Bit by bit, the chatter stopped. Felicity held her breath as the familiar beat kicked in, followed by the haunting synthesiser, momentarily disguising the true nature of the song.

The music built slowly and Felicity once again started to sway. The stage illuminated with a bang as the keyboard player tapped out the frenzied introduction and a huge cheer erupted from the crowd as they moved in unison like a wave ready to crash onto the beach. Felicity struggled to see over the undulating mass that shifted backwards and forwards, side to side, with the beat.

"Wait until you see the hips moving," Sophie shouted over the music. "Sammy recorded *Top of the Pops* when A-ha was playing so he could learn the moves, just like an eejit," she laughed. "I told him he looks like he's having a fit."

Felicity had never seen *Top of the Pops* or A-ha perform, so she had no idea what to expect.

For the duration of the 35-second introduction, the cloud of neon lace blocked her from seeing as Sammy stood gripping the mic stand, one hand tucked casually into his stonewash denims. Had she been able to see, Felicity may have noticed that Sammy was wearing a replica of Morten Harket's leather waistcoat, painstakingly made by his mother, Tess, from an old leather jacket she'd picked up in the charity shop. It was open, giving way to a firm hairless chest. Lucie had burst in on him shaving it in the bathroom the day before, resulting in her convulsing with laughter at first and then being reduced to tears when he'd kicked her in the shin.

Now, his solid abs contracted as he expertly moved his hips from side to side in time with the beat. Had Felicity ever been allowed to watch the popular music TV show and seen Morten Harket on it, she might have guessed from the similarities of the two performances how many hours Sammy had spent in the confines of his bedroom. She'd have seen him holding Tess's sweeping brush in place of a microphone stand, thrusting his hips from side to side and pointing at an imaginary audience, his lip curled. She was about to voice that Sammy was indeed the walking image of Morten Harket, as Lucie put it, and as the neon screams in front of her were now suggesting.

"Here it comes!" Lucie screamed.

Just as his wrist, banded by at least twenty black leather straps, borrowed from the laces of his father's workboots, reached up to take hold of the microphone, Lucie grabbed Felicity by the hand and heaved her to the very front. The crowd parted and she stood there exposed as Sammy Maguire locked eyes with her and started to sing.

Felicity stared back. The likeness was uncanny. She'd seen pictures of Morten Harket before – even ran her finger over his little face looking out at her from Lucie's magazines that she'd borrowed. She watched Sammy now as he reached up and flicked his full fringe off his face, probably just like he'd practised in the mirror at home. Felicity stood stock-still, spellbound. She could hear the blood rushing in her head, feel the heat of the room around her, as she watched him purr out the lyrics.

His lips curled into the rehearsed smile as he took a breath, his voice deepening at first and then soaring to unusually high levels for a man. His eyes bored into hers, the quirky smile remaining fixed on his lips as he reached his crescendo, throwing his head back as his voice pitched.

Felicity forgot the crowd of people behind her, forgot Lucie beside her, and forgot herself as she stood frozen, staring, hands by her side. Her blonde hair glistened against the colourful changing lights as Sammy Maguire sang the entire song to the statuelike form in the black tube dress, cinched in by the red plastic belt. All she could see was him, singing to her, as everyone else in the room faded into the smokey atmosphere. They were alone, just the two of them. Was she imagining it? No. For once, she felt visible, present – tethered to his unwavering line of vision, savouring her own special performance – willing it not to end.

It took only three minutes and forty-five seconds for Felicity to get lost in Sammy's brown eyes. To hear the lyrics of a song that she'd listened to many times, in a new way. In a way that when he sang the lyrics "Take on me, Take me on?" she found herself fixing her eyes on his and wanting to scream, "Yes."

Lucie had been so intent on getting the Ha-yeah drummer to notice her that she hadn't seen the fission of electricity that visibly ran between her older brother and her best friend. She turned towards Felicity just as the song was winding down and witnessed a look she'd never seen before: determination.

"Fliss!" she squealed. "Are you all right?" she asked, following Felicity's line of vision, which rested firmly on Sammy. "You look like you've seen a ghost!"

Felicity shook herself back to reality and looked at her friend, an enormous smile on her face from someone who hadn't seen a ghost but instead had caught a glimpse of her future.

"You never told me . . . you never said. Why didn't you

say?" Felicity gushed. "Take on me? Yes, please. I mean, he's gorgeous."

"What *are* you on about, Fliss?"

"Your brother! I . . . I . . . I didn't know. How have I never met him before? Wow."

"Eww, Fliss, seriously? He's a complete idiot. He's had more girlfriends than I can count. Mum says he's like the singer Tom Jones, a Lothario – don't go there!" Lucie waved her hand in dismissal. "Besides, he's nineteen. He's too old for you," she continued, knowing full well that her own drummer interest was twenty and wild horses couldn't keep her from trying it on with him.

"Let's take a breather," Lucie said finally, dragging her uncooperative friend towards the back of the room to break whatever spell Sammy and his bare-chested sorcery had placed on her.

Felicity looked over her shoulder to see Sammy following her gaze as he sang the lyrics to the next song, which began with "Touch me . . . " What she'd have given to reach up onto the stage and oblige! What had just happened? She could hardly breathe. She'd seen the look in his eyes, she was sure of it. She'd barely spoken to a boy before, let alone wished she were up onstage caressing a glistening chest beneath a leather waistcoat. She turned once more towards him and saw him point and wink at her before the crowd swallowed her.

They spent the rest of the set at the back of the room, Lucie trying to distract Felicity by introducing her to some friends and a few of the lads from the Estates, who were just as taken by the blonde beauty as Sammy had been. None of them recognised her as the reverend's daughter. Lucie was careful to introduce her as just Fliss, in the hope that no one would put two and two together. Not that they would have, since the local teenagers had never really seen her. Even though the town was small, Felicity was never seen hanging around the chip shop or the pool hall, where the young romances of Knockmore usually blossomed.

Felicity tried to appear interested but spent the entire time craning her neck towards the stage, where Ha-yeah had moved on to Duran Duran's "The Reflex" and had blasted out her favourite U2 song, "I Still Haven't Found What I'm Looking For". Well, she'd found what she was looking for all right and was impatiently waiting for them to play "Take on Me" for the second time, when hopefully she'd get to meet him.

Lucie had told her that the DJ would then come on and there'd be a disco, after which they'd all throng towards the chip shop before strolling home. Felicity looked at her watch and peered up over the crimped heads to where Sammy was still crooning away to the hypnotised girls.

After the last chords of *their* song rang out, she turned to Lucie, who was being chatted up by a guy whose hair was gelled into a quiff at the front and then spilled down his back in a cascading wave.

"I'm just going to go to the loo," Felicity mouthed, trying not to disturb her.

"I'll come with you," Lucie offered, stealing a glance at The Mullet beside her, hoping he'd stay exactly where he was. She'd forgotten all about the drummer already, her attention now focused on this vision in a lemon shirt and pale denim.

"No, stay. I'll be right back," she winked at her friend.

Felicity shoved her way through the crowd and waited in the line of giggling girls, crossing their legs and hopping up and down excitedly, chatting about the band and the hot lead singer while simultaneously trying not to wet their pants. She kept an eye on the door that led to the stage, expecting Sammy to burst through it at any minute and take her in his arms. Or at least in her dreams. And what a dream!

By the time it was her turn in the stall, she was anxious that he'd already left and she'd missed her chance. She caught a glimpse of herself in the mirror, her cheeks flushed with excitement, life suddenly full of possibility, and then she paused, her face dropping. Who was she kidding? Why would he be interested in her when he could have any one of the girls in this room . . . ? She was so used to feeling unloved, annoying, *a stain on her mother* that it was hard to imagine anyone would actually want her. She shook her head and fixed her slightly drooped hair before walking back through the door into the lounge.

Lucie was waiting for her just where she'd left her. The Mullet, whose name was Sean, had gone to get them a drink and Lucie was starting to get frantic as to her friend's whereabouts.

"Jesus, where were you?"

"I'm sorry, the queue was huge," Felicity said, looking over her friend's head for any sign of The Leather Waistcoat.

"It's okay. There's someone I want you to meet. He's a friend of Sean's – he's really nice."

Lucie shoved her forwards towards Mr Nice, who was standing against the wall, one hand tucked into his maroon jeans, the other holding a pint of beer, from which he was slurping thirstily every few seconds. Felicity couldn't help noticing the strange colour combination of his Friday night finery. His denim jacket was the same colour as his jeans and he wore an orange T-shirt underneath, displaying the remnants of beer that had missed his very full lips and splashed down his front, staining it in places.

The Mullet nudged Mr Nice, whose eyes were out on stalks as she approached. Mr Nice quickly wiped his mouth with the back of his hand, ready for the big introduction to the finest thing he'd ever seen coming out of the toilets of Lennon's. Felicity was just extending her hand towards him, when a crisp white tank top stepped in front of her and blocked her union with the rubbery lips.

"Oh." She stepped back, briefly losing her footing under her kitten heel and wobbling to one side before being caught by a hand wrapped in countless bands of black leather.

He grabbed her around the waist and brought her to a sudden stop just inches from his face. She swept back her hair, which had fallen over her face, and was left staring directly into the smiling eyes of Sammy Maguire. For the second time that night, she was spellbound.

"Easy, tiger," he laughed as she collected herself.

"I'm . . . I . . . I'm . . . " she stammered.

Up close he was even better looking. He'd removed the leather waistcoat and changed into a white T-shirt following his set, which perfectly matched his beautiful white smile.

"I take it you're Felicity?" he asked. "I'm Sammy. Lucie's brother."

"Yes, Felicity Montgomery," she said, wondering why she'd given both names and flushing.

"Yes, Felicity Montgomery."

She heard her name on his lips and cringed. It was so old-fashioned, so formal and stiff as it escaped his upturned mouth. She wished she could be anyone else right then – someone who lived in an ordinary house, with ordinary parents, with an ordinary life and an ordinary name. She wished her name was Mary or Ann and that meeting Sammy tonight could be the start of a beautiful adventure, instead of the complication it was sure to be, for the unloved girl with the hideous name.

"I've heard a lot about you, Felicity Montgomery, but never seen you. Until now that is. It's a pleasure to meet you." Sammy shook the hand he was already holding, his eyes never leaving hers. "Can I buy you a drink?"

She nodded, briefly catching Lucie's glare, who fervently shook her head in warning. Ignoring her, she followed Sammy to a secluded corner of the lounge and they sat in one of the red leather booths. The other side was taken up by a couple in a passionate embrace. Felicity didn't know where to look as the couple hungrily snogged the faces off each other. Sammy directed her face to him, steering her chin with one finger until she was once again staring into his brown eyes.

"Right here," he said, pointing his two fingers towards his eyes, guiding her vision away from the pair.

The other couple looked as though they were slowly melting into the booth, pressing so hard against it that Felicity was worried they'd be swallowed into one of the open foamy wounds, where the red leather had burst open to reveal a custard-coloured foam.

"I'll be back in one second," Sammy shouted over the music, heading off to retrieve some drinks from the bar.

Felicity tried to collect herself while trying to avert her eyes from the passionate display across from their table. She took a few deep breaths, managing to slow her racing heart to a safe level that wouldn't result in her being removed from Lennon's on a stretcher. It's just Lucie's brother, she told herself. It's just chatting, you can do this.

Sammy returned a moment later with two glasses of Coke and slipped into the booth beside her.

"Do you not drink?" Felicity asked.

"Nah, I've seen too many fellas from home wasting their lives on the gargle," he said, shaking his head. "Besides, me and the lads have big dreams for the band. I'm training to be a mechanic and I love cars, but it's not my thing. I want to sing. It's like I become someone else when I'm up there and I hear the music . . . a different version of myself," he added, looking down at the table. "It's hard to explain . . . " He drifted off.

Felicity knew what he meant. She was sure some of the lyrics of the songs she listened to at home had been written especially for her. They called out to her, preventing her from turning to stone, keeping the air twirling around in her lungs. She looked across at him. He was turning a beer mat over and over in his hand and sensing her watching him, he looked up. She almost jumped. She couldn't explain it, couldn't understand the physical feeling of being so close to him. She could feel it in her chest, but there was something more. It was as if they were meant to be together and he'd been always been waiting for her.

"I get it," she whispered.

"You'd be the first," he laughed. "Everyone else seems to know who I am before they've even talked to me."

"I get that, too," she smiled.

"I promise this isn't a line, but I feel like I know you, like I always have, or always should have." Sammy looked at her, searching her eyes, and she knew he felt it, too.

"When I was singing back there, I felt like . . . like we were meant to meet."

Feeling braver, Felicity reached over and gently placed her hand on top of his, and he smiled – one that went beyond his mouth, reaching his eyes.

The couple beside them suddenly righted themselves. The boy reached out and took a huge gulp from the pint of beer in front of him on the table, while the girl wiped at her lips, smudging the last of the shocking pink lipstick across her cheek. She adjusted her top and pulled down the elastic tube skirt that had ridden up in the heat of the moment.

Sammy caught Felicity's shocked face and they erupted into giggles.

"Come on," he whispered. "Let's go outside."

Felicity followed him through the pub, checking for Lucie all the time and finally spying her in a darkened corner, wrapped safely around The Mullet and holding on tight to the back of his shimmering hair. Madonna's "Crazy for You" was playing and Felicity watched the young lovers of Lennon's circling the floor. She'd listened to the song so many times in the dead of night, longing to be wrapped in someone's arms while Madonna sang about "strangers making the most of the dark". And here she was now, allowing herself to be led outside by Sammy, the warmth of his hand sending an electric current through her arm.

"Let's sit down." He gestured towards a low wall near the back of the car park. "Are you warm enough?"

"Yes, I'm fine," she shivered, without knowing why, and he put his arm around her.

"So, Felicity Montgomery, and again I don't mean this to be a line," he said, holding his hand up, "but where have you been all my life?"

She laughed. "Right here. I've been right here. Well, apart from being practically locked up," she said sadly.

"What do you mean?" Sammy asked gently.

"Well," she began, and for no other reason than he was the first person she felt she could tell, she told him the full story.

Felicity Montgomery

Then – 1978

To Felicity, it was the summer of dreams – filled with innocence and a fresh promise of hope. Each day was a new adventure and the two new friends spent every afternoon together, exploring the sizeable gardens of Knockmore, climbing trees and grazing knees under the sun. Tess was warm and kind, and Lucie was a fresh bundle of energy cartwheeling through the house, injecting it with long overdue vibrancy, so much so that gradually Felicity stopped waking with the empty feeling in her heart that Nelly's passing had left.

Tess was always cooking or baking and they barely noticed Margot's looming presence.

"Shush, girls, keep it down now," Tess would scold, smiling after them as they ran through the hallway giggling quietly, conscious not to wake The Beast and disturb the surge of warmth that filled the house.

Once school finished for summer, Tess and Lucie would arrive on the driveway each morning to see Felicity up and dressed and waiting impatiently for them, ready for the day's activities to begin. In the evenings, she and Father would eat together and then head off in the car to the beach outside Knockmore, where they'd sometimes swim or walk, chatting together happily. And for the first time, Felicity felt warm.

"Look here," Lucie said one day while they collected treasures in the garden, ready to put into the old tin box Tess had given them that morning to keep them occupied.

Felicity bent down next to her by the old oak tree, near the back of the orchard.

"It's a fairy door," Lucie told her.

Lucie reached her hand right into the hole at the base of the trunk and squealed, making out as if something were pulling at her arm. Felicity gasped, jumping backwards and losing her footing.

"Felicity! I'm joking."

"Lucie, you frightened me!" She righted herself and crawled over to peer inside the old oak.

"Mam told me about these. It's where the fairies live. It'll be our secret. We can hide our treasures in here," Lucie said, pleased to have found a secure hiding place for the tin box filled with their valuables, consisting of feathers, shiny paper, chewing gum, leaves and their best pictures. "Now we have a secret," Lucie told her, placing the shiny box at the back of the gap and covering it with leaves to conceal it further. "Come on, let's climb the wall."

"Now we have two secrets," Felicity replied, knowing she'd be murdered if she was discovered climbing out of the grounds of the house but doing it anyway, always feeling braver with her new friend in tow.

They sat in the field, plucking at the long grass and plaiting it together.

"Have you ever heard of someone called Florrie?" Felicity asked, finally asking the question that burned inside her.

186

"Who's that?" Lucie replied, concentrating on the plaiting.

"Well, I think it's my aunt – Mother's sister. I saw her once, when she came here, but Mother doesn't see them. She says she rose up from them, leaving them behind. Where she came from must be very far down the hill," Felicity continued innocently. "Florrie's very friendly. She wears blue on her eyes and she smells like lemons."

"Do you mean Florrie Hughes, she's friendly? Yes, it must be her. She's married to the sergeant," Lucie said.

"The sergeant? The one who came to the house when Nelly fell?" Felicity couldn't believe it.

"Yes, she's friends with Mam. They play bridge together every week."

"Oh."

"She's nice. Why don't you see her?"

"I'm not sure really. Mother doesn't see a lot of people. She used to see Mrs Kidney a lot, you know, from the butcher's, but Mother said she was too interfering. I liked her. She was always laughing."

"Well, that means you have cousins. I know she has a boy – I'm not sure of his name. And there's Mary, the little one."

"Cousins," Felicity whispered, surprised by the revelation. "I didn't know." She stopped to pick another strand of grass. "Do you know Rosie then, too? She's another sister."

"I'm not sure about a Rosie. I'll ask Mam."

"Will you help me to find out more and we can keep our discoveries with our treasure?" Felicity suggested.

"Ooo, like spying?" Lucie liked the sound of a new game.

"Yes, let's be detectives, with a case to solve."

"You know, I think my brother could help us to find out more. He's always running away from Sergeant Hughes!"

Felicity laughed. She didn't know much about Lucie's brother, Sammy, except that he was annoying and smelled like socks. But regardless of the sock smell, she'd be happy for him to be a detective, too.

"Lucieee . . . Felicitee . . . "

They heard Tess calling them, so they quickly jumped back over the wall and stood at the gate of the orchard, pausing expectantly.

"Ready?" Lucie said. "Steady . . . Go!"

And they were off, racing up the garden to where Michael was sitting at the table waving at them and Tess was emerging through the back door with a plate of sandwiches. They looked like any other family enjoying a meal on a summer's day as they chatted easily together, unconscious of the twitching curtain in the room above them, not knowing someone was watching. Someone who'd almost recovered from the embarrassing incident of being caught sound asleep while her elderly housekeeper lay dead in the hallway.

Time was indeed healing them all, but it was Felicity who was blossoming most. Michael was thrilled with the positive influence that the Maguires were having on his once sullen and withdrawn daughter, and the change in the household was truly infectious.

"You'll have to show me how to do those cartwheels, girls," he laughed as they spun by him on the grass.

"You try, Daddy!" Felicity giggled.

"I think I'll watch for now," Michael replied, sitting back proudly.

It was wonderful to see Felicity being a child, she was so rarely allowed to be herself. Margot pushed her heavily academically, perhaps to ensure she was given the chances she hadn't been. But he suspected it was more to prove her worth as a mother, by producing a child who excelled in every arena – every arena except, of course, socially. Margot had all but kept Felicity under lock and key her entire life and her social aptitude had suffered severely up until now. But the Lord works in mysterious ways, and perhaps the passing of Mrs Walsh and the new additions to the household were all part of a higher plan. He didn't wish Margot ill, but he was certainly enjoying watching Felicity emerge from her shell and grow in confidence.

"Felicity, would you accompany me somewhere after lunch? Lucie, too, if Mrs Maguire will allow?" Father asked.

He'd already cleared it with Tess and she looked over and nodded at the reverend.

"It's all right with me. Go and wash your hands, girls," she told them.

Tess had known when she accepted this job what she'd be up against. She'd known Nelly Walsh her whole life and while the old lady had never gossiped about her position in the big house, Tess had gleaned from her over the years that Margot neglected Felicity emotionally and that the reverend was all but terrified of his wife. Tess had known Maggie Treacy too, as youngsters, been friendly enough with her at one time, but now she was more familiar with her younger sister, Florrie, who was the polar opposite of Margot. Kind and youthful, Florrie could light up any room.

"You'll keep an eye out, won't you, Tess? There's something I just can't put my finger on with that child. I worry," Florrie had told her.

189

At first, Tess had worried about Felicity too, noticing how withdrawn and shy she was, but as the months passed, she felt sure there was nothing major to be concerned about.

"I've got to go and see someone just outside town. Come along, girls. Let's have an adventure," Michael said now, standing up from the table, wiping his mouth and taking a final gulp of tea from the informal mugs he'd become accustomed to drinking from.

He hadn't consulted Margot on his plan – had grown quite brave during her rehabilitation – and he was excited to see how the afternoon played out.

The trio took off in the Triumph, the girls squealing with excitement and waving at passers-by out of the rear window of the car. The wind blew in through the window and Felicity's hair whipped around her face in the back of the car. Michael watched his daughter through the rear-view mirror, free from worry and filled with light. They drove through the town and out on the winding road, past the two trees that signified that they were leaving Knockmore.

"Girls, this is Mr Power," Michael said after they arrived at an old farmhouse and were greeted by a kind-looking man, patiently awaiting their arrival. "This was his father's house, but Mr Power senior sadly passed away last month and the house is being sold," he explained.

"Hello, girls," Mr Power smiled as he tipped his cap at the two expectant faces, both covered with freckles and the remnants of sticky jam sandwiches.

"Sorry for your loss, mister," Lucie piped in.

"Yes, Mr Power. I'm very sorry, too," Felicity added, less versed in her outspokenness, dropping her gaze reverently to the ground with unease.

"Thanks, girls. That's fierce kind of you to say," he smiled at them. "But I have a small problem and the reverend here thought you two might be able to help."

"Yes, of course. Certainly, sir," Felicity offered, wondering what it could be.

"See, my old da, he had a little dog who now needs a home. I'd take her myself, only the missus would have my guts for garters. Oops, sorry, Reverend," he coughed. "Would you like to meet her?"

It took Felicity a few moments to understand what he meant and she looked from Mr Power to her father in utter confusion. Michael smiled broadly and nodded at her encouragingly.

"Fliss, a dog!" Lucie nudged her, jumping up and down.

"Oh, yes. Yes, please," Felicity gushed.

Mr Power led them into the small farmhouse, through the dark hallway, into a dimly lit kitchen, where there was a basket placed beside the hearth with a black-and-white dog curled up inside. The dog, clearly distraught by her owner's abandonment, barely lifted her eyes. The look of her was enough to poke at Felicity's soft heart and she immediately dropped to the floor beside the basket to take a closer look.

"See, she's been a bit down in the dumps since my da passed on. I think she needs a friend, someone to mind her. She's only two – still young," Mr Power said.

"Oh, I know how she feels," Felicity said as she gently reached out her hand towards the black-and-white ball of fluff. "Hello," she whispered, gently stroking the dog's soft fur.

"Her name's Daisy," Mr Power said. "But you can change that if you like."

"Daisy," Felicity repeated as Daisy's ears pricked up and she cautiously emerged from her basket to sit and nestle into Felicity.

"I think she likes you."

Felicity looked up at her dad with eyes that said it all. "Really, Daddy?"

"Really," he confirmed and Felicity's heart spilled open for the dog who needed her just as much as she needed it.

It didn't take long for Daisy to settle into the new-found ease of the vicarage, where the two little girls and their faithful friend embarked on a world of adventure. Daisy, a collie, was extraordinarily smart and thrived with the constant entertainment that the girls provided. Felicity no longer dreaded the time when Tess and Lucie would take their leave to walk back down the hill towards the Estates. Felicity would then curl up with a book in the makeshift den that she and Lucie had created under the window in the kitchen. With the afternoon sun streaming through the panelled glass, Daisy would crawl into the crook of her bent legs and snooze while Felicity lost herself in a book.

In the evenings after dinner, Felicity and her father would take Daisy for a walk through Knockmore, stopping to chat with people as they made their way up past their church. They'd often sit on the bench there and look down over the town. Felicity would squint her eyes and try to see the Estates, hoping she might be able to see Lucie out playing on the road.

"Are we different, Father?" she asked one evening.

"From what, my child?"

"From the others, the ones down in the town, the Catholics. Mother said we were different up here, better." She looked up at him.

"Oh, well no, not better, Felicity," he replied after a

moment. "A little different, perhaps, in our beliefs and I suppose our traditions, but not better. The Lord created us all the same, Felicity. It's what we do with our lives that matters. How we treat others," he answered, disappointed in himself that Felicity had ever been subjected to such entirely unchristian views.

The last few months had been a gift, spending time with her. It had been wrong of him to stay in the background. But he was so often distracted by his work and by Margot. He'd pray for the strength to be a better husband and father, knowing that one would come easier than the other.

"Come along, Felicity, let's get back. Mother asked to see you this evening. She's feeling much better. Isn't that tremendous news? The doctor thinks she should be back on her feet in no time."

He didn't miss the shadow passing across his daughter's face.

"Yes, very good news, Father," Felicity replied woodenly, feeling something squeeze her insides.

She'd hardly seen Mother lately. She was sometimes summoned and would sit nervously at the end of the bed before being brushed away as soon as Margot grew tired. But from the confines of her room, Margot had begun to sense a change of atmosphere in the house. Her rehabilitation was disturbed by snippets of joyous notes that drifted up the stairs, or floated up from the garden, weaving between the ivy next to her bedroom window. And most recently the din of a dog barking and children playing had started to arouse her from her depression-soaked coma.

Felicity felt the change as soon as she entered the room. For a start, the heavy drapes were open and the windows ajar. Mother was sitting bolt upright in bed, her usually unkempt hair, which hadn't felt the bristles of a brush in months, combed down.

"Felicity dearest, sit. Good evening, Michael," she cooed at the reverend.

The pair sat either side of the bed, equally nervous of the sudden transformation.

"What a lovely evening. Where have you been?" Mother enquired through narrowed eyes.

"We took a walk, dearest, to the church and back," Michael offered.

"How pleasant. Just the two of you?"

"Daisy too!" Felicity chimed in, forgetting herself.

"Daisy?" Margot's eyebrows lifted, the tight smile remaining on her lips.

Felicity looked to Michael, who'd fleetingly forgotten his very recent request for strength from the Lord and left Felicity to answer.

"My dog. Father got her for me last week . . . she's very good and very soft . . . " Felicity's voice trailed off as her mother's smile faded.

"A dog? Michael?" Margot's eyes flashed towards the reverend.

"Well . . . um . . . yes . . . a parishioner needed to be dug out of a hole with a dog that needed rehoming. Mr Power senior – you remember him, nice old man – well, he passed away, may he rest in peace. And the dog, well, like I said, she needed a home and um, I thought perhaps Felicity could do with a little friend to, well, keep her company – while you were unwell," he said, stumbling over his words.

"Funny, I thought I could hear incessant barking. I assumed it was from a neighbour. What a funny way to assist my recuperation," Mother laughed hollowly.

"Oh no, Daisy never barks. Well, she does bark but hardly ever," Felicity piped up, bravely defending her new friend.

"Well, I see there have been even more additions to the household, like your cheekiness, young lady." Margot stared at Felicity.

"I'm sorry, Mother," Felicity whispered, her eyes and shoulders instantly drooping.

"Perhaps it's learned behaviour?" Margot asked. "From that Tess and her tag-along child. How you gave them a position here, Michael, is beyond me. Common as muck, that family." Margot's chest puffed out dangerously.

"That's enough, Margot!" Michael stood up. "I won't have you speaking ill of the Maguires. They've cared for Felicity and the house beautifully, and I value Mrs Maguire's employment immensely. It's enabled me to continue to run the parish."

Michael's face was now puce with the effort and Felicity was so visibly taken aback that she sank so far down, she almost disappeared off the end of the bed.

"Michael!" Margot shouted but then exhaled dramatically and fell back against the pillows. "Please leave, I'm exhausted," she puffed.

Michael tumbled out of the door past Felicity, whose feet couldn't carry her quick enough. He headed towards the parlour to pour himself a shot of whiskey, usually reserved for the most stressful of situations, and Felicity disappeared into the kitchen to curl up with Daisy. Both were individually lost in their thoughts, which shared a common theme: sooner or later, all good things must come to an end.

"I've found out lots of things," Lucie told her, opening the tin box and taking out their detectives' notebook.

"That's good," Felicity said, distracted.

She was tired. Mother was now insisting that Felicity visited her every evening, wanting to know every detail of every day.

"Earth to Felicity, come in."

"Sorry, I'm here. Tell me everything you know." Felicity sat up, ready to hear the latest findings.

"Well," Lucie began. "Florrie lives in Station House with Sergeant Hughes and her kids. There's Dermot – he's ten – and Mary is five. She goes to Mass every Sunday and always buys the paper afterwards."

"Oh!" Felicity said, her interest aroused.

She wondered what it would be like if Florrie were her mother instead, or at least if she could meet her and talk to her, but for now, she felt happy just knowing she was out there. The tin box that resided in the fairy door of the oak tree was like a doorway to another life, one she longed to crawl through. She'd have liked to take a potion, like Alice in Wonderland, and vanish into the tree. But not without Lucie. Their friendship had grown over the summer, and she loved Lucie and Tess so much, but the summer was ending, she knew that, and before long she'd only see them for few hours in the afternoons.

"And Rosie has one daughter. I don't know her name. They moved to England for work, so she's not around any more," Lucie continued.

"I'll be sad when the summer's over," Felicity said suddenly.

"Let's make a pact," Lucie replied, "that we'll always be friends, no matter what. We could be blood sisters."

"I'd like that, but I'm worried that when Mother gets up again, she won't let us play. She never lets me play," Felicity said sadly.

Lucie nodded. She'd overheard her mam taking about Margot. She'd listened in at the back door as Mam chatted over the wall to her neighbour.

"It's the depression she has. That's why she's in bed – must be like the flu," Lucie said. "But she'll be up soon, my mam said. Said she knows from the way she's always giving out that she must be getting better. Said it was a pity the bed didn't swallow her," Lucie revealed.

"And that'll be the end of the fun, Lucie. It'll be back to lots of school work all the time."

"We'll find a way. We can leave notes for each other in the fairy hole. Our secret." Lucie pulled out a pocket knife borrowed from her brother to carve their names in the tree and bravely made a little stab at the palm of her hand before watching a blob of blood squeeze out. "Now you." Lucie passed her the knife.

Felicity winced as she closed her eyes and jabbed at her hand before opening her eyes and seeing a successful drop of blood colour her palm. They spat on their hands then for good measure and joined their hands as one.

"Friends for ever," Lucie said.

"For ever," Felicity repeated before collapsing onto the grass beside Daisy, who was snoring away happily. "Hey, you notice anything funny about Daisy?"

"Yes, she sleeps a lot, lazy girl. Isn't that right, Daisy?" Lucie said, rubbing Daisy's ears.

Daisy briefly lifted her head upon hearing her name before exhaling loudly and rolling onto her side for her second snooze of the hour. Yes, indeed, Daisy had started to sleep a lot lately. She'd also taken on a rather round form for such a young and active dog, which of course wasn't apparent to the two little girls laughing and giggling on the grass beside their doorway to freedom. It wasn't until Felicity casually mentioned it to her father that evening and the reverend kneeled to examine their household friend that she discovered the cause.

Michael stood up and exclaimed, "Felicity, I think the Lord has blessed our friend here. It looks very much to me as if Daisy's going to be a mother!" Michael laughed as he watched his daughter's eyes fill with delight. "And sooner rather than later by the looks of it!"

Felicity couldn't wait to tell Lucie the next day. The excitement was more than they could bear. The vet was called and confirmed that Daisy was indeed pregnant and must have already been by the time they'd taken her in. The vet had no way of knowing exactly when the birth would take place, of course, but it appeared to be imminent.

On the vet's advice, Felicity and Lucie set up some warm, cosy bedding in the outhouse and provided Daisy with plenty of water and food. They watched as Daisy increasingly escaped the warm sunshine and took refuge in her little sanctuary. All they had to do was wait patiently, which was proving very difficult for two excitable nurses in training.

"Now we won't be able to keep them, Felicity, but we'll find them good homes," Michael explained.

"Yes, I know, Daddy. I understand."

It was enough that she had Daisy and would have puppies for a short time. Even Tess seemed excited by the impending arrivals at the big house and always made sure to keep Daisy a little meat after dinner to ensure she was in good health for the birth.

Everyone was elated by the news except Margot. The

girls' excitement had woken her several times and when she questioned them over their constant squeals arising from the garden, Michael calmly informed her of the news.

"Well . . . um . . . dearest, it's tidings of joy. It seems Daisy is to have pups," he told her that evening.

Felicity watched from behind her father as Margot's face tightened and her nose upturned.

"Puppies! What a bother. Make sure you deal with it, Michael, when the time comes. And I don't ever want to hear or see those dogs, do you understand?"

It was the first pregnancy to occur successfully in Knockmore House and while the others were blissfully unaware, it wasn't lost on Margot. The thought of it made her reel with anger, bringing back all the feelings that she'd unsuccessfully buried, the secret that she could never tell. That the pregnancy of a *dog* could awaken those feelings after many years made the bile rise in her throat.

"Yes, Margot, I'll find them good homes. Fear not," he smiled.

"Please leave. I have a headache from all the noise."

Margot watched the pair of them skipping from the room together. What she wouldn't give to shout the truth at them, to scream that Michael hadn't been man enough to provide her with a child and instead was nurturing some common whore's child from the Estates, and a Catholic one at that.

She was fed up being in bed now, fed up with this mood. She needed to gain control back. She was sick of watching them play happy families. Post-traumatic stress, the doctor had called it. What would he know of what she'd endured in this house, filled with disappointments, filled with idiots?

She'd had the dream again. She'd been having it for

years. It always upset her. She rubbed at her head, trying to clear it. What a few months it had been, all started with that blasted woman launching herself off the landing. She'd probably done it on purpose.

And now here she was like an outsider in her own home, with life carrying on without her and that Tess bloody Maguire delivering her meals with an enormous fake smile plastered on her face, taking over her house and her family. Oh, she was sure Tess was enjoying seeing how the other half lived all right, pretending she was the lady of the house. And Felicity with all the freedom in the world . . . "Blossoming," Michael had said, "out and about all the time." No. It had to stop. It wouldn't do at all.

Felicity Montgomery

Then – 1978

"I think it might be time," Felicity told her father that afternoon.

The mother-to-be had spent much of the day panting and pacing in the outhouse, fluffing and circling her bedding in preparation. By the time Tess and Lucie were heading home that afternoon, Daisy was settled in her bed, resting for the ordeal that lay ahead.

"I'm going to miss it all!" Lucie huffed.

Lucie begged her mam to let her stay, but Tess insisted that it was best to leave Michael and Felicity to deal with it alone, and they'd return early the next morning, hopefully to some happy news.

"Good luck." Lucie hugged her friend goodbye and bent to kiss Daisy.

"Don't worry, Lucie," Michael told her. "We'll be keeping an extra close eye on her this evening."

Michael and Felicity spent late afternoon with Daisy, sitting by her side, but by seven o'clock, with nothing much happening, they paid their usual visit to Margot.

"Well, I may as well be talking to myself! Is no one listening to me?" Mother asked, feeling restless and fidgety.

"Sorry, dearest, other things on our minds." Michael tried to focus. "What were you saying?"

"Nothing. Forget it. You can go."

She dismissed them and they hurried back to Daisy, who in their absence had bravely delivered two tiny pups, black-and-white like her with small pink noses and curled-over ears.

"Look, Daddy!" Felicity picked them up. "A boy and a girl. Well done, Daisy."

She could hardly believe it and Michael was just as excited by the new additions. They sat and watched, fascinated, as one by one throughout the night, Daisy delivered a pup. She'd lick each one clean and the process would commence again. By the time the fifth pup arrived, it was almost two o'clock in the morning.

"I think that might be her lot, Felicity. Perhaps it's time you got some sleep," Father suggested, sure that Daisy's job was done.

"Okay, Daddy."

Felicity yawned and stood up reluctantly. She was just about to leave, when Daisy started to pant once more and with that, a final pup emerged.

"Another one!" Felicity squealed proudly.

Although this time, obviously exhausted, Daisy didn't begin the same process of licking and cleaning.

"I think something's wrong, Daddy."

Without faltering, Felicity reached down, tore open the amniotic sac around the pup and cleared the fluid from its nose.

"Come on, little guy," she whispered as she began to rub him vigorously, willing the life into the only all-black pup. "Come on, that's it, good boy," she repeated.

The pup started to wriggle in her hand and, thankfully, she noticed soft snuffles as his tiny nose sucked in his first taste of air. Felicity looked up at her father, who was watching in awe at his daughter's instincts and smiling down at her with admiration.

"Well done, Felicity," he whispered proudly. "Six pups safely delivered, thanks to you. Perhaps you'll be a vet someday."

Felicity held the little black pup close for a moment before holding her up to Daisy and letting her sniff him. Felicity stood and threw her arms around her father uncharacteristically.

"Thank you, Daddy," she muttered into his chest. "Thank you for this."

She didn't have the words to express the feelings that that summer had ignited in her – the sense of belonging, of mattering, of being. The entire evening had been a fascinating and incredibly bonding experience for father and daughter as they witnessed the miracle of life unfolding before them. Michael returned her embrace, also feeling the magic that the summer had instilled in them – a simplistic charm that had opened his heart to the possibility of happiness once more.

By the time Lucie and Tess arrived the next morning, Daisy was lying proudly in her bed with her six offspring feeding away contentedly. The girls watched the pups scramble over each other and crawl about blindly, twisting and falling over each other in the basket.

"I have something for the new babies," Tess offered, holding up the different-coloured ribbons she'd brought to tie around their little necks, so they could easily identify which was which.

Felicity and Lucie spent the whole day naming and renaming them, then gently cuddling them and rewarding Daisy with treats. An air of celebration hung in the air and when Michael arrived home for lunch, Tess had baked a Victoria sponge and placed six candles in the cake to celebrate the pups' birth.

"A birthday cake for the birthday pups," she announced.

"Now, let's see what you've called them," Michael added. "Perhaps we can do a little blessing," he suggested as they sat in the garden, minding their own business, enjoying the celebration.

The girls presented each pup one by one, announcing their name and giving a bow as they revealed the chosen name. There was Buster, Wilbur, Custard, Lily, Florrie and of course Lucky, the brave little pup who almost didn't make it. He was their favourite.

"Well, I've never seen the likes," Michael told them. "Without even thinking, Felicity reached down, cleaned him off and rubbed him to life. A miracle!" he exclaimed as he retold the story of Felicity saving Lucky's life.

They all clapped while Felicity took a confident bow.

"I don't know about you, but I'm exhausted," Michael told Felicity after Tess and Lucie left for the evening.

"Yes, I'm a little tired too, Daddy," Felicity agreed. "Could we visit the pups one last time before bed?"

"Oh, I think it would be wise to tuck them in. Come on," he winked, standing up from the table after supper.

Felicity picked up each pup in the dim light of the outhouse and with great care, kissed each little nose and whispered into their velvety fur.

"See you tomorrow, little pup," she promised.

Michael, feeling exhausted from the activities of the

night before, went to his room and was asleep almost before he uttered amen. Felicity, however, still filled with the excitement of the day, settled herself on the rug in her room, with sheets of paper and her colouring pencils, and set about drawing each pup from memory. She planned to stick them up the next day on the dreary wall of the outhouse, to brighten up the puppies' nursery.

She'd just finished Wilbur's portrait and was moving on to Florrie, when she barely heard the door of her room open, she was so ensconced in her work. But feeling the air change, she turned to see a form in the doorway. The light from the hallway behind disguised the features and Felicity gasped as it advanced into view to reveal Mother, smiling suspiciously at her.

"Mother!"

"Good evening, Felicity." Mother walked past her and sat on the end of her bed.

"What are you doing up, Mother? Are you well?"

"Most well, thank you. Thanks to your little party today. Quite the joyous occasion. I saw from the window."

She'd sat there earlier, watching with disgust, observing Felicity cartwheeling across the lawn, cheered on by Michael, whose nose had turned pink in the sunshine, like the strawberry-tinged cream that oozed from the cake. She'd seen Tess smiling at the frizzy-haired child, running about feral-like, her arms spread wide. They were happy – happy without her. Happy like she could never be. They were free.

"I'm sorry if we woke you, Mother." Felicity sat up and smoothed her skirt out, remembering to push her shoulders back and imagine a string pulling her head upwards, just as Mother always told her.

"What have you got there?" Margot asked.

205

"Drawings of the puppies, Mother."

"Bring them here."

Margot extended her hand impatiently and Felicity awkwardly got to her feet, trying to arrange the drawings before handing them over.

"Hah!" Margot laughed. "Are you sure these are dogs? They look like blobs to me. Oh and look, you've called one Florrie. Whose idea was that?" Mother said, looking at each one before tossing them to the floor.

Felicity's face flushed red as she bent to pick them up.

"And what do you propose to do with these dogs, might I ask?"

"Well, Father's going to find good homes for them, when the time comes." Felicity looked down at her feet, her voice quivering.

"Is that right?"

"Yes, he's going to ask around and see who'd like one."

"Hah, who'd want a blob like that?" Margot gestured towards the pictures that were shaking in Felicity's hands. "You know what happened to pups like that in my day? The problem was fixed, Felicity. We'd wipe our hands of them," she spat. "Your father is the head of the community, but you, you selfish girl, could never understand what a busy man he is and how important he is.

"I've watched you all summer dragging him out, letting his duties slip. There I was, sick in bed after poor Mrs Walsh's incident, all but forgotten by you, and there you are laughing and skipping about with those people! Those rough urchins from the Estates. Didn't I tell you, Felicity? We're different – better."

Felicity didn't know what to say as uncontrollable tears started to spill down her face.

"I'm sorry, Mother. I'm sorry. I'll find someone to take the pups. I'll ask Tess to help me."

"You'll do no such thing! People like us don't ask for help from people like them. You've let your father down, giving him idle rubbish to deal with."

Margot stood up and marched from the room, leaving Felicity sick to her stomach. She hadn't forgotten Mrs Walsh, had she? Had she dragged her father out? She hadn't meant to. Felicity heard the key to her door turn like she'd heard many times before – the familiar "clink, clink" that signalled her isolation – and she sank to the floor, curling her knees up and hugging them tightly to her, rocking gently back and forth to soothe herself.

"You're one of us, you're one of us, you're one of us," she whispered to herself until the words that had often offered her comfort started to calm her breathing.

Felicity got up and went to the window, hoping to find a star to wish upon – to wish that everything could return to the way it had been just an hour before. She looked up at the brightest star and was just about to squeeze her eyes tightly shut in preparation, when she saw a figure moving in the garden below. She pressed herself against the windowpane, straining to see who it was.

As it started down the lawn, the moon gradually illuminated the scene, revealing Mother striding purposefully down the garden towards the orchard, a coal sack in one hand, a shovel in the other. Felicity stood on tiptoe to try to see what she was doing. Had she found out about their treasures? Did she know about the fairy door?

It was impossible to see the orchard from the house, so Mother couldn't possibly know about the tin box and its secret contents. But what was she doing? Felicity started to panic and rushed to her door to try to open it. She knocked loudly, hoping to wake Father. Running back to the window, she saw another movement. Daisy had emerged from the outhouse and was wandering the patio below, sniffing about and wailing in the dim light. Felicity banged on the window, calling her name.

She stared out at the garden for what seemed like hours before seeing Mother emerge from the darkness and wander back up the lawn, this time with only a shovel in her hand. Margot stopped before she reached the patio, resting the shovel on the ground and looking up to where Felicity was standing frozen behind the glass. The moon shone down on her like a spotlight in the centre of a stage, like the leading player in her performance with an audience of one.

Margot smiled up coldly at her before dramatically lifting her hands and slowly wiping them together several times, her eyes never leaving Felicity's. Satisfied with her demonstration, Margot picked up the shovel, walked towards Daisy and lifted it before bringing it down in one swift movement on the dog's head.

Felicity heard a yelp and everything went black.

Felicity Montgomery

Then – 1987

Sammy rested his hand on Felicity's as she spoke, listening as she told him her secrets, things she'd never uttered out loud to anyone before, ever. He watched her speaking, her eyes fixed on the ground, staring ahead, remembering, her voice a whisper in the empty car park.

"Did my mam know? Did Lucie know?" he asked, shaking his head slowly from side to side in disbelief. "I just always thought you had this perfect life, living up there in the big house."

Felicity shook her head in response.

He'd thought she had it all – the perfect house, the perfect life. "Does your posh friend not want to come round and slum it with us down here for the day?" he used to tease Lucie when she spoke about Felicity.

"That's enough, Sammy," Tess would scold him. "You don't know what you're talking about."

But he'd thought he had. All he saw was a wealthy family, living in a big house, and a woman who treated his mother like crap, unable to understand why his mam continued to work there. He hadn't realised. Of course, he knew how fond his mam was of Felicity and Lucie adored

209

her, but her life seemed far from tragic to an outsider looking in.

"People see what they want to see, Sammy, but you have to be careful to look beyond," Tess would tell him whenever he asked about the Montgomerys.

"But that Margot one treats you like shit, Mam. Why do you take it?"

She'd ruffled his hair and said, "You can only be treated like dirt if you are dirt. Besides, I like keeping an eye on Felicity. I'm fond of her. If you knew her, you'd understand."

He was beginning to get the picture only now as he listened to Felicity speak. His father, Paddy, had told Tess for years not to get involved, but when her position there ended, he put his foot down.

"It's not your business any more. We don't know what goes on behind closed doors," Paddy told her whenever Tess got worked up over it.

Only Mam must have known, or guessed at least, what was going on and now Sammy knew, too.

"I can't believe she killed the dog."

Sammy was almost shaking with anger when Felicity finished telling him what had happened that summer. He remembered it now. The dog and its six brand-new puppies taken in the dead of night. They'd gone on about it for weeks, devastated by it. Lucie had spoken about nothing else for the rest of that summer.

But he knew the truth now. He almost wished he didn't. Sammy now sat silently, staring ahead, trying to make sense of it. How could he have got it so wrong? He didn't know what to say to her, suddenly at a total loss for words.

It was less than an hour since they'd left the smoky

atmosphere of Lennon's and sat on the wall outside side by side, but the gap between them now felt huge. Felicity could feel the heat of Sammy's hand over hers and suddenly felt the temperature rising to her face.

"I'm sorry. I don't know why I told you all that," she said at last, unable to meet his eyes.

What had she been thinking? She'd gone and ruined it now, like she ruined everything. He'd asked her so many questions and once she'd started, she'd found herself unable to stop. Maybe it was the can of cider from earlier, or maybe it was just him, but the floodgates had opened, and the years of frustration and isolation had forced everything to come spilling out. She hadn't meant to. She hardly knew him and yet . . .

"I'm sorry," she repeated.

If her mother ever found out, she'd never be allowed outside the house again. In fact, if she found out where Felicity was tonight, she was sure that Margot might bring that same shovel down on Felicity's head.

Felicity removed her hand from under his. "I should go . . . I need to go . . . Tell Lucie I had to go," she said, standing up and starting towards the gate, briefly disorientated by her surroundings and wondering which road would bring her back to Knockmore.

"Felicity, stop." He was right behind her. "What are you doing? Where are you going? Wait. Please."

"I just . . . I can't . . . I've said too much. Please don't tell anyone what I said. It's my problem. Please forget I said anything . . . I . . . "

But before she could finish, Sammy took her hands in his and stepped closer. She wanted to push him away, to run as fast as she could from it all, but she stood frozen to the spot, feeling his breath against her face as he inched closer to her, his cheek brushing off hers.

She fixed her eyes on her feet, afraid if she met his eyes, it would be too painful ever to look away. They stood for what seemed like hours, their breathing growing ragged. She wondered, could he hear her heart beating through her chest? Then, unable to stop herself, she looked up. Her eyes met his, finishing the story. Without needing to speak, he was right there, where she needed him to be. He held her gaze, silently answering her questions, his eyes steadying hers as he leaned forwards. Her body was pulled towards him and he wrapped his arms around her, silencing her worries with his mouth. It almost hurt. It felt so right, it ached.

"Felicity . . . Fliss, there you are!"

Felicity looked up to see Lucie, closely followed by Sean. He was weaving along behind her unsteadily, his mullet now looking better than Lucie's hair, whose face was now almost hidden within the masses of red-and-blonde frizz.

"I was worried. What have you been up to?" Lucie said, looking from Felicity to Sammy, her eyes settling on his with a scowl.

Felicity broke away, dropping her hands to her side.

"Where were you?" Lucie asked again, placing her hands on her hips.

Felicity didn't look up.

"Right here, Lu, what's your problem?" Sammy answered, his tone growing frosty with the unwanted interruption from his sister. "I've got to help the lads put the gear into the van," he said, turning towards Felicity, his voice softening. "Will you wait?"

"No, no way," Lucie piped in. "Mam made me promise we'd walk back together. Fliss is staying with me."

"Whatever." He ignored her, looking at Felicity instead. "Will you wait?"

"I'd better stay with Lucie and I don't want to upset Tess."

"Okay,' he grinned. "I'll catch up. Start walking, slowly. I'll be five minutes, okay?" Sammy took Felicity's hand and gave it a quick squeeze, followed by a look that made her stomach do an Olympic-worthy blackflip.

"Okay," she whispered, glancing over at Lucie, who was momentarily distracted by Sean, who was desperately trying to get her phone number.

Felicity took the opportunity to reach up boldly and kiss Sammy on the lips, lingering for just a second longer than necessary, just long enough to stop him in his tracks.

"Wow," he said, closing his eyes before breaking into a heart-wrenching smile and running off to catch up with the lads.

"What in the name of Jaysus are you up to, Fliss?" Lucie asked, linking Felicity's arm and breaking into a brisk walk.

"What do you mean?" Felicity asked innocently, trying to keep the smile off her face but finding it impossible to relax the muscles in her cheeks.

"He's no good for you, Fliss. A total dipshit. I told ya."

Felicity laughed at the blunt description and stopped to face her friend.

"I know he's your brother, Lu, but I don't know . . . I can't describe it. It's like I've known him all of my life. When he kissed me . . . "

Lucie rolled her eyes and made a barfing noise, sticking her tongue out as far she could for extra effect. Felicity giggled but continued, lost in the events of the evening.

"When he kissed me, it was like I just knew. It just felt right." She took Lucie's hands in hers. "Please, Lu, I don't know what happened tonight, but something did. Try to understand. Please, for me."

"Oh, Fliss! Please be careful. Promise me," Lucie said. But she'd already seen it – the look that passed over her friend's face – and she knew that no matter what she said, no one was listening. "I mean, you deserve a fella, but Sammy? Really?" She continued walking. "Of all the lads staring at you tonight, you pick him! Mam will freak," she said over her shoulder as Felicity ran after her to keep up.

"Please don't tell Tess," Felicity begged.

"I won't. But it's written all over your face. Just be careful," Lucie repeated. "Sammy makes you feel like that because he's had a lot of practice, you know. It's all show with Sammy, nothing behind it. I don't want you to get hurt."

Felicity nodded. She could hear her, but Lucie was right, she wasn't listening.

"How was Sean?" Felicity asked, changing the subject.

"Well, it was all going well until he headed into the toilet and came back stinking of barf then tried to kiss me again! Honest to God, Fliss, some of the lads around here . . . Did he really think I was going to kiss him with barf dribbling down his chin?" Lucie asked seriously.

Felicity erupted into fits of giggles. "Oh, God, Lucie, that's disgusting."

"Disgusting all right. Lucky, though, that that's when I came to look for you, only to see you getting face-sucked by my brother. Sure, that nearly made me puke myself."

The girls had to stop for a moment as they doubled over in laughter.

It was just then that Sammy came sprinting after them.

"What's wrong with you? I thought one of you was barfing," he said, which set them off again.

It took them ages to reach the corner of the Estates because of the laughing fits and the fact that Felicity was now finding it impossible to walk in the borrowed patent kitten heels. Sammy rested his hand protectively on her back to steady her as they made their way past the houses.

Felicity looked around in awe at this place she'd heard about all of her life. The houses were close together like they were all holding each other up, supporting each other. She couldn't ever imagine feeling lonely in a place like this. The front doors were all painted different colours, and they each had different gates and plants hanging outside, distinguishing one from the next.

When they reached the corner, she could see Tess waiting, the front door open. She was standing there clutching her dressing gown tight to her chest with one hand. Tess was out of the door before they were even inside the gate, throwing her arms around Felicity.

"Fliss, little one! Are you all right? I've missed you. Are you okay? Let me look at you." Tess stood back, taking in the striking beauty who now towered over her, helped by the loan of the shoes. "You look so grown up," Tess gasped. "Like something from a magazine. But you always were gorgeous," she smiled.

Felicity would have fitted right in among the pages of the magazines that Lucie left strewn all over the sofa in the sitting room. It had always shocked Tess how the reverend and plain old Maggie Treacy had created such a beauty.

"Margot's jealous of her. I'm convinced of it," Tess told Florrie once. "That's why she dresses her in those itchy navy woollen dresses, like a toddler. It's all to try to contain her beauty."

Well, it appeared Margot had lost, Tess thought now as she looked at the blossoming young woman before her in the tight black dress, hair tumbling down her back.

"I'm sorry, love," Tess said, dabbing at her eyes. "It's so good to see you."

Felicity hugged her tightly.

The same feelings of regret that Tess always had at having let Felicity down suddenly swept over her. Her husband, Paddy, was always telling her to steer clear of it all, warning her not to take on other people's problems. They'd argued about it and eventually, she came round to his way of thinking. They had their own two children to worry about. Besides, what could she have done? Taken her to live with them? She'd thought that Michael was on Felicity's side, would protect Fliss from Margot, but it seemed that while the reverend had found his spine, he'd lost it again just as quickly and she hated him for it. Enough now, she thought to herself. She's here now, that's all that matters.

Tess ushered them all into the kitchen, where she had sandwiches, tea and cake laid out, and she watched fondly as all three tucked in hungrily.

"Well, how was it?" Tess asked Sammy.

Felicity sat in the tiny kitchen staring with disbelief at a family chatting and laughing and joking with each other.

"Oh yeah, Sammy aka Morten Harket was out in full force tonight, Mam, all the eejits ogling him. I wanted to grab the mic and tell them all about the smell in his football boots!" Lucie teased and Sammy took a swipe at her.

"Now now, you two, play nice. Anyhow, any girl would

216

be lucky to be with my Sammy." Tess squeezed his cheek lovingly with one hand and ruffled his heavily gelled hair with the other.

She almost missed the look that passed between Sammy and Felicity, but not quite.

Felicity's eyes met Sammy's and he smiled at her, ducking from Tess's outstretched hand.

"Watch the hair, Mam. Morton Harket wouldn't let you ruin his quiff," he said, picking up the plates and starting to deposit them in the sink.

Tess followed him and gave him a hug. "Careful there, sweetheart." Tess whispered a warning in his ear, flicking her eyes towards Felicity.

God knows Tess loved her son, but he was far too good-looking for his own good, far too confident and talented, and she was sick of answering the door to sullen-looking girls who became obsessed with him after his interest in them quickly faded, as it always did. Tess had asked him about it before, wondered why none of the pretty girls were enough to hold his attention. He was nineteen years old and no girl had ever made it past the two-week mark.

"They're just not right for me, Mam. Yeah, they're pretty, but they don't get me. I'll know when I meet the right one," he'd told her.

Lord above, Tess had started to wonder if he was the *other* way inclined. Not that it would matter to her, she loved her kids for who they were, but sooner or later, Sammy would have to stop playing the field and settle down a bit, surely. But Felicity Montgomery was one game Tess didn't want him to play. He was sure to hurt her and she couldn't live with that, not after all the hurt the poor child had already experienced in her short life.

217

Pretending he hadn't heard, Sammy made his way out of the room, turning at the door. "Goodnight, fans," he bowed, never taking his eyes from Felicity, whose face turned beetroot red.

"Now, girls, I've made up an extra bed in your room, Lucie. Paddy's already in turned in and he's up early tomorrow, so try to keep it down. Fliss, are you sure no one's going to come knocking down the door in the middle of the night for you? Just so we're prepared," Tess asked. She'd assured her husband, Paddy, there'd be no trouble accompanying young Fliss.

"No, Tess. Father's away and Mother, well, Mother hasn't been great lately, you know . . . "

"Oh, I do, little one, don't worry. I don't like lying, just so you know, and I won't be making a habit of it, but I'm glad you're here with us for tonight, anyway," Tess said, turning away before the lump that had formed in her throat escaped into a sob.

"Thank you, Tess. It was the best night of my life."

"I'm sure it was, love," Tess said, knowing that it probably had been and it was the saddest thing she'd ever heard. "Now, I don't know about you, but I'm falling on my feet. I'll be asleep before my head even hits the pillow." She kissed them both. "Get yourselves to bed."

They chatted excitedly, tucked up in bed, still laughing about Sean and the other antics of the evening, but it wasn't long before Lucie drifted off, leaving Felicity alone with her thoughts. The noise from the band was still reverberating through her ears and she was still buzzing with energy – picturing him singing, him catching her, him putting his hand on hers, him kissing her . . . It went over and over in her mind on repeat while she stared at the ceiling.

218

His voice, his touch . . . Oh, God, she couldn't stop it! How he'd listened to her . . . his face when she'd told him about her life. Where had it all come from? She shouldn't have said so much. She suddenly felt sick and sat up quickly in bed. She looked at Lucie, gently snoring, her hair over her face, the glitter from her eyeshadow falling onto her cheeks like stars.

Creeping out onto the landing, she tiptoed to the bathroom, quietly closing the door behind her. She kneeled by the toilet, afraid she was going to throw up. The softness of the carpet felt comforting under her knees and she breathed slowly until the sickness passed. She ran the tap, putting her wrists under the cold water, letting it cool her and calm her thoughts.

She'd never felt the way she'd felt tonight. Would she ever feel it again? Knowing it was all she now needed, what had been missing all along . . . well, it made her hungry for more. She'd have done anything to freeze time. To slow it down and reverse it, so she never had to feel any other way.

Felicity opened the door and looked up to see him standing in the doorway of his bedroom, watching her, still wearing his white T-shirt and jeans. But he looked different – his earlier confidence gone, momentarily faded. He held out his hand to her and she noticed it shook a little.

Without thinking, she took it and stepped through the door to his bedroom, seizing her chance to pause time. He touched her face, smoothing her hair and tucking it behind her ear. She instinctively pressed against him, drawn to him, unable to stop herself, and he took her in his arms and kissed her. It was urgent, as though he, too, sensed this break in time, reserved only for them.

He hadn't known how to act earlier, how to help her,

but he knew now and she let him. She knew she'd already crave what she'd been missing when he stopped, but for now, all she could feel were his lips on hers.

She slipped off her nightdress and stood in front of him nervously. He touched her, cupping her breasts, caressing them, and she gasped. He pulled his T-shirt over his head and took her hands, placing them on his smooth chest, just like she'd imagined when she heard him sing.

He felt it, too. Every touch went through him like an impact, a shock, a blow to every nerve ending.

Her body blazed next to his and they fell onto the bed together. He lay over her, searching her eyes, and then he moved towards her and she wrapped her legs around him. There was no going back now as they melted into one another – every memory, every feeling, every heartbeat split into the before and after. The before fading, the pain diminishing, and the after filling her with a light that she didn't even know existed.

"What about your dad?" he asked her sleepily after a while, wrapping himself around her. "Didn't he know what was going on?"

She didn't answer for a while. "He knew some. I used to think he cared about me, but he stopped too, just like everyone else . . . "

But he didn't hear her. He was already asleep, dreaming of her.

Felicity Montgomery

Then – 1978

Felicity woke the next morning, confused.

"You're very hot, little one, do you feel sick?" Tess asked.

Felicity felt Tess's hand on her forehead and slowly opened her eyes to see the concerned look on her face, then she remembered.

"Tess . . . the puppies . . . I saw . . . " she started.

Her eyes caught a movement, hovering over Tess's shoulder, where Margot was standing, one finger held to her lips in a silent warning.

"What did you see, little one?" Tess asked.

Felicity reached round to the back of her head and rubbed at the place where a lump the size of an egg had erupted.

"You've had a fall, love, but you're all right now. What did you see?" Tess asked again.

"I . . . I saw . . . I . . . " She stopped, unable to finish.

Tess placed an ice pack under her head. "There, love. You poor thing." She couldn't decide if she was more shocked to see Margot up and about, or by the news that there had been a burglary last night at the vicarage and both the puppies and Daisy were gone.

"But who would do such a thing?" Lucie had cried when Michael had met them in the driveway that morning, looking ashen-faced. "Why?" she'd shouted.

"Well . . . I . . . um, called the sergeant and he told me it happens all the time," the reverend explained. "They broke the lock on the outhouse. Perhaps it was someone looking to steal gardening equipment or bicycles and they happened upon something more valuable – to us, at least. It was Margot who heard the commotion. Then poor Felicity fell out of bed and bumped her head. Margot had to wake me, but by then it was too late – quite the night." He shook his head.

"Another thing . . . " he'd said, pausing, looking directly at Tess and then over his shoulder to where Margot was standing at the front door, arms crossed, watching them talk.

"Oh," was all Tess had managed, following his line of vision.

Margot approached the bed now. "Leave us now, Tess, please. I want to speak to Felicity alone."

Tess bent down quickly to kiss her forehead and mouthed, "It'll be all right."

"Shut the door, please," Margot called after her.

Margot sat down on the bed, her weight nearly toppling Felicity on the floor as the mattress sagged to the side.

"Now, Felicity, you've had an awful shock with that terrible fall," she started. "You were dreaming. Whatever it was, it must have been quite terrifying. Was it?"

Felicity nodded, her eyes wide.

"And I have to tell you some more sad news. Someone broke into the outhouse in the night and took both the puppies and Daisy. I'm sure they plan to sell them. Puppies are valuable to some. How very sad."

"But I saw you. I saw . . . "

"Please don't babble, Felicity," Margot tutted. "You saw *nothing*. Remember that. You saw nothing."

"But you hit her . . . the shovel, the coal sack," Felicity whimpered, trying to sit up.

"Oh dear, you must have hit your head very hard. I was in bed all night. I've been unwell, remember?" Margot raised her eyebrows. "I heard some noises outside and then I heard you fall. Father had to be woken to lift you." She placed her hand on Felicity's. "You have quite the imagination, Felicity. You wouldn't want to let that get away with you," Margot said, squeezing her hand so tight that Felicity was sure she could feel her bones cracking.

"Ouch!" she squealed, wriggling her hand free.

"Do you like Tess and that girl coming here? Would you like them to have to leave because you're making up wild stories? Maybe it's them, filling your head with wild thoughts?"

"No, please. Please don't send them away. Please."

"Or much worse, Felicity. You could be locked up, locked away with all the other precocious children who conjure wild stories. Now," Margot said, smoothing out her woollen skirt as she stood and righted Felicity. "Let's not speak of this again. Understand? A bad dream is just that. Now rest. School starts very soon and you need to be right for your studies."

But Felicity knew what she'd seen.

She saw Mother go down the garden with the coal sack, wriggling with the lives already buried inside it. She saw Mother lift the shovel and bring it down on poor Daisy's head. She'd tried to stop her, but the room had started to whirl. She'd fainted, but not before her heart had splintered apart there and then, flying in every direction so that it would be impossible for anyone ever to glue it all back together. One tiny, almost invisible fragment had shot out of the window and landed deep in the patch of earth beside the ill-fated dogs.

Felicity started to cry, allowing a river to flow down her face. She couldn't understand it. She couldn't make sense of it, but she knew what she'd seen and she was scared.

"Can I see Lucie?" Felicity begged Tess the next day when she came upstairs with her lunch. "Please, I need to talk to her."

"I'm sorry, pet, but you must rest. Try to eat the soup – it'll make you feel better," Tess encouraged. "Can you talk to me?"

Felicity shook her head. Should she tell? She couldn't risk them being sent away. Everything had changed in a few days, the atmosphere in the house now heavy, a sudden pressure pushing out from behind the walls.

Tess bent again. "Tell me, Fliss. What is it? Tell me," she said, willing her to speak.

"It's nothing."

Tess stood up. "I'll come back later," she promised.

"Could you ask Father to come and see me?" Felicity whispered and Tess nodded.

Perhaps if she could see Father alone, she could tell him what she'd seen and he'd fix it – make Mother go away again. It could go back to the way it was before – just the two of them. He'd only been to see her once the day before, with Mother close behind him.

"I'm so sorry, Felicity," he'd told her. "I'm as sad as you

are." He'd hugged her then. "I've asked Sergeant Hughes to keep an eye out – perhaps they'll be found."

Felicity was almost hopeful for a moment before she remembered that they'd never be uncovered unless the ground where Mother had buried them was somehow upturned.

"Let's not give false hope," Margot had piped up. "A case of missing puppies is hardly the correct use of police time," she'd laughed and Felicity had felt sick.

"Now, I'm off to a tea party tomorrow, hosted by Mrs Kidney. I haven't seen her in so long. She said it's to welcome me back into society," she'd chuckled. "I'll be needing you to rest, Felicity. Father has an important meeting tomorrow and you're to have no visitors. Do you understand? I've told Tess the same. Total rest."

Felicity had nodded. She'd thought of nothing else for the rest of the day. She lay awake that night thinking about it and was still wondering what to do the next day, when she heard the gravel crunch in the driveway. Felicity rushed to the window on the landing to see Father getting out of his car. He'd know what to do. He looked tired as she watched him stroll into the house, then a few minutes later she saw Tess and Lucie leaving for the day. She rushed back to her room then heard his footsteps on the stairs and watched as the door handle turned.

"Felicity, how are you feeling?" Father asked. "Tess said you wanted to see me."

"Yes, I wanted to . . . "

"Actually, I wanted to talk to you, too." He sat on the edge of the bed and put his hand on hers. "They've found Daisy, but it's not good news," Father said. "I'm afraid she's dead."

Felicity didn't move. Did he know?

"She was found in the field behind us," he continued.

"She must have got in and been kicked by one of the horses. Terrible shame. No sign of the puppies, though. Let's hope they're safe," he added.

Felicity stared ahead. He didn't know.

"Sometimes these things happen and there's no reason." He patted her hand.

What should she do? She knew what she'd seen. She didn't want Tess and Lucie to go away, and nor she did she want to be locked up. But then maybe it would be better than being locked up here. She couldn't lie any more. It was the right thing to do. It was what her teacher always said – what Mrs Walsh used to say and what her father would tell his parishioners on a Sunday. "If you tell the truth, you can't go far wrong," that's what he always said and she owed it to Daisy.

"But there *was* a reason!" she began. "I saw it. I saw what happened." She took a breath and told him, her body shaking as she did.

He could hardly understand her through the tears.

"What?" Father stared at her, shocked. "No. No, Felicity." He shook his head. "It can't be. You must be mistaken." He watched her little face willing him to believe her as she roughly wiped the tears from her face with her sleeve. "No, you must be mistaken," he repeated.

Felicity stared at him silently.

He couldn't think. What was she saying? There was no way Margot would do such a thing, was there? Was Felicity lying? But why would she lie? He could see by how upset Felicity was that she believed the story, there was no doubt about that, but could she have dreamed it? He'd grown to love her more than anything else in the world over the summer, finally been allowed to get to know her, and what

226

he knew was that she was good and kind and honest. Could this be some form of stress manifesting itself? Could this be a result of Margot's treatment of her? Was Margot crazy? Had the months in bed and the depression made her psychotic? Felicity's eyes pleaded with him.

"This is a grave accusation, Felicity. Are you sure?"

"I'm sure."

"Come with me."

He stood and she followed him through the house before making their way to the outhouse. Michael stepped into the darkness, looking about for anything untoward. Once their eyes had adjusted, he noticed the shovel wasn't in its usual place, lined up on the wall beside the other tools. Instead, it was nestled behind the coal bunker at an angle suggesting it had been placed there at haste.

He pulled it out and made his way back towards the light. There was a small amount of dried earth stuck to the rounded tip – not unusual for a shovel – but otherwise nothing else looked out of place. He was about to put the shovel back and thankfully deem the whole thing a misunderstanding – and then he saw it. There, on its edge, was a smudgy red streak and nestled in the small lump of dried earth were a few stray black hairs.

Michael dropped the shovel and sprinted towards the orchard. The ground by the wall was as it always was: hardened muck covered with offerings from the trees above. He walked along the perimeter wall searching for clues before his eyes settled on the old vegetable patch, which had in recent years been sadly neglected. The earth had been newly turned and he clearly observed the darkened ground, sticking out like a sore thumb compared to the paler dry earth nearer the trees.

"Good God!" Felicity heard him say.

He dropped to his knees, frantically clawing at the ground with his hands, throwing the soil to the side. Felicity watched as Father unearthed the corner of the coal sack, just as she'd described. He put his hands to his face.

"Good God, no. What on earth? Oh my God. Oh my God . . . "

"Daddy?" Felicity crouched beside him and reached her hand towards his.

He took it and held it.

"I'm sorry, Daddy. I couldn't stop it. I tried, but I couldn't stop it." His eyes filled with tears and not knowing what else to say, she asked, "Will we pray?"

"Yes, my love, let us pray," Father said, taking both of her hands.

They prayed together, holding each other tight. They prayed for Daisy, murdered in cold blood and thrown over the wall. They prayed for the innocent pups, suffocated by hatred. And Michael prayed silently for strength, to face what he knew he could no longer deny. He begged the Lord to guide him, to help him do the right thing, knowing it was all he had left to do.

"I'll need to talk to her alone this evening, Felicity, you understand?" He couldn't bring himself to say her name.

They covered over the pups' grave and returned to the house downtrodden.

"Yes, Daddy, but I'm scared. Mother said she'd send Tess away, send me away."

"I won't let that happen. I'll fix it. You have my word. I'll come to you afterwards. I'll tell you what happened, I promise."

The house was in total silence when Margot swept into

the hallway of Knockmore that evening. She was in high spirits, having been received most favourably by Mrs Kidney and the small band of women in attendance at her "welcome back" tea party. They'd briefly spoken about Mrs Walsh and her untimely death, and Margot was appreciative that her time spent in self-appointed captivity had proved her *devastation* at the old lady's sudden passing.

Yes, she felt wonderful.

She removed her hat, placed it on the mahogany table by the mirror and smiled to herself. The last few days had been hard, but taking control back was essential and she felt in charge once more. She felt strong. Everything had been left to fall to pieces. Felicity was practically running wild and clearly had Michael wrapped around her little finger. No, it wouldn't do. It was all to protect them really – that was always the goal. To protect her secret – and the secret must be controlled, at whatever cost.

She just needed to figure out how to get rid of Tess and her child. It was too risky having them poking around all the time. She'd felt so angry that day, looking down at them and those silly puppies from her window. She almost hadn't known what she was doing until it was done. But it was the right thing to do. She'd dealt with it, just like she dealt with all the problems life threw at her. She placed her gloves on top of her hat and turned to see Michael standing in the doorway of the parlour.

"Margot, a word, please?"

He spoke quietly and she wondered what parishioner had passed away now. He took it all to heart. He needed to learn not to be so very attached.

"Make it quick, Michael, I'm tired," she said, crossing

the hallway impatiently in preparation for another sob story.

She watched him as he sat at his desk and she sat down in her reading chair as he slowly began. She grew more and more incensed as she listened.

"Preposterous, Michael! The child is psychotic," Margot laughed, trying to remain calm.

She hadn't imagined for a moment that Felicity would tell him anything. She'd underestimated her, believed she'd said enough to warn her. Perhaps she should have been clearer.

"Margot, I'm giving you one opportunity to tell me what happened. Felicity was worryingly certain about what she saw."

Margot looked at him sitting in his chair, watching her suspiciously. How dare he! There was no way she was going to let herself be buried with those puppies and let that child get the better of her. She'd deny it as she always did. It had seen her well this far.

"How dare you even suggest such a thing!" she shouted, struggling to dispense the claims.

Not only had she underestimated the girl, but she'd also underestimated the relationship between father and daughter – one that she'd allowed to blossom . . . another mistake.

"I see what's happening here. The child is delusional. I've always thought it. And you've allowed her crazy imagination to thrive by subjecting her to the lower classes and their habits." She was on a rant now and not even a shovel to the side of her face could have stopped her. "All along I've tried to raise her in such a manner that she understands her stance in the community. She *is* different. We *are* different. But you've allowed—"

"Enough!" Michael picked up a book and slammed it down hard on his desk. "Enough," he whispered, exhausted by her tirade.

"What you have raised is a prisoner. What you have raised is a child so afraid of you that she shakes when you walk into the room. What you have raised is a child who doesn't understand who she is, let alone where she belongs. You tried to keep me away from her, cocooning her here in a strange solitary world, and I let you. God forgive me, I let you," he shouted. "But what I saw this summer, what I witnessed is a kind, gentle girl with real compassion for others.

"We *are* different, Margot. We are different in that there's no real warmth in this house, like the warmth I see in all the other households in Knockmore. You are different. You deceived me. Let on to be someone you weren't. But I see now.

"Maybe I always knew but didn't want to believe it. I thought I was wrong. Lord knows I prayed I was wrong. But I see it was all a game, all a way for you to better yourself from where you came." He stood over her now, looking down at her. "But let me tell you, where you came from isn't what made you. Where you came from are real people with real feelings and love. All that lies within you is hate. Pure hatred." He stopped for a moment, out of breath from the exertion that had laid dormant for years, before gathering himself. "But how you could take the lives of God's creatures in cold blood is an abomination." He shook his head, worried his emotions would fail him now.

"How dare you! How—" she started to argue.

"Save your breath, Margot. I found them. I found where you buried them. There's no point in further denial.

231

And for what? That's what I can't understand. For what? To hurt her? To hurt me? To prevent us from being happy? I'm going to the archdeacon tomorrow to ask for his advice on how best to proceed. But I can't let you hurt an innocent any more. I won't let you. She's my flesh and blood, and that's all that matters."

Margot closed her eyes and took a deep breath. "Where is she now?" she asked, a sudden calmness taking hold of her.

There was no point in denying it, but she wouldn't let him win. The archdeacon would have her removed, possibly committed, and she'd come too far to go backwards.

Michael ignored her, still trying to catch his breath.

"Where is your flesh and blood now?" Margot repeated, standing up.

She knew what she had to do. There was nothing else for it.

"She's in her room. Leave her be. She doesn't need to hear any more," he said as she approached him.

"No, she doesn't need to hear this, but you do. Sit down, Michael."

He sat, exhausted, not knowing what she was going to tell him, what far-fetched excuse she was going to offer. But he'd never have guessed, not even as she stood over him and told him – not in a million years.

She could have delivered her story in so many ways. She could have pleaded that she'd been misguided, fuelled by inadequacy. She could have told him about the regret she felt, the shame of what she'd become, but instead, she delivered it as a threat.

Michael sat shaking his head, unable to understand what she was saying, refusing to believe her cruel words. He listened as she made her secret his. The secret she'd carried for eight years. The secret that left a young girl so distraught that she took her own life because of Margot's actions: a parish priest blackmailed, a family left distraught, and a baby stolen from her mother and passed off as their own. It was more than he could bear.

"And so help me God," she said through gritted teeth. "I'll tell everyone that you knew all about it, Michael. That the great Reverend Michael himself planned it all with Father Nugent. You wanted a family so much and you saw your opportunity. You'll be the one locked up! You'll be the one destroyed. And Felicity will be left homeless, disgraced. Would you do that to her? Would you? And all because you couldn't give me a child, you gormless, weak, weak man. You promised me a different life to this!" Margot screamed.

Michael closed his eyes as he heard her threats, hoping that she was lying, praying it wasn't real, that it was the invention of a deranged mind. But he knew before she'd finished that his hands were tied. It would ruin him, ruin the community, destroy his position. He wished he didn't know now, that she'd never told him. He'd have been happier to live in ignorance.

He thought now of the planning that must have gone into it all and of the cruel actions of a woman filled with enough hatred to execute it. It was insane, but it all made sense now. Her contempt for the child she couldn't bond with, her lack of maternal instinct, her aloofness, her sensitivity over Felicity's looks. "Sent from heaven," people would say about Felicity and now he knew. Felicity had been sent from heaven and landed straight in hell, and there was nothing he could do to stop it – nothing at all.

Enough lives had been ruined already. What was the sense in destroying more? There was no way he could have pre-empted what was coming earlier that day when he'd kneeled and prayed for strength. If he'd known, he'd have bitten his tongue and begged for forgiveness instead – forgiveness for being another person to let Felicity down. He rose then and walked towards her.

"You will never speak of this again," Michael said, pointing his finger at her chest. "You will never utter it to another living being. You will make yourself scarce in this house. Do not interrupt me!" He held his hand in front of her. "Felicity will never hear about this, ever, or I will tell the story no matter what the consequences. You are dead to me, Maggie Treacy. We're married only by name.

"You will continue your duties looking after the church and accompanying me to service, but I forbid you to consort with the other ladies lest you let slip your little secret. You will allow Tess to continue working here with her daughter in the afternoons, keeping the house. I think that is reasonable to ask," he finished. "Now, get out!"

"No longer your flesh and blood, Michael, no longer yours. Never was," Margot spat before turning on her heel and slamming the door.

Michael slumped to his knees. Felicity wasn't his. What had Margot done? She'd taken everything and torn it to shreds, buried it for ever. He was nothing but a coward. He'd never be able to look at Felicity's sweet face again. Not because she wasn't his – he'd have loved her regardless – but because he'd let her down.

Always do the right thing and you'll never go far wrong.

Deep down, he knew he hadn't done the right thing. He hoped by allowing Tess and Lucie to stay, it would be enough to save Felicity, because he couldn't now.

He'd won the battle, but Margot had won the war.

Felicity Montgomery

Then – 1978 to 1987

Father hadn't fixed it. He'd come to see Felicity in her room before he went to bed – a promise is a promise, after all – but he hadn't fixed it.

Felicity had heard the raised voices seeping upstairs as she'd waited, shocked to listen to her father, with his even temper, shouting at Mother. She'd sat pinned against the door trying to hear what they were saying. Trying to decipher the muffled tones that drifted through the wood. Then she'd waited to hear Margot shouting back and it had come eventually, after what seemed like for ever.

Had she admitted what she'd done? Felicity was terrified the entire time. Frightened her mother would storm into the room at any moment, grab her by the hair and lock her up for ever. But then she'd heard the door slam and footsteps on the stairs. She'd scrambled into bed, pulling the covers up over her head, barely breathing.

But Mother never came. It was Father who quietly opened the door a little while later. Felicity peeked over the covers, her little body trembling as he'd tried to explain.

"There are some things that we can't understand, Felicity. There are some things that we shouldn't try to comprehend. But know that it's all part of God's plan," Father had said, sitting on the end of the bed, staring at his feet, his shoulders drooped.

"I know it's hard for you to understand, but I'm going to ask something of you now, Felicity, that you'll find hard, that you'll question. But you must have faith that it's the right thing to do. Someday, I hope you'll understand that life isn't always easy. Sometimes we must do what's best for everyone."

His hands were clasped tightly together and his eyes fixed closed, afraid to meet her gaze as she waited for him to make it better.

"Yes, Daddy."

"I'm going to ask you to promise with all of your heart never to speak of this incident to anyone again, ever," he finished.

He finally met her eyes and she read the anguish in them as she tried to understand. He looked so sad as he pleaded with her and she saw it, recognised it. It was how he'd looked when she saw him by the vegetable patch earlier that day.

"Daddy?" She reached her hand towards him but he shook it off. "Daddy?" she repeated as he stood up.

"Please, Felicity. Don't make this any harder."

"But Daisy, the puppies?"

"I'm begging you, Felicity. I'm begging you to forget what you saw. Please, for me?" He didn't insult her by trying to convince her she was mistaken – didn't try to tell her she was delusional. "You have to trust me."

"But she'll lock me up, send Tess and Lucie away. She told me. Please, Daddy. Make it go away." Tears sprang to her eyes as she pleaded.

"No, Felicity. You have my word, no one will send you away, and Tess and Lucie can stay. But I promise you, this is the only way I know how to make it go away. You have to trust me," he told her, taking advantage of her good nature, knowing she'd do anything to prevent him from feeling pain – the same pain they both shared.

Felicity looked up at him, understanding that he was hurting, too. She could feel it.

"I will. I trust you, Daddy," she answered, nodding sadly.

"Thank you, Felicity, thank you for trusting me."

There was nothing more to say. No other way to explain that he'd betrayed Felicity – betrayed the trust he didn't deserve. After Margot had left him in the parlour, he'd tried to convince himself that he was protecting her, but deep down Michael knew there was only one person he was protecting: himself. He turned then to look at her before he left.

"I'm sorry, Felicity. So very sorry. More than you'll ever know."

"I forgive you," she whispered and he felt the words like a knife.

Lord knows, he'd never forgive himself.

After that, everything changed. Whatever events led them to that summer in 1978 – when for a time everything had seemed so perfect – whatever twist of fate had enabled it to reach a climax also allowed everything to come crashing down around them. There were no winners after that summer. They'd all lost.

Michael threw himself back into the Church, working long hours and avoiding home. Felicity often wondered as the years passed what had changed that night, what had happened. Perhaps what he'd seen was too much for him to handle. Maybe he was annoyed with Felicity for telling the truth. She wished she'd said nothing. She'd ruined it all by telling him. She'd never repeat anything again, she swore that much to herself – not even to Lucie.

Felicity learned to accept her existence, relishing the stolen moments of happiness over the years with Lucie and Tess, when Mother had a *headache* and took to her room. She managed to conceal herself from her mother's tempers by throwing herself into her studies. They were rarely all together as a family, except on a Sunday, when they'd all go to church together and she'd listen to her father preach about love and forgiveness and acceptance. And she'd try to believe that her life was all part of God's plan – if the plan meant three ruined lives, existing together but alone, that is.

Father made an attempt of sorts to make amends when she was eleven years old, when he arrived home with a dog.

"I got this for you," he'd smiled awkwardly. "Thought maybe it's been time enough."

It had been so long since he'd spoken to her that she'd jumped when he walked into the kitchen. He was holding a sandy-coloured scruffy-looking dog under his arm.

"It's a male . . . so . . . well . . . no . . . you know," Father said.

"I'm not sure. Won't it, you know?"

How could she put it? Won't it send Mother into a thunderous rage, causing her to bludgeon another dog in the night with a shovel? She still thought about it, even though she wasn't allowed to talk about it.

"No harm will come to him. I can assure you," he told Felicity, handing over the dog who'd never be Daisy.

238

Father never looked at the dog again after that. Lucie suggested they call him Scruff and they did like him, but both had never really got over the so-called disappearance of Daisy and the pups. Besides, Scruff was far too independent and didn't need them to entertain him. He made his own fun, stealing and burying things. None the less, he was a companion of sorts to her, she supposed – someone to talk to.

If it hadn't been for Tess and Lucie, who continued to arrive every weekday after school for a few hours, Felicity was sure she'd have shrivelled up and died. Tess recognised the change after that first summer, too. Something was different. Felicity withdrew again and the reverend was scarcely about, although at first she put it down to Margot being up and well again.

As soon as Margot was back on her feet, Michael had all but vanished from the house and disappeared from his daughter's life. Tess understood his reluctance to be around Margot, but the relationship that Tess had so admired between father and daughter that summer had withered almost as soon as it had bloomed. Then again, she could see why. Margot stamped her authority everywhere, always making her presence felt whenever the Maguires were there. She issued ridiculous tasks to Tess and was continually trying to prevent the girls from playing together, but Tess was well able for her.

"Will I clean the chandelier next?" Tess retorted one day after Margot had asked her to remove and hand wash the heavy drapes in the parlour.

That had shut her up for a few days. No, Tess wouldn't be bullied by her. She needed the job, but not that much – and the real reason she stayed was for Felicity. She'd long suspected that Margot was prone to hitting her. She'd spotted a few bruises over the years, but try as she might, she could never get Felicity to tell.

"You can tell me anything, little one. I'll always try to help you," she'd said one day after noticing a sizeable bruise on her arm.

"I fell. Silly me," Felicity always replied, quickly changing the subject, and Tess would return home weighted down with guilt.

"You can't get involved," her husband told her. "It's enough that you're there for her, that's what counts."

She knew he was right, at least she hoped he was, and the friendship between the girls filled her with joy.

They'd managed to stay close over the years, even though at times Margot made it impossible. But the fairy door had helped. Lucie would sneak out to the tree while Felicity was undertaking her lengthy study sessions and leave her funny notes, which Felicity would retrieve as soon as she could get away for a few moments, generally under the guise of trying to find something that Scruff had pilfered.

Lucie still kept Felicity up to date on all the sightings of Florrie and of all the goings-on in the Estates in her notes – everything they didn't get to discuss during the week under Margot's watchful eye. It was like reading a comic book and it entertained Felicity throughout many lonely hours. As the years crept by and Lucie reached various milestones, Felicity reached hers alone and through listening to Lucie's accounts of what growing up should be.

Felicity was developing quickly into a young woman, growing more and more beautiful as she did. When her breasts began to show, Margot ridiculed her. When she got her period at eleven, Margot called her a slut and locked her in her room. But whatever abuse Margot threw at her, Felicity accepted it, staying firm in her resolve never to tell. By the time she was fifteen, Felicity towered over her mother in every way.

Margot knew then – realised who it had been all those years, who it was who'd been appearing to her in her dreams, watching her, haunting her. Margot looked at Felicity one day and noticed that same face staring back at her. She'd dropped the book she was holding in her hands in shock, suddenly understanding who it was who'd been visiting her in her sleep all along. Felicity was her mother's daughter all right. There was no denying it.

"Felicity's got so tall," Tess said one day on the rare occasion that Margot was having a good day and some element of conversation passed between them. "She reminds me so much of someone. I can't think who it is – it'll come to me."

She never got the chance. Tess was dismissed the next day. Felicity tried to object. She'd even gone to her father about it, but he didn't want to hear. But there was one positive, she supposed, when the physical abuse was replaced by drinking. It made Margot quieter and often saw her collapsing in a comatose state in her room for hours. It turned out Maggie was her father's daughter too, in every way.

Felicity was so lonely during that time. But she was thankful for the drinking. After all, without it, Michael would never have encouraged her to volunteer at the Brownies to get her out of the house, and she'd never have been reunited with Lucie and Tess.

In a way, it was the drink that drove Felicity straight into Sammy's arms.

Felicity Montgomery

Then – 1987

"Jeez, Lu, talk about scaring me to death."

Felicity had forgotten where she was for a moment, almost jumping out of her skin when she woke to see Lucie peering down at her from her bed, to where Felicity lay curled up on the camp bed below.

"Sorry," Lucie giggled. "I was willing you awake with my eyes," she said, opening her eyes wide and staring intently at her.

"That's terrifying," Felicity laughed and rolled onto her back.

"Well, how do you feel this morning?"

Felicity had sneaked back into Lucie's room after Sammy drifted off to sleep and had thought of nothing else all night, only falling asleep what felt like moments before. But she wasn't going to tell Lucie that. Felicity put her hand to her face and could still smell the delicious fragrance of his aftershave lingering on her fingertips, making her stomach flip.

"Great," Felicity sighed and fluttered her eyelids.

"Fliss, what *is* up with you?" Lucie said, tossing a pillow at her face. "I hope you're not still thinking about

Sammy. I'm telling you, he's a loser. You need to find a decent lad. You know, one who'll treat you right."

"Sammy would treat me right!" Felicity threw the pillow back. "Anyway, where and when exactly am I supposed to meet someone else?" Felicity turned on her side to look at her friend. "Come on, Lucie, give him a chance."

"You think I don't know my own brother? Love 'em and leave 'em, that's his motto!"

But Felicity didn't care. This was different – this was real.

"Anyway, chances are I'll never even see him again after today. Last night was like a military operation and who knows when my parents will go out together again. It was a one-off, Lu. At least I still have Brownies."

Felicity smiled despite herself, knowing she wasn't out of the woods yet and still needed to get home safely before she was missed. She couldn't mess it up now, or she'd lose the small bit of freedom she'd gained. And she had a reason now, more than ever, to hold on to it.

"Talking of which, I'd better get moving."

"Oh, come on, the wicked witch can't keep you locked up for ever. You'll be eighteen next year and then you'll be free to do whatever you want," Lucie said.

"Yeah, you'd think."

Felicity shook her head. They'd already discussed what plans had been laid out for Felicity as soon as she finished school. Lucie had been shocked, but Felicity had accepted that it was just how it was going to be – or at least she had until now.

Margot had arranged a position for her to train as a librarian in Knockmore after she finished school and sat the state exams at the end of it. Felicity had studied so hard, knowing already that she'd ace them, giving her the points to do anything her heart desired. What she wanted more than anything was to be a vet, to head off on the bus to the university in Dublin and never look back, but she knew it would never happen. Some dreams just don't come true.

"And how do you propose that to work, dear?" Margot had laughed at her, the tinkly sound ringing in Felicity's ears. "A vet? I've never heard the likes! And good luck to you affording the fees alone. No, no, it won't do. What you need is a good solid position. Besides, your duty is here in Knockmore, with your father."

"Daddy? You once said I'd make a good vet, could we consider it?" she'd asked.

But she was talking to his back, as he left the room. What was the point? He didn't care. Her father – whatever had happened between them she'd never understand. He hadn't been cruel to her over the years, not like Mother. Instead, he'd been . . . well, he'd been nothing at all. Almost acted as though she didn't exist. Aside from the small gesture on her seventeenth birthday, giving her Scruff, he'd all but abandoned her after that summer. What was it? She'd never know . . .

Sometimes she'd catch him looking at her, a sad smile on his face, but as soon as she looked up and smiled back, he'd look away, his features returning to neutral. She'd never stopped loving him as he had her. Felicity half expected him to come to her one day and tell her he'd been wrong, that he was sorry, that he should have done something after what Mother did. She did forgive him though, knowing there must have been a reason. There had to have been.

"I have to go to work," Tess said, bursting into the room, breaking her thoughts. She planted a kiss on each of their foreheads and stood back. "Look at my girls, getting all grown up," she smiled.

Felicity grinned back.

"Can I count on you to get up and out of the door? Fliss, you'd better get going soon, little one." She squatted down beside the camp bed, placing her hand on Felicity's cheek. "Mind yourself. Try to get back to see us again soon, won't you? I'm always here if you need me. You know that, don't you?"

Felicity closed her eyes, savouring the tender moment, never wanting it to end, wishing she could stay here in normality instead of going back.

"I do, Tess, thank you for everything."

"Come on, let's get breakfast. I'm starving," Lucie said.

"Morning, you two." Sammy was already up, sitting at the kitchen table, wearing black jeans and a sweatshirt with a zip at the front, zipped right down to reveal the same firm chest that Felicity had buried her face in last night.

Felicity could feel her face starting to burn before she even sat down, remembering the night before.

"Hi." She could barely meet his eyes.

He looked so mature sitting there, his legs resting on a kitchen chair and his arms behind his head, and she felt like a child, in her borrowed nightdress and fluffy socks. Felicity pulled the nightdress down over her knees, all the confidence she'd felt the night before now evaporated. He didn't look up and she began to wonder if Lucie had been right. It had been clear last night that it wasn't his first time and she was now mortified by how forward she'd been. Maybe he thought she did that kind of thing all the time.

"Help yourself, Fliss. Don't mind the weirdo sitting at the table. He goes away eventually." Lucie grabbed a slice of toast off the counter and with her other hand, she smacked Sammy playfully on the back of his head before heading to the door. "I'm going for a shower. Try to behave."

Sammy was on his feet before Lucie even reached the bottom of the stairs. He pulled Felicity to standing and took her in his arms, giving her no time to hesitate.

"Are you okay?" he asked, smiling down at her as she melted into his arms, curling her body into his and inhaling. "I couldn't even look at you. Thought I'd scream if I couldn't kiss you," he said. He pulled her chin towards him so that he could see her face.

"I'm okay now," she smiled, reaching up to meet his lips.

She was better than okay – she'd never felt this good in her entire life.

"Spend the day with me!" Sammy kissed her again, unable to stop himself.

"I can't," Felicity said, looking at the ground, wondering how she was ever expected to return to normal.

"Why not? What's the worst that can happen?"

Felicity stepped back, dropping her hands and breaking the delicious contact.

"You don't understand. I'm not like other people. I don't have that kind of freedom. Please don't make it harder for me than it already is," she pleaded, upset that he didn't seem to understand after everything she'd told him.

He went to put his hands around her waist but she shrugged him off.

"Don't. I can't be the girl you need and sooner or later you'll get tired waiting around for me."

She always ended up driving everyone away. Maybe if she stopped whatever it was between them now, it wouldn't be so painful when he disappeared as they all did.

"Hey, I won't," Sammy replied, taking her hand. "I'll see you when I can. We'll find a way. I understand."

The words reminded her of what Lucie had once said the day they cut their hands and became blood sisters.

"Well, there might be a way," Felicity said, remembering the fairy hole in the oak tree that had been her door to freedom. "There's a tree, an old oak, just over the back wall of my house. It was how we communicated when we were kids. Lucie used to leave me notes in it."

"Clever girls," he laughed. "So that's how you did it. I'm even more impressed by you now. So, I guess we'll be getting back to nature," Sammy grinned and she kissed him. "But I'll be needing to see you, too. I can't live without this," he told her, holding her tight, nuzzling her neck.

"Well, I could maybe squeeze you in for a half an hour before the Brownie meetings on Thursday evenings and Saturday mornings," she giggled.

"Where do I sign up?"

He kissed her then and for a moment she felt as though she were floating on air.

"We might need a little help though, an ally of sorts," Felicity suggested. "Now, who could we pick?"

They both looked up to see Lucie walking into the room, her hair wrapped in a towel, watching them suspiciously.

"I don't like the sound of this, guys."

Lucie shook her head as they revealed their plan to her.

"What if you get caught, Fliss? Are you going to risk being locked up? I don't want to lose you again. This is going waaay too fast for my liking." Lucie put her hand

247

over Felicity's. "You guys have only just met and you want to run the risk of losing everything for that saddo?" Lucie gestured dismissively towards Sammy.

Felicity giggled. "I know it must be hard for you to understand, Lucie, but it doesn't feel like we just met."

She didn't want to tell her friend that they'd already spent the night together. She wanted that to be her and Sammy's secret for a while longer. Sammy reached over then and touched Lucie's arm.

"Lu, I've never asked you for anything before. Never will again. But I care about Fliss too, and I want the best for her, I do. Please do this for me – for us."

The last bit of the sentence was delivered with his eyes locked on Felicity's, who was smiling back tenderly.

"Oh, for God's sake. I'm like an extra in *Romeo and Juliet* here, and that did *not* end well."

Lucie looked from one to the other, genuinely taken aback by her brother's public declaration. He almost sounded . . . desperate.

"All we're asking is that you cover for Felicity from time to time. Maybe keep watch. Just an extra pair of eyes to give us a chance to see each other," Sammy pleaded.

"Okay, okay, enough, Romeo. I'll help you – but mark my words, this will end in tears."

She sounded so like Tess that they all erupted into giggles.

"Bloody typical," Lucie said. "You go out one night and fall in love at first sight, and I meet Sean of the Puke." She threw her eyes to heaven. "Now, you two have half an hour before we're due back at the scout hall and Margot comes looking for you. I'm going for a walk – let the games begin," she winked.

There was no question where they'd spend their time. They ran upstairs and Felicity threw herself on his bed, landing on her back with a bounce and laughing as her hair fanned out around her. He was on top of her then, pinning her hands above her head, kissing her, and she arched her body towards him, anticipating what was coming next and impatiently wanting to get there.

It was different from the first time, less rushed, more expert, and when they finished, he kissed her nose.

"Now that I have you, Miss Montgomery, I'm never going to let you go."

She clung to him, her long legs wrapped around him, and for once she hoped her wish would come true. She was in too deep already, her fears blinded by what she felt and her mind whirling with possibilities.

"Be careful," Felicity warned him. "Things don't always work out the way they're supposed to with me. I don't want to get hurt."

"I'm afraid I might be the one to get hurt here," Sammy replied, looking at her so seriously that she started to laugh.

"Don't worry, I won't let you go, but right now we have to get dressed before Lucie finds us. She'll kill us."

Reluctantly, they unfurled themselves from each other. She threw on the pair of stonewash jeans and a black T-shirt she'd borrowed from Lucie and glanced in the mirror opposite his bed. She liked the way she looked in these clothes. They made her feel normal, young, just like everyone else. She wished she never had to take them off, but she knew she'd have to as soon as she retrieved her Brownie uniform from where they'd stashed her bag behind the church hall the previous day.

"You look even lovelier than you did last night. How is

that possible?" he said, standing behind her and admiring her reflection while struggling to keep his hands off her before she playfully swatted him away.

The jeans made her waist tiny and the T-shirt hugged her in all right places, perfectly accentuating her figure.

"Come on, guys." They heard Lucie calling from downstairs.

He kissed her one last time.

"I promise you, we'll make it work. At least we'll try to. Okay?"

Felicity nodded.

As the three of them made their way through the gate and up Farmleigh Estates, feelings of dread began to creep back in. She clung tight to Sammy's hand, knowing that the next time she'd see him would be Thursday evening – a lifetime away.

They were almost at the end of the road, almost home free, when someone grabbed Felicity's shoulder.

"Oh!" She jumped and turned, finding herself face to face with a woman she'd never seen before.

She looked a little like Mrs Walsh had, with her headscarf tied around her head, a few strands of wiry grey hair escaping beneath it.

"Annie. Annie. Is that you?"

The woman's face was pale as if she'd seen a ghost. Felicity stared at her, confused, shaking her head.

"No. I'm not Annie."

"Oh. I could have sworn. I'm so sorry. So sorry," the woman mumbled, covering her mouth with her hand and hurrying away.

"Who was that?" Felicity asked, just as taken aback as the woman had been.

Sammy put his arm around her protectively. "Oh, that's old Mrs Slaney. I wouldn't mind her. She's as mad as a brush."

"Don't be mean, Sammy. She's a nice old lady. But Mam said she was never the same after it all."

"After what?"

"She lost her daughter, seventeen years ago. Never got over it. I remember because Mam says it was around the same time I was born. Mam said for ages after she used to call in to see me as a baby, said it was a tragedy. Her daughter sliced her wrists in the bath. Rumour has it she was up the duff."

"I guess seventeen years ago that was the worst thing that could happen to a girl. Lucky we're in the eighties now and the world isn't so backwards. Although I'd be killed if that happened to me!" Lucie laughed. "Can you imagine Margot? Jaysus!" she finished, nudging Felicity.

"The poor lady and that poor girl." Felicity shivered. It didn't even bear thinking about. "What did the woman call me? Annie, was it?"

Felicity Montgomery

Then – September 1987

Felicity stuffed the note into the pocket of her school skirt and quickly replaced the tin box in the tree, checking over her shoulder all the while. She'd waited all afternoon for the opportunity to escape and it finally came in the form of one of the church's do-gooders, who'd unexpectedly called to discuss the upcoming harvest festival service with Mother.

"I won't be long. Continue with your calculus and I'll try to get rid of her. You'd think after almost twenty years decorating the altar she'd be able to do it herself. Incompetent old biddy," Mother muttered, leaving the room, Felicity's heart almost beating out of her chest.

Now or never, Felicity thought, creeping out of the French doors of the dining room onto the patio and sprinting towards the orchard. By the time Mother returned, she was back at the table, the French doors locked and the note burning a hole in her pocket. Her face was only slightly flushed from the exertion, but her heart was still hammering at the thought of reading the letter that night, alone in her bed, and dreaming of him. She still couldn't believe it had only been three weeks since they'd met. It seemed like it had never been any other way. Every time she thought about that first night together and their glorious little secret, it gave her goose bumps, sending delicious shivers up her spine.

"Felicity, please pay attention. You're starting to irritate me immensely and we know what happens when I get irritated," Mother said.

"Yes, Mother, sorry, Mother. I was thinking about a test I have tomorrow at school. Just going over the answers in my head."

She couldn't concentrate on anything, always having to check herself to make sure she wasn't staring off into the distance at school or while she was studying with Mother. She knew she had to act calmly to avert suspicion, but the more Felicity saw of Sammy, the harder she fell. She couldn't eat, couldn't sleep. And she could barely breathe when she knew she was going to see him, setting off a little earlier than usual for the Brownie meetings to meet him at the back of the hall behind the trees for fifteen minutes of heaven while Lucie kept watch.

"Guys, this is getting weird. I'm like a flasher hanging around in the bushes waiting on the two of you," Lucie complained after the first couple of weeks.

Felicity had been so nervous that he wouldn't turn up the first night they'd arranged to meet. She'd felt sick the entire day with anticipation, worried that what Lucie had predicted for them would come true.

"Oh my God!" Felicity had shrieked as he'd grabbed her around the waist, pushing her against a tree and kissing her before she had time to speak.

She'd kissed him back, inhaling him, savouring the moment. There was little time for words, not wanting to waste a moment of real time. But there were words, plenty of them, scribbled on the notes they exchanged, hidden inside the tree: *I can't stop thinking about you . . . I want to be with you . . . I've never felt this way before . . . When you kiss me . . . When I hold you I want to . . . I'll wait for you . . .*

Felicity had read them a thousand times, closing her eyes, holding the paper to her chest as if she could feel his touch through the page. She'd imagined him whispering the words to her and slowly peeling away her clothes, caressing her with his mouth, kissing her breasts, prising her legs open and . . .

"Felicity! What *are* you doing staring out of the window? Come on. Finish this problem. It's almost dinner time," Mother said, roughly pushing Felicity's head back towards her calculus.

Felicity's mind plummeted back to earth. It was only Tuesday – two more days before she could see him again. She needed to concentrate, just for a little while longer, knowing that dinner time was code for Mother's first legitimate drink of the day, chased by several more, alone in her room. It would give Felicity the chance to read the note and scribble a response before sneaking back out to the secret postal service tree.

"Sorry, Mother, I'm almost finished," she said, hurriedly deciphering the problem and closing the book. "All done."

"Good. Remember, this is a big year for you and you *will* get top grades in the Leaving Certificate Examination."

Of course she'd get top marks, there was no doubt about that, but what was the point? A trainee librarian in Knockmore hardly needed high scores – although lately, her mind had started to churn with possibilities.

"What would *you* like to do?" Sammy had asked her.

"It doesn't matter – it's already decided."

"Just humour me," he'd smiled down at her.

"Well, I want to study to become a vet, but it'll never happen."

"You keep saying that, but it can. It might. They can't keep you for ever. Didn't you ever think of leaving? When you've finished school? You don't have to stay," he'd said, holding her tight around her waist and kissing her tenderly.

"She'd never let me go."

"But she can't keep you, either."

Felicity supposed not. she'd never really considered it before. There was never anyone to make her believe she could make it on her own, or anyone to make a life with, and now, suddenly, there was.

"I'm sure she'll have me married off by the time I'm twenty-one to some neighbouring reverend's son or someone who's someone."

"Over my dead body!" Sammy said, looking shocked. "Reverend Twenty Chins' son can join the queue! No, you'll be mine one day, Felicity Montgomery, all mine," Sammy had said, pretending to bite her neck like Dracula. "And I'll drive you to vet school every day in my limo while I'm taking a break from my world tours."

It was a lovely dream. Was that all it would ever be? Sammy made her feel brave, as if she might be able to conquer the world. He'd ignited the possibility of a possibility in her and she held on tight to it, knowing that for now it was all they had.

She took the note from her pocket now and carefully unfolded it:

Fliss,
I've missed you. I hate the wait from Saturday to

Thursday. It's too long. Mam asked was there
something wrong with me. I seemed in bad form. I
wanted to tell her I've never been better. But I
couldn't. I'll tell you, though. I've never been better.
I have another gig in a few weeks. Do you think you
could make it again? Could we make a plan? I want
to start making other plans with you . . . I love you.
Sammy

I love you. He loved her! It was the first time anyone had
ever said it to her. She kissed the page. Felicity loved him,
too. It seemed crazy, but she did. She took out a pen and
tore some paper from her folder:

Sammy,
I know. The days go so slowly and the time when
I'm with you even faster. I think about nothing else.
I want to be with you, to talk to you, to . . . That
night in your room, I felt as though I were breathing
for the first time. I love you, too. I can't wait to tell
you to your face. Maybe I'm ready to talk plans. I
didn't think there was ever another life for me but
this one . . . perhaps I was wrong.
Felicity

She lay back on her bed, smiling to herself. It would be a
few hours before she'd be able to sneak out to deliver it so
that it would be there in time for the morning. Lucie had
taken to jumping the wall in the mornings to fetch the note
before heading to school.

"I'm using it as exercise," Lucie told her, "and leverage.
I have Sammy doing most of my chores at home, so I have

more time to study. It looks like we're all getting a little something extra from the arrangement!"

Whatever it was that was going on with that pair, it was bigger than anything that had ever happened in Lucie's life. Lucie was growing more and more concerned with each passing week that it showed no signs of fizzling out, as she'd been so convinced it would. But for now, she needed the extra time to study. She, too, had a dream of her own for when she finished school, a simpler dream of studying nursing up in Dublin. She'd already applied and had been accepted – all she had to do now was get the points. Unlike Felicity, she wasn't escaping, though.

"I'll be devastated leaving, especially Mam, but it has to be done. Anyway, it looks like I'll have to leave Knockmore to meet a fella. There's only the shite lads left now," Lucie had laughed.

"And I'd do anything to leave," Felicity had said, staring ahead.

"Well leave, then. We're all saying it to you now. Maybe you'll start to listen."

As soon as all the lights went out, Felicity took her cue, sneaking down the stairs and quietly out of the back door. Having spent so much time at home, trying to be invisible, she knew every creak in every loose floorboard and could safely navigate her way to the back door in the kitchen without making a sound. Even the dog didn't look up at her as she crept past him and opened the door, always ensuring to put the latch on.

She was out of the door quickly, running in the shadows, and had the note delivered in record time. Felicity had written two notes that night: one for Lucie and one for Sammy. She was so grateful to her friend and didn't want it to affect their friendship, so she'd written a little love letter of sorts to her as well:

> *Lucie,*
> *I know! We're ruining your life! But I can't thank you enough. For everything. I won't bore you with the mushy bits . . . but I love you. You're my best friend. Always have been, always will be.*
> *Your blood sister,*
> *Fliss*

The words had flown out of her easily that night. It was like she were floating in a bubble of joy. She slipped back through the door, the adrenaline pumping through her veins, stopping for a moment to listen, making sure she hadn't been heard before stealthily continuing to her room by floorboard hopping.

She hadn't been heard. The silence of the house was almost deafening.

Margot had enjoyed a glass of wine with dinner, followed by two cups of vodka, taken from the bottle she kept hidden in her closet. She'd passed out earlier than usual that evening, waking briefly with a mouth as dry as the desert. She'd pawed at her bedside table for the glass of water, knocking it to the floor in the search. Then she'd stood to try to pick it up, pausing briefly when some movement caught her eye in the garden below. She'd tried to focus, but everything was blurry. Then she'd shaken her head before giving up on the water and lying back down on the bed. What was that? But her eyes closed before she could register what she'd seen.

Felicity Montgomery

Then – October 1987

Felicity felt the butterflies swirling almost as soon as she woke. It was two months to the day since she'd met him and in that time, everything had changed. But tonight, she was going to get to see him again and she could hardly wait.

Felicity's body tingled with both nerves and excitement. She was aching to be touched by him in the way he had that first night. It was almost too good to be true.

"Two months is a proper anniversary," Lucie told her. "One month is nothing, but if you make it to two, well, that's an achievement, especially with Sammy. He's never made it past two *dates* before."

Felicity had been thrilled. She loved listening to Lucie tell her how lovesick her brother was as they whispered in the corner of the Brownie meetings.

"He talks about nothing else – well, to me at least. He doesn't even stay out after his gigs like he used to. Straight home to us on a Saturday night. Up in his room listening to love songs. I even caught him listening to 'Glory of Love' last week and looking a little glassy-eyed," she giggled.

Felicity laughed, secretly delighted. She'd listened to the

Peter Cetera song herself, over and over on the cassette tape he'd made for her, found stuffed into an envelope in the tree. Not even Lucie knew about that. He'd delivered it himself. After all, he had somewhat of a reputation to uphold around his little sister, not wanting her to know how deeply he was already in; although she'd deciphered that herself.

"Mam thinks he's finally been rejected by some yoke. Said it'll do him a power of good. If only she knew! She'd kill him."

Felicity felt bad. She didn't want to upset Tess; hated the thought of her disapproving, especially since it felt like the whole world was already against them.

"Are you okay, Fliss?" Lucie asked her the night before. "You're a million miles away."

"Sorry, yes. I'm just excited for tomorrow and seeing Sammy."

"You look a bit pale, are you sure?"

"Yeah, I'm great," Felicity assured her. "It must be the remnants of the tummy bug I had last week – still not fully over it."

"Yeah, I'd say it's more lovesick you are." Lucie clutched her heart and started singing the lyrics of the power ballad "Glory of Love" before stopping and pretending to barf into the bin.

Felicity couldn't believe it when her mother revealed that she had to attend a dinner with her father on the very day of their two-month anniversary. Talk about fate. Her parents rarely went anywhere together, but the dinner hosted by the archdeacon and his wife was one that couldn't be missed.

"A boring fiasco, but it must be done. You'll be alone in

the house. Make sure you lock the doors and use the opportunity to get some extra study in. Perhaps I should ask Mrs Kidney to sit with you, but we'll be late and I don't want to have to endure all of her tedious questions when we return," Mother told her.

"I'll be studying and going to bed early. I still feel a little ill," Felicity answered.

It wasn't until later that she realised it was the perfect opportunity for her to be alone with Sammy – alone in her bed. Felicity felt her stomach flip again in anticipation – three hours alone with him. Three perfect hours. She hadn't been able to think about anything else for days. Tonight was going to be amazing.

Felicity grabbed her bag from the hall and flew out of the front door, dashing across the road to school, for once forgetting to count her steps as she went. How she was going to get through the day was anyone's guess. At least it was starting with double biology and not maths.

"Okay, class, please take out your books. We'll be revising today – human reproduction. Yes, yes, settle down. Less laughing, please." The teacher threw her eyes to heaven.

Felicity giggled as the class unanimously cheered at the chosen topic. Another twist of fate, it seemed, especially considering what she intended to do later that evening. Perhaps she'd get a few pointers. Felicity opened her book.

"Okay, let's begin with the female cycle . . . "

Felicity zoned out. She knew all this back to front already, had revised it only recently. Maybe she could afford to daydream instead.

"Miss Montgomery, are you with us?"

"Yes, miss."

She tuned back in just in time to hear the teacher highlight the early signs of pregnancy.

"Absence of menstruation, tender breasts, feelings of nausea . . . "

Felicity was suddenly alert, listening as if she were hearing it all for the first time. Nausea. There it was. The absence of menstruation. Oh my God! Surely not? She'd been so caught up in everything lately that she hadn't noticed. But it had been . . . how long now?

Felicity took out her notebook and started scribbling as the colour slowly drained from her face. She listened to the teacher talking, describing everything she'd been feeling of late. Oh my God. Oh my God. No. By the end of double biology, she'd noted in her book that it was in fact ten weeks and four days since the day of her last period and she had a solid feeling – no, she was almost sure – that she was carrying something that was approximately the size of a prune.

It was all she could do to make it to the end of the class without vomiting all over the table. She picked up her books and ran to the girls' toilets before emptying the contents of her stomach into the toilet bowl as reality hit her like a punch in the gut. She was pregnant. She was sure of it. It made sense. She'd been feeling it for weeks without knowing what she was feeling.

Her hand drifted to her stomach as she sank to the cold floor in the toilet stall and tears started to stream down her face. How could she not have thought of it? How could she have been so stupid? And Sammy . . . oh my God, Sammy? She couldn't focus.

Of course she knew how it had happened, but she didn't think it could happen so quickly. She'd heard Mother's rants over the years about how long it had taken to conceive her. How Mother had prayed for years and years for a baby.

"It takes work to get what you want, Felicity. Nothing comes easily," she used to lecture.

Nothing comes easily, except when it's not what you want. Felicity had no idea that once, or even twice was all it would take to *work* – to place a bun or at least a prune in her oven. What was she going to do? She couldn't tell anyone – not even Lucie knew that she'd done the deed with Sammy. She couldn't tell her, and definitely not Mother. Mother would kill her with her bare hands, or worse still, she'd kill Sammy or have him locked up.

She rested her head against the wall, digging her nails into her arm to calm herself. Tess would be so disappointed in her for ruining both her life and Sammy's. And surely Sammy wouldn't want anything to do with it. Would she be sent away? She had to do something. Could she run away? Could she hide the baby?

No. She'd seen what had happened to that girl in Longford. She'd heard her mother discuss it and say she got what she deserved for her sinful behaviour. That poor girl had given birth alone and died. The baby had died. No. She had to face it. She and the baby were in it together, alone. The poor baby. Her baby. She had a baby growing inside her and she had to do what was right for the baby. She'd done something terrible, but it wasn't the prune's fault. Think, Felicity, think.

Thoughts whirled around in her head, backwards and forwards for what seemed like hours, and there she sat on the toilet floor, beyond the bell ringing to signal the start of the next class.

She willed herself to stand. Stand up, Felicity. Walk to the office. Tell them you're sick. Get home. She could fake a relapse of the sickness she'd had last week – that would buy her some time. She walked robotically to the office.

"Miss, I don't feel well. I think I have a bug," Felicity told the secretary.

"Oh, Felicity, you do look pale." The secretary took one look at her now grey face. "You'd best get home. Is there someone there?"

"Yes, Mother's there."

"Well, quick as you can across the road," she smiled kindly, wanting to get rid of her fast.

She had two young children at home and didn't want to be cleaning up vomit for the next week. Under normal circumstances, she'd have phoned ahead, but she'd just been applying the second coat of Shimmering Veil varnish to her nails and didn't want to risk smudging it in the rotary dial. Besides, Felicity lived just over the road and she'd watch her from the window. Which she would have done, of course, had she not knocked over the bottle of nail varnish and rushed to get a tissue, thus ruining her nails and the desk in one swoop anyway.

Felicity left school on autopilot and headed towards the gate, where two magpies had landed and sat watching her. When a third glided down and sat beside them, she automatically recited the poem in her head: one for sorrow, two for joy, three for a girl . . . Three for a girl! And then it suddenly came to her. She knew where to go. Maybe she'd always known that it was there for her, if she needed it. She had to try at least.

Felicity walked through the gate, but instead of crossing the road, she headed right, down the hill, past the church and into town. She walked quickly, hanging her head, hoping that some busybody wouldn't notice her. Every inch of her body was trembling as she inhaled deeply then exhaled, her hand resting on her belly, feeling the air puffing in and out. There was no other way – it was this or nothing.

After reaching her destination, she knocked on the door then stepped back and closed her eyes. When she opened them, a shocked face stared back at her.

"Felicity, it's you! What are you doing here? How did you know where I lived? Are you all right, child?" Florrie looked her up and down, trying to take in the apparition at the door.

Florrie hadn't laid eyes on her since she was a child and she never thought Felicity would show up here, not in a million years. But my God, she was beautiful, even more so in the flesh. They were right – she was nothing like her stern-faced mother, nothing at all.

"Come in, Felicity," Florrie said, glancing up the road first before ushering her through the door and down the hall to the kitchen. "Sit, please. I'll make tea."

Florrie started to fuss about, boiling the kettle and taking out cups. Felicity sank into the pine chair and sat with her hands on her knees. She looked around at the small kitchen, taking in the children's drawings taped to the wall, the patterned lino, the floral curtains, the shiny brown kitchen cupboards. It was colourful and bright and homely.

She ran her hand over the intricate design on the back of the kitchen chair beside her, tracing the violin-like design with her fingers. It was so like Tess's kitchen and it suddenly made her feel lonely – yearning even more for the life she knew she was missing.

Florrie's back was to her and she suddenly felt embarrassed, not knowing why she'd come here. She didn't know this woman. She only thought she did. She'd thought about her so often over the years that perhaps she'd created a character like from a book, a fairy godmother of sorts. But now, sitting here in Florrie's kitchen, she felt awkward and stupid and petrified. Fresh warm tears welled in her eyes. She shouldn't have come – this wasn't a fairy tale and no one could save her.

"I always hoped you'd come," Florrie prattled on. "Wished for it, I suppose. You see, things were difficult with Maggie, I mean Margot, and she didn't want me in her life, but I did try. Do you remember at all?"

Florrie turned then to see Felicity sitting, shoulders slumped in despair, tears freely rolling onto her hands, which remained locked together on her lap.

"Felicity, child, what is it?" Florrie dropped to her knees and took her hands.

Felicity looked up at her.

"Has she done something? Has she hurt you? I always feared she would. Knew she would. I told Jim, I told him, I did. I even went to a solicitor to see if I could get visitation rights to you. But I tried, Felicity. Lord knows I tried. Oh, God, what has she done?" Florrie hung her head.

"You did? You went to a solicitor?" Felicity asked, looking up at her, astonished there had been someone all along who'd cared – who'd tried – and it was enough for her to know that she'd come to the right place. The tears continued to pour, spurred on by the warmth that she could feel once again from the colourful aunt. She opened her mouth to speak, but all that came out was, "Help me."

Florrie folded Felicity into her arms as if she'd always

known her and let her cry until the sobbing turned to sniffles.

"What is it? I'll help you," Florrie told her.

Felicity fixed her hair behind her ears and screwed her fists up tight inside her school jumper.

"I met someone. I got out for a night. I lied and I went out with Lucie – you know Lucie?"

Florrie nodded.

"And I met a boy and well, I fell in love."

Florrie smiled, relieved that the problem was more than likely a case of unrequited love and not something more sinister.

Felicity continued, "And well, *we* fell in love and . . . " She started to sob again.

Florrie put her arm around her. "It's all right, love. We can fix anything."

Felicity looked up at her with pleading eyes. "You can't fix this."

"Now, Felicity, whatever it is, I'm sure it seems huge. Will your mother not let you see him?"

"She doesn't even know about him. Please don't tell her."

"Well, what is it, child?" Florrie asked gently.

Felicity took a breath. "I'm pregnant."

"Oh, God." Florrie stood up, shocked. She hadn't expected that.

Felicity saw her face and instantly regretted telling her.

"I'm sorry, I shouldn't have come. She's going to kill me. I don't know why I . . . I'll go." Felicity started to gather her coat from the chair beside her.

"Stop that. Come here." Florrie hugged her tightly. "It's all right, love. You just gave me a shock is all."

"I can't let her send me away. I won't let her take my baby," Felicity sobbed into Florrie's hair.

"It's all right. Let's take a deep breath and sit down." She pulled out the chair for Felicity, who slumped back down. "Have you told your boyfriend?" Florrie asked her softly.

"No, no, I can't tell him. I won't tell Mother about him. I've seen what she can do to people. I don't want to hurt him. I won't have him hurt."

The thought of Sammy started the tears again.

"But he's the father, Felicity, and he needs to know. You say he loves you? Give him a chance. If he does love you, he'll stick by you," Florrie said, rubbing Felicity's back in circles, trying to calm her.

"But it'll ruin his plans. I'd ruin it for him." Felicity looked up at Florrie.

"Tsk, Felicity. What about your plans? He wasn't thinking of your plans when he got you pregnant, was he? I'll wring his neck if I find him," Florrie said protectively.

"No, Florrie, please," Felicity pleaded. "I've no plans to ruin. I have nothing and no one," she said sadly.

Florrie put her arm around her again. "All right, all right, let me think. Do you know for sure?"

Felicity shook her head. "No, but I'm almost sure."

"We'll need to have it confirmed by the doctor first. You may not be. It could be a false alarm and it was just one night. It's not as easy to get pregnant as you think," Florrie smiled.

Felicity couldn't help but smile back. "You sound like Mother," she whispered and Florrie laughed.

"Well, we are sisters, or at least we were once upon a time. Maybe you're not pregnant."

But Felicity already knew she was. She didn't know how she was so certain, she just was.

"She's going to kill me," Felicity said quietly.

"She won't. I'll make sure of that. I can speak to Maggie. I'm not afraid of her," Florrie said.

"She'll throw me out."

"Well, you can come here and live with us and . . . "

The door to the kitchen opened and Felicity shot out of the chair like a bullet when she saw the sergeant standing there.

"It's all right, Felicity – it's just Jim, my husband. Jim, this is Felicity, as in Montgomery."

Florrie met his eyes and issued him a visual warning.

"Ah! Jaysus, Florrie, have you gone and kidnapped her?" Jim exhaled slowly, ignoring her. He removed his hat and placed it on the kitchen table before sitting down. "No offence, Felicity, it's nice to see you," Jim said, taking in the scene. "As I always say, 'the unexpected moments are sometimes the sweetest', or perhaps even 'there may be trouble ahead'. Should I be worried?" he asked, looking at the tear-stained face of the pretty blonde girl who'd miraculously shown up unannounced in their kitchen.

"A word alone in the living room, Jim?" Florrie raised her eyebrows to him before turning to Felicity. "Felicity, let me talk to Jim. Don't be worrying. He's on our side."

The pair left her alone with her thoughts, which continued to run in circles. She was terrified the sergeant was going to march her straight home to Mother, and she was mortified at him finding out that she was pregnant and what he might think of her, but she trusted Florrie. She had nowhere else to go. She was on a moving train and there was nothing she could do to stop it now. She just had to go with it and try to hold on for dear life. But she was about to learn, if indeed she was pregnant, that it wouldn't be her biggest hurdle.

"Good timing is invisible, but bad timing sticks out a mile," Jim Hughes said when he opened the door to the kitchen a few minutes later. "Now, Felicity, can I speak plainly?" he asked a little more gruffly than intended and Felicity flinched.

He smiled at her then, taking his time before he spoke. There was very little that shocked Jim and this wasn't the first nor the last girl he'd see who'd gone and got herself in trouble. The fact that it was the reverend's daughter was uncomfortable, but the fact that it was Margot's daughter was almost amusing. He was a big believer in what goes around comes around. In fact, over the years Jim Hughes had amassed a quote for just about every situation he'd encountered as the sergeant of a small town.

Jim would have enjoyed seeing the smug smile drop from the reverend's wife's face when she found out that her daughter was just as low as all the other young ones in town, but he felt sorry for the poor girl. He knew how much Florrie had wanted to help Felicity over the years and he was aware that she saw this as her big moment. Jim wasn't going to deny her. He'd do anything for Florrie, would happily take on the girl for a time, and he was well able to handle the village gossip, but the real problem here was timing.

"As I said," Jim continued, "the problem is your timing. You're seventeen, is that right, Felicity?"

Felicity nodded.

"And when do you turn eighteen, Felicity?" he asked, leaning back and balancing the chair on its back legs.

"The seventeenth of June," Felicity said, wondering if he was going to arrest her for being underage.

"See, the problem here, Felicity, is that until you turn eighteen, you're technically a minor and unless you have your parents' permission, you can't leave home. So unless they let you off to live with the *likes of us*, we have a problem."

Jim watched her face fall.

"And I know your mam, Felicity, and I'm not sure she's going to make this easy for you." He smiled in a way that looked more like a wince.

"Please, let me stay with you. Please, she'll kill me. I . . . I can't explain it. She's worse now, worse than before."

Felicity started to sob uncontrollably and even Jim was taken aback by the outburst. He sat up quickly and looked over at Florrie.

"Hush, Felicity," Florrie soothed as she put her arms around her.

"Does she hurt you, Felicity?" Jim asked, wondering if the situation was worse than he'd first imagined.

"No," Felicity lied. "It's hard to explain. She's horrible."

Felicity's hands were shaking and Florrie eyed Jim across the table.

"Felicity, are you worried for your safety?" Jim asked again, his tone softening.

"No." She'd never tell. She'd never tell again.

"Okay, love, here's what we're going to do. Now listen," Jim said, unable to cope with the tears and making a mental note in future not to come home for lunch. "Florrie here is going to take you to the doctor out of town and have it confirmed. We can make an appointment for next week. It's early days, she told me, so we could be making a storm in a teacup here, if you get me. In the meantime, you just lay low at home. Don't go doin' anything stupid, do you hear me?" Jim raised one eyebrow at her. "Okay?"

"Yes," she nodded.

"Let's just have it confirmed and we'll take each step as it comes. But you might want to start thinking about telling the father. That's another thing – was it, you know, was it consensual? Like, were both of ye okay with it? You weren't forced, like?" he asked uncomfortably, stumbling over the words.

"Yes. Yes, it was consensual," Felicity nodded.

"And do you know who the father is?"

"Jim!" Florrie swiped at him. "For God's sake, Jim!"

"I'm just checkin', Flo. You never know and he should be stepping up. Tell him. It's the right thing to do. There are plenty of eejit young fellas in this town, but they're not all bad," Jim said before a thought came to him. "And you know your parents with their connections might be able to send you away to have the baby and find it a nice home. That happens, you know. And then you carry on with your life, Felicity. You'll have more kids when you're ready." He trailed off, seeing her face change.

Yes, there it was, he could see it – she'd already made up her mind to keep this baby.

"It'll be tricky, though. If I'm right, that baby will be born just before you turn eighteen. Timing is everything, you know," he said again. "Tell him. Sooner rather than later. 'The truth hurts for a little while, but the lie hurts for ever.' Tell him," he nodded knowingly.

"I'll think about it," Felicity agreed. "Thank you." She hugged Florrie tightly.

"I'm glad you came, Felicity," Florrie smiled. "But you'd best get home. When can you come again?"

"I can skip Brownies on Saturday and come here – you can tell me when you have the doctor's appointment. Thank you, Florrie. Thank you so much."

"No need to thank me – you're one of us."

She hugged her niece and thanked God for finally bringing her to her, even under these circumstances.

Felicity ran home. Mother was probably still in bed, so she had time to slip in and get into the dining room to study. Not that there was much point now. She'd be sent away for sure and instead of doing her exams, she'd be having a baby. She still couldn't believe it, but she knew it was there inside her. She could almost feel its presence now. She was going to fight for this baby as no one had ever fought for her, but she was so afraid. She prayed for strength, wishing there was someone out there looking down on her, guiding her.

Felicity felt as if she were the only person in the world who'd ever felt this way, ever had to deal with this situation, not realising that there was someone else who'd made a similar discovery seventeen years before. There was a girl just like her who'd tried to fight for her baby but suffered at the hands of greed – a girl called Annie, whose long blonde hair had swept out behind her as she ran home distraught after discovering she was carrying a baby that she, too, would have done anything to save.

Felicity sat in the dining room, her face in her hands, the solace consuming her. What was she going to tell Sammy? She couldn't see him that night. He'd know something was wrong and she couldn't tell him. She knew how important his dreams were to him and he had talent enough to make them happen, but she loved him enough not to tie a noose around his neck and lock him to her for ever.

She'd bought herself a couple of weeks now until the pregnancy was confirmed and then she'd have to deal with it – face her parents and tell them the truth. Maybe they'd let her go to Florrie and Jim, who she knew would help her until she could find a job and leave Knockmore. She'd be almost eighteen then and she'd find a way for her and the baby. She was sure she could do it.

She scribbled a note for Sammy. He was supposed to climb the wall and look in the tree for the key to the back door. She'd planned to send him on a treasure hunt to find her, which would end in her bedroom. She'd intended to have their song playing – it would have been perfect.

Felicity focused her mind on the prune inside her and folded the note before heading to the tree. She looked up at the autumn leaves drifting down around her, spiralling in the air before landing at her feet, and she felt empty. She'd have done anything to change what had happened, well at least adjust the timing, as Jim had said. What she and Sammy had shared wasn't like anything else she'd ever known and she was sure she'd never feel it again.

She had no regrets – none. But she had to get Sammy far away from her now before she ruined him, too. Felicity placed the note in the tree and ran back to the house before she changed her mind. Her parents had already left for the evening and she was grateful to be alone. She ran upstairs, pulled the curtains and threw herself on the bed, sobbing. She wouldn't look out of the window. She didn't want to see. Instead, she cried until she slept, knowing that when she woke, it would be done – but also knowing that some things could never be undone.

Felicity Montgomery

Then – October 1987

Felicity hadn't come to the Brownie meeting, either. What was going on?

Lucie was sure she'd be there tonight, so she could find out what had happened after Sammy returned home crestfallen the night before. He'd walked straight up the stairs, slamming the door to his bedroom behind him. Moments later the sound of music vibrated through the ceiling and Tess glanced over at Lucie.

"Know anything about that?" Tess gestured her head towards the noise.

"Nope." Lucie shook her head and shrugged.

"I'd better go and check," Tess said, resting the iron down and folding the shirt she'd been ironing.

"I'll go, Mam. I'm sure it's just girl trouble."

Lucie put down her French book and headed upstairs.

"What the hell is going on?" she asked, flinging the door open without knocking. "Turn the music down. What's happened?"

"Piss off, Lucie. Get out!" Sammy shouted.

He was lying on the bed, legs tucked up under him like a huffy teenager and looking at a piece of crumpled paper.

Lucie ignored him and closed the door behind her.

"Sammy, come on, why aren't you with Fliss?" she asked.

He flung the piece of paper at her and watched as she smoothed it out and read.

"Really?" she said. "This was a mistake . . . don't contact me again . . . I'm sorry . . . need to focus on my exams." She read bits of it aloud, looking confused. "That doesn't sound like Fliss," she said finally, handing the note back to him. "She's mad about you. She couldn't wait for tonight. Did you knock on the door? Was the car gone?"

"Yeah, the car was gone." Sammy crumpled the note again and threw it at the wastepaper basket, missing. "No, I didn't. It's clear, Lucie – pretty clear that she never wants to see me again," he said sulkily.

"You're an idiot," Lucie said, picking up the note and throwing it at him. "Haven't you been listening? What's pretty clear is that something happened. What, though?"

Sammy sat up. "You don't think it's the crazy mother, do you?"

"Hmm, maybe. But more reason to check, no? Why didn't you check?"

His face dropped.

"Look, it's probably nothing. I bet she's fine," she said, not wanting to upset him further. "But you should write back. Let me go and talk to her tomorrow night at Brownies and see what's going on. Maybe it's nothing, just a two-month anniversary wobble," she laughed unsurely.

"Thanks, Lu. I've got to be in work early tomorrow. Could you deliver a letter in the morning?" Sammy asked, reaching for the pen and paper beside his bed.

"Sure," she smiled, thinking it would be easier if all this went away and things could go back to normal.

Lucie watched him starting to write.

"Hey! and remember that song that you were playing, you big sap, 'I am the man who will fight for your honour'?! Maybe do that," she laughed, closing the door, assuming all would be well by tomorrow and the star-crossed lovers would work out their little spat.

But then Felicity hadn't shown up at Brownies and Lucie was worried.

Straight after the meeting she'd run round to Felicity's house, expertly jumped the wall and stuck her hand inside the tree for the tin box. The note she'd put there that morning was gone, which at least meant that Felicity was mobile, but there was no note in there for Sammy. Lucie replaced the box and peered over the orchard wall at the house. The lights were on. Maybe Felicity was sick. She'd have to tell Sammy now that she never replied and he'd have another tantrum. But what could she do?

Felicity looked out of the window in her room. Had she seen movement in the garden? Maybe she was just hoping she had. She'd received Sammy's note earlier. She'd sworn she wouldn't look, but Mother had been in bed most of the day after the night before, so she'd checked.

Fliss,
Don't do this. I can't live without you. I refuse to live without you. I know it's only been a couple of months, but I want to be with you. I thought I wanted to travel the world, but I've found the world in you. Please tell me how to make it right. All I

want is for us to be together, for ever. There will never be anyone else. If you want me to climb up the wall and rescue you, I'll do it right now. Just say the word, Fliss. Come back to me. No matter what it is, we can figure it out together. Talk to me.

Take on me,

Sammy

It was all she wanted to hear and she'd cried after she read it. Maybe she'd tell him about the baby once she'd been to the appointment with Florrie. Perhaps it would be okay, somehow. But she needed some time. Sammy would have to be patient with her. She quickly wiped her eyes and almost smiled before a shrill voice interrupted her thoughts.

"Felicity! What are you doing in there? Come out at once!" Margot called.

Felicity opened the door and walked straight into her.

"Sorry, Mother."

Margot tutted and looked at her suspiciously. "What's wrong with you?"

"Nothing – a bit of a head cold, maybe. I'm fine," she sniffed, trying to conceal her tears.

"A head cold this week. A tummy bug last week. Pull yourself together." Mother yanked her arm hard, roughly brushing against her breast.

"Ouch!"

Felicity flinched, her arm instinctively covering her breasts, which recently felt as though something had crawled inside them, taken up residence and was clawing to get out. Felicity had never felt anything like the pain. She went back to the dining room and sat down.

Margot stopped in the hallway, her eyes narrowing.

Something wasn't right. She couldn't put her finger on it, but something was off and she intended to find out what it was. Just like Sergeant Hughes, Margot also loved a good quote, and one of her favourites was "Give a man enough rope and he'll hang himself."

Felicity Montgomery

Then – October 1987

Today was the day. Today she'd know for sure.

Felicity had managed to avoid everyone for the last week, knowing she just had to hold it together until the doctor's appointment. It was the second Saturday in a row that she hadn't turned up for Brownies and she knew it wouldn't be long before someone came looking for her. She was running out of time.

"I've arranged the appointment for next Saturday morning," Florrie told her the week before when she'd run down into town to her aunt instead of going to the church hall, where she knew Lucie would be waiting for her.

Felicity had telephoned the Brownie leader to tell her she was sick and wouldn't be back for a few weeks. At least that would keep Lucie at bay for a time. She felt terrible lying to her, but there was no other way for now.

Just being in Florrie's company managed to ease the constant feeling of panic that rested in the pit of her stomach. Florrie had been even happier to see her last week and even Jim had welcomed her in with a pat on the back, relieved she'd turned up as she said she would.

"We'll have just enough time to get to Balinstill, see the

doctor and have you back on time before you're missed," Florrie assured her.

Felicity sat in the passenger seat of Florrie's little red car, staring out of the window, watching Knockmore fly past before the view turned to a blur of constant green on the winding road. Felicity closed her eyes, her mind returning to Sammy. She missed him so much – wished it were him sitting beside her now. She'd waited her whole life to feel something, to be living, and now here she was caught in real life and its events. It was almost funny. The persistent rollercoaster of queasiness in her stomach had started to pass over the last two days, replaced instead by nerves, but then again, the feelings were so similar that it was impossible to decipher what was what any more.

She'd had to put on two bras that morning, the pain in her breasts was so severe, and she couldn't be sure, but she thought her waist looked a little thicker already, even though she'd eaten very little over the past few weeks.

Florrie glanced over at her. "Are you okay, love? It'll be over soon," she said kindly, knowing that the worst was yet to come if she was indeed pregnant – and Florrie strongly suspected she was. Felicity would need all her strength to face what lay ahead.

"Now, Mum," the doctor said, returning to the room after several minutes and a full examination of Felicity. "Take a seat, please."

They both sat down, grateful to remove the weight from their shaking legs.

"I can confirm that you are indeed pregnant and by my calculations, I'd say you're bang on twelve weeks," he announced, looking over his glasses at them. "You are now over the hump of it. The first twelve weeks is often the hardest. The due date is approximately the tenth of May," he said, quickly counting the weeks on his desk calendar and nodding in agreement.

Felicity looked over at Florrie, who placed her hand protectively on her knee. Felicity didn't cry – she'd already known – she just stared at Florrie.

The doctor looked from "mum" to daughter.

"I take it this is an unplanned pregnancy, considering your age?" he asked carefully.

"Yes, Doctor," Florrie answered.

"And is there a particular young man involved?" he asked, raising his eyebrows.

Felicity nodded.

"Well, then I suggest you inform him and see if he steps up to the plate."

Felicity caught Florrie's eye, who nodded silently in agreement.

"Now, if that's all. I'll see you next month for a check-up and we'll get you registered with the hospital. Plenty of time yet," he said, standing up all businesslike. Then stopped and walked to the front of the heavy mahogany desk. "Listen," he smiled kindly. "My mother always used to say that sometimes the best things in life happen when we least expect them." He patted her shoulder. "That and timing is everything."

Felicity looked at Florrie and they burst into uncontrollable laughter, much to his confusion. Florrie thanked the doctor in between snorts then they made their way out of the office and back to the car.

"Looks like Jim isn't the only one who loves a saying," Florrie giggled, feeling a strange release from finally knowing.

"No, I suppose not," Felicity laughed.

There was a lighter mood in the car now as they drove back to Knockmore. It was done. She knew for sure now.

"I'm sorry to bring it up, but what next, love?" They'd just pulled into Station House and Felicity needed to get back home. "Are you going to tell him? Will you tell me who he is at least?" Florrie encouraged.

Felicity shook her head. "I'd like to tell him first, Florrie, if that's okay. I feel I owe it to him. But I'll tell you then. I promise."

"And your mother? What will we do about her?" Florrie couldn't imagine how Margot was going to react.

"Yes, I'll have to tell them soon. Just let me do it one step at a time."

Felicity knew what was ahead but bit by bit, she was beginning to think she could handle it.

"Okay, love, but you need to do it soon and make a plan. I've told you, you're welcome here with us. We have a spare room. It's small now, but there's enough room for a bed and . . . a cot." Florrie squeezed her hand. "You're over the hump now, love, but this baby is coming like it or not and before long, you won't be able to hide it. Best rip off the bandage now and I told you, I'll come with you to talk to her if you need me to."

Felicity nodded. "You know, Florrie." She looked down as she spoke. "I remember that day you came to the house when I was little. I remember it so well. It kept me going when . . . when . . . " She paused, trying to choose her words carefully. "When things weren't great. And then Lucie, she helped me years ago to find out who you were and we sort of spied on you." Felicity's face turned red. "It's how I knew where to find you."

Florrie folded her into her arms. "Well, I'm so glad you did. It's going to be okay, love. In the end, it's always okay."

Felicity Montgomery

Then – November 1987

Margot paced the floor in her room, backwards and forwards. She felt addled.

Felicity seemed to have recovered from whatever dreaded virus she'd contracted from that little group of snotty-nosed children. It was Felicity's final year in school and she should be focusing all of her energies on her exams, not on extra-curricular activities. But her marks at school were consistently high. Margot was almost willing Felicity's grades to drop, so she could put a stop to Brownies, hating the thought of her out and about mixing with God only knows who. It made her nervous, but Michael had insisted.

"Her work will suffer," she'd warned him. "And do you think it's wise having her around all *those people*?" Margot had said when he first suggested it.

"It will arouse more suspicion if we keep her locked up here, Margot," he'd said, immediately understanding to what she was referring. "Besides, she's almost an adult and if anyone were going to put two and two together, they'd have done so by now."

He hated talking about it. It was a subject that was kept off-limits since Margot told him the truth about Felicity.

Lord knows, he'd spent much of the last nine years in constant fear of being found out, but Father Nugent had died years ago before Michael even knew the truth and that dreadful nurse had disappeared, never to been seen again. He prayed it would stay that way.

"If her studies suffer, it's over."

Margot made him promise and he had, knowing they wouldn't. God, she hated him – could barely stand to be in the same room as him. He'd ruined everything when she told him what she'd done all those years ago. It had felt good watching him squirm, knowing he was too weak ever to do anything about it. She'd felt powerful at that moment until he'd issued his threats to her, all but confined her to the house, trapping her further in her misery. Her only respite nowadays was the drink or four she enjoyed in the evenings, spending every day counting the minutes until she could feel the alcohol numb the pain once again. She'd had very little to think about for years. Nothing to occupy her suspicious mind with – until now.

Margot had been watching Felicity for well over a week from a distance, backing off a little to allow her to slip up, but all she'd noticed was that Felicity seemed quietly content, humming away to herself. Her school work was still impeccable, her appearance unchanged except at times she looked a little drawn, but she'd been unwell, of course. Then this morning she'd walked in for breakfast and Margot had almost gasped. That face. There it was again, looking at her. She was a beautiful girl, she hated to admit it, usually trying to find fault in her features, but this morning she'd looked radiant, positively radiant. Felicity had eaten a massive bowl of porridge, chatted cheerily to Margot and asked to be excused for school.

Margot continued to pace.

Felicity would be heading off soon for her stupid Brownie meeting. Under normal circumstances, Margot would be pouring her first drink around now, waiting to feel the clear liquid burn her throat, slow her bloodstream, but tonight she'd refrain, at least until Felicity was home. Perhaps it was nothing. Maybe it was an overactive imagination in an underactive life. She'd soon find out. She could be patient when she needed to be – she'd proved that before.

It was as if a switch had flipped in Felicity that morning. She'd woken up and the butterflies were gone, replaced with an insatiable hunger. Since Saturday she'd let the news slowly wash over her, absorb into her, become her, and she'd almost decided it was time to tell Sammy.

He had a right to know and no matter what happened, she still had the support of Florrie and Jim. Felicity hoped Sammy would stand by her. She imagined Sammy coming to rescue her and she could picture them together with their baby. It made her feel calm as she gradually accepted her fate. What was done was done, what would be would be.

Felicity smiled to herself. She'd go to Brownies tonight and find out the lay of the land from Lucie, then she'd get a note to him. She wanted to tell him before she told anyone else and then she'd need to face her parents. But there was still time for that. Surely they wouldn't send her away. She was almost an adult. They couldn't keep her here for ever. She was sorry she'd let them down, but she was sure this was the right thing to do.

"Where the hell have you been?" Lucie sprinted towards her as soon as she saw her coming up the lane.

"I've been worried sick. No note, nothing. What's going on?" Lucie placed her hands on her hips, waiting for a response. Now that she knew Felicity hadn't been locked up by Margot, she was furious with her. "Well?"

Felicity looked around for Sammy.

"He's not here. Not that I blame him," Lucie said, her anger visible.

"I'm sorry . . . I . . . " Felicity started.

"What is it, Felicity?" Lucie asked, softening. "Sammy is up the wall. I can't sleep. What's wrong? They said inside you were sick."

"I am. I mean I was. I'm fine. There's just been a lot going on."

"Like what?" Lucie placed her hands back on her hips, waiting.

"Like just a few things. But it's okay. I'll tell you soon. I just need to talk to Sammy first."

"You're scaring me, Fliss."

"I'm sorry. I know. Is he okay? Does he not want to speak to me?"

"Speak to you! He's seriously lovesick. I'm worried about him, we all are. Mam thinks he's on drugs and he's had me checking that bloody tree fifty times a day for word from you. I swear, if I have to stick my hand in there one more time, I might get sucked inside and never be seen again."

"I'm sorry."

"He's really bad. Dad even took him for a pint to try to get him to tell him what's wrong. Mam said it was a dark day when Paddy Maguire would part with money to get to the bottom of a problem."

Felicity laughed despite herself before answering.

287

"I never meant to hurt him. I never meant for any of this – and I did get his letter. I just needed time to think, to figure something out."

Lucie threw her arms around her. "I'm worried about you – please tell me."

"I know, Lucie, and I'm sorry. I'll tell you soon. I just need to talk to him first. I'll write a note as soon as I get home and put it in the tree. Tell him to get it tonight as late as he can. I need to talk to him in person on Saturday. It's important. I'm sorry I can't say more, but please trust me. This may be hard to hear, Lu, but I am in love with your brother and he loves me back. I know he does. Make sure he gets the letter," she smiled. "Please."

Lucie linked her arm into Felicity's and rested her head on Felicity's shoulder.

"I know you are and yep, he loves you, too. But please fix it all soon. I'm just scared something weird is about to happen."

Margot heard the front door close and listened as Felicity took the stairs two at a time up to her bedroom – and then silence. Margot had been waiting in the dark in the parlour, watching from the window in the shadows, looking for anything untoward. But Felicity came up the driveway alone, right on time. Satisfied, Margot went to her room for a drink, taking out her secret stash and pouring herself a large helping before sitting and swirling the clear liquid in the glass.

Maybe her mind was playing tricks with her. Perhaps she was overthinking it, but there was something about the way Felicity was acting that wasn't quite right and she continued to swirl the drink, thinking back over the last few weeks. Maybe she'd taken her eye off the ball again. Margot thought about the bit of freedom that Michael had insisted on, the recent illness, the irritating calm that had descended on her daughter, the silly humming she'd witnessed as she'd lurked behind doors watching. There was something familiar about her behaviour.

Margot's mind drifted back to a time she'd all but forgotten, wiped from her memory. But there it was. Her sisters, lying on the bed, talking about their teenage crushes. She could picture Florrie tumbling onto the bed on her back, clutching her heart, pretending to die with pain. And there was Rosie, saying that she'd never eat again after her boyfriend had gone off with some slut.

Margot sat up. That must be it. Someone must have turned Felicity's head. She must have encountered some ruffian along the way. Some little hooligan must have set their eyes on the reverend's daughter and Felicity, so impressionable, was pining after him. Was she even attending the Brownies meetings? She'd check tomorrow, alert Michael if she had to.

Well, she'd be sure to turn her head back. There was no way that she'd allow Felicity to make a show of them – no way she'd let that girl pull the wool over her eyes. She'd stay patient and alert – lock her up if necessary. Margot was sick of Michael asserting his pathetic authority. She'd lost control once before, been taken by surprise, but she wasn't going to let it happen again.

Margot sat in the darkness for what seemed like hours, observing the low-hanging moon in the black sky, glistening against the drizzling rain that had started to fall. She'd almost nodded off, when she was startled by a creaking noise. She brushed it off as the sounds of the old house and settled her chin into her chest once more, but there it was again.

She looked out of the window, a movement in the garden catching her eye. There was something familiar about it. Had she seen it before? But when? She couldn't remember. She moved to the side of the window, hiding from the light, and peered out. Then she saw it. It was Felicity, she was sure, going through the gate to the orchard. What was she doing?

Margot looked about for her shoes, getting ready to follow her and confront her. Maybe she was meeting someone down there. She'd go and catch them in the act. But when she glanced out again, she saw Felicity making her way back to the house. Margot remained motionless, listening, and almost heard nothing at all except the gentle click of Felicity's door. What was going on? Had whoever it was not shown up?

Margot waited a few minutes before taking her shoes in her hand and leaving her room, creeping past Felicity's, where the light was now out. She glanced over at Michael's permanently shut door, knowing there was no point in rousing him. She'd go and have a look around, see if she could see anything untoward.

She pulled her shoes on in the kitchen and grabbed a knife from the drawer, just in case, before making her way down the garden. It was dark and she waited for her eyes to adjust before calling "Who's there?"

No one answered.

She looked around for anything unusual, but the night offered her nothing. The rain was getting heavier and she was just about to turn to go back to the house, when she saw the footprints in the ground and followed them to where they stopped by the oak tree.

Perhaps Felicity had acted too hastily earlier that evening when she'd delivered the note destined for Sammy. Maybe she was excited at the prospect of a fairy tale reaching its conclusion, or perhaps she was clumsy because of the rain. But Felicity had put the note in the tin box and quickly thrown it into the mouth of the tree before running back inside. The corner of the old biscuit box caught Margot's eye now, so she picked it up and opened it.

All Felicity needed to hear from Lucie was that Sammy still cared. It was all she'd needed to understand. As soon as Lucie told her he was distraught, she'd been sure of her decision to tell him about the baby. She wasn't going to force him into anything, but instead she'd give him the opportunity to choose. She'd rushed home after her Brownies meeting and straight to her room, where she'd poured her heart out to him on paper. She'd have liked to tell him in person, but she was too afraid. At least this way he could see it on paper and think about it before she saw him on the Saturday:

I know this might be hard for you to hear and I know this isn't what you want. At first I didn't want to tell you. But I can't make it go away, Sammy. I can't make it disappear. I'm pregnant, Sammy – twelve weeks. It was the night we met. I've cried so many tears, I can't cry any more.

I know what I have to do. I'm going to keep it. I'm going to raise it alone if I have to. I've been on my own my whole life, Sammy. But I'm not any more. There is love growing inside me, at last, and I want to hold on to it. I'm not asking for anything but know that I love you. I'm scared, Sammy –

291

scared of what she'll do when she finds out – but you make me feel strong.

You once asked what I wanted from life. Well, it's this – this is what I want. I have to get away from her now. I have to get away before she kills me or sends me away. I'm so sorry for everything over the past few weeks. I'll meet you on Saturday. If you're not there, I'll know. It's okay. Do what's right for you. Either way, I'll love you for ever.

Fliss

x

She left out the bit about Florrie and Jim, not wanting anything but his feelings to influence his decision. When she'd finished, she'd waited until it was safe and sneaked out in the rain, making sure to be quick.

Afterwards, she'd slept instantly, finally feeling a release of pent-up emotions, knowing that when she woke in the morning, he'd know. It was in his hands then. She dreamed of him that night. She dreamed about their baby. Her, Sammy and a little girl who looked exactly like her.

"There was nothing there." Sammy stood over her.

Lucie switched on the bedside lamp.

"Jaysus, Sammy, what the hell? You're dripping wet."

His eyes were wild as he stared back at her. She glanced at the clock radio. It was 3 a.m.

"You're shivering. Have you been out there all this time?"

"There was nothing there," he repeated.

"I don't understand. She said she needed to talk to you this Saturday after you read the letter. Maybe she forgot.

Let's wait until Saturday."

"Yes, Saturday," he said. "Did she say anything else? Anything, Lucie?"

"No, she wouldn't tell me – said she needed to tell you first. I think they might be sending her away to college maybe. I can't think what else it could be."

"But that's not that bad. Why all the drama?"

"I don't know, Sammy. I told you, no matter how much we think we know about her life, we don't."

"Yeah, I suppose. Okay, thanks, Lucie," he smiled sadly.

"It'll be okay, Sammy. Honestly. I'm sure she's fine. She seemed happy tonight. But it's hard with her parents. Just give her time. Maybe she couldn't get out this evening. I'm sure that's all it is."

Felicity Montgomery

Then – November 1987

Margot hadn't slept a wink after reading the gripping bedtime story she'd discovered in the tree. Instead, she'd tossed and turned all night. Margot almost admired Felicity for being able to pull it off, twelve weeks of deceiving them, of playing them for fools. Yes, she almost admired her. She'd raised quite the adventurous spirit.

At first, she couldn't believe what she was reading, but then again, what had she expected? It was like history repeating itself, she supposed. It was probably always going to turn out this way – a whore from a whore – and that's all Felicity was, a whore. Well, there was no way she was going to let some slut's daughter be the one to bring her down finally – and after all she'd done for that girl! She'd given her every opportunity to have a better life, living in the lap of luxury.

Margot had heard whispers of ways to induce miscarriage back in the Estates. Perhaps she'd make her drink a bottle of castor oil, have her soak in a bath of gin, or throw her down the stairs – good enough for her. She wasn't going to waste a bottle of gin on her, mind. No, history was about to repeat itself in more ways than one.

There was only one way to deal with this. Margot would arrange for Felicity to go away to finish her studies, confident she could organise a nice doctor and his wife, perhaps, to adopt the child. What a hassle this would be! Margot would need to make plans soon and have her gone. It was bad enough looking at her face as it was, but a lovesick pregnant teenager wouldn't do at all. Felicity could come back once she'd had the baby and given it away, but she'd pay for this embarrassment.

She wouldn't tell Michael.

She'd involved him before and look where that got her. No, she'd deal with it. Everything ran smoother when she dealt with the problems. All the upset over the years and for what? Margot shouldn't have bothered. Perhaps it would be a relief to have her gone. Maybe Michael would come round then. It would be far more comfortable for them all if she were gone.

How Felicity got through the day she'd never know. She was up early ready to check the tree before school, but Margot was dressed before her, stalking about the house, making it impossible to get out. She waited the entire day, chewing at her nails, wondering, hoping that Sammy had received her letter and replied. Then finally she got the chance.

"I'm going to lie down. I have a headache. Father's out for the evening and I doubt I'll be up again. Could you make something to eat yourself?" Margot asked later that day.

"Yes, Mother. I hope you feel better."

It took all of her willpower to wait until Mother was upstairs and sound asleep before she slipped out of the back door and ran towards her destiny. Taking a deep breath, she bent down to open the tin box containing the blueprint for her future.

"Looking for something?"

Felicity almost jumped out of her skin. She turned to see Mother standing over her waving a note in her hand.

"Mother. I . . . I'm . . . " But she couldn't finish, the words sat on her tongue.

"The stammering again, Felicity, please. Stand up straight. Just because you're a slut doesn't mean you should look like one," Margot spat.

Felicity pulled back her shoulders, ready for the verbal attack, but instead, Margot came at her unexpectedly, pushing her into the tree with full force. Felicity stumbled, losing her balance, and fell to her knees.

"Stand up. Felicity!" Margot shouted.

Felicity slowly stood, fighting back the tears. Margot launched at her again, pushing her to the ground.

"Stand up!" she shouted again.

Felicity stood, clutching her belly protectively, and stared defiantly at her mother, all the hate and all the hurt suddenly bringing her strength. Margot launched herself once more and stumbled as Felicity sidestepped her.

"Slut!" Margot shouted. She righted herself, brushing the leaves off her skirt, and threw the letter at Felicity. "Read it to me! Read it now, you whore," she screamed.

Felicity took the letter that never reached Sammy and started to read. She read until her voice broke. She trembled as she spoke of the moments they'd shared aloud. How they'd made a baby, how she loved him, wanted to be with him, how she could see them together, how she needed to get away from here before she died, how her mother would kill her, but she was ready and . . .

"Enough!" Margot put up her hand to stop her. "Beautifully put," she clapped. "I'll make one of your wishes come true. You *will* be leaving here and you *will* put the baby up for adoption. That's the only choice," she said coldly. "You're still a child, Felicity. In the eyes of the law, you're a child, so you don't get a choice. Who else knows about this? Did you tell anyone? Did you go to the doctor?"

"No one. No one knows," Felicity lied. "I took the bus to Balinstill last week," she whispered. "Saw a doctor there. I didn't give my real name."

"How industrious of you, Felicity, you sneaky, sneaky little slut. Well, I'll have it taken care of before lover boy finds out."

"I won't let you take my baby." Felicity stared her down.

"But you don't have a choice." Margot approached her and stared intently into her eyes then slapped her hard across the face.

Felicity's hand shot to her cheek, stunned.

"That's for doing this to your father." She smacked the other cheek. "And that's for doing it to me," she said. "Sammy? I take it that's a Maguire? You couldn't stay away, could you? Now go to your room," she spat. "I've arrangements to make. And if I hear anything from you, I'll have your little boyfriend arrested for rape. You wouldn't want that, would you?"

Felicity Montgomery

Then – November 1987

Sammy was there an hour before Felicity was due at the church hall and he waited an hour after she failed to show up.

"I don't get it. I'm going to check the tree again and have a look at the house, see if I can see anything," he told Lucie.

But there was nothing there.

Sammy made his way up the road towards Knockmore House, walking past slowly and peering through the gates. It took all of his willpower not to march up the driveway and bang the door down, demanding to see her. But he didn't. Instead, he returned home, downtrodden, to Lucie, where they sat on the end of her bed trying to figure it all out.

"Maybe we should tell Mam," Lucie suggested finally.

"I can't, Lu," was all he said.

Margot had seen him walking by the gate several times and stopping as if he were about to attempt a confrontation but couldn't decide whether he should or shouldn't. Eventually, he'd left. That was all she needed.

"Where's Felicity?" Michael had asked her that morning.

"Didn't I say? I had to call the doctor yesterday. She has a terrible dose. He's confined her to bed. Total rest, he said, for at least a week." She finished buttering her toast.

"Oh dear. Should I go and see her?" Michael asked, looking concerned.

"No, no, Michael. Don't be ridiculous. It's highly contagious and you can't afford to be ill at this time of year when so many others need you."

She smiled sweetly. That would keep him away. He was terrified of any illness. She'd tell him, in time, but she needed to make some calls first and find out where best to displace her. He wouldn't have a choice in the matter if the arrangements were already made. It was his fault. She'd be sure to mention that to him. He gave an inch and Felicity took a mile. What a mess.

So far, Felicity had been quiet, sulking in her room. But Margot made sure to keep the door locked, just in case. As soon as Margot had mentioned the word "rape", it had taken the pep out of her step. She'd be sure to use that threat again to keep her pliable.

Margot had given her very little to eat yesterday and today, but even that had come back untouched. She could stay there hungry until she came round to her way of thinking. It shouldn't take long.

Felicity Montgomery

Then – November 1987

There he is again. Margot was sure he'd have given up by now. She peered out of the window at the young man stalking past the gate – not a bad-looking boy, rough-looking, though. Felicity obviously went for looks and not breeding. He was starting to irritate her, but it would all be over by Monday and Felicity would be gone, for some time.

Margot had secured a place for her in a school in Dublin with the nuns. They'd been very understanding. Felicity would still be able to sit her exams and deliver the child as if it had never happened. And the stupid girl had always said she wanted to go to Dublin – now was her big chance. Careful what you wish for, Felicity. The nuns would arrange a suitable adoption and then she'd come back to Knockmore.

The baby was due at the start of May and her exams were in June. It was a tight turnaround, but she had youth on her side and she'd have to get on with it. Good enough for her. She'd tell everyone that she'd been accepted into a specialist scholarship programme. That would go down well.

"I've to do some paperwork in here, Margot."

She turned to see Michael at the study door.

"How's Felicity?"

"Yes, still unwell. A bad fever. She should be fine after the weekend. Best leave her be. I'm just going to check on her."

Felicity hardly knew what day it was. Had it been a week? She was exhausted. She tried to sleep, but images of Sammy and her baby and her mother, of Tess and Lucie, her father, the puppies, kept flashing into her mind and she didn't know what was real any more. Had it really happened? The door to her room was still locked. She'd tried at first, but she knew she couldn't risk it. She couldn't risk *her* hurting Sammy. Perhaps Father would come to her. But how could she tell him, and would he do anything? He hadn't before. She knew what Mother was capable of and she wouldn't stop now. She'd seen the hatred in her eyes when she'd hit her. No, Felicity wouldn't let her hurt them all.

Felicity thought about Sammy, holding on to his image in her mind. He didn't even know about the baby. He wasn't coming – no one was. Only Florrie knew and Felicity had told her she'd get word to her when she was ready.

Felicity tried to sit up in bed, but her arms gave way from under her and she collapsed back on the pillow. She felt so weak, had barely eaten anything aside from a few sips of water, and her mind felt muddy. Her hand travelled to her belly, where she could feel the tiny swell of her baby nestled inside her. They were going to take it. She was going to be sent away. Sammy would go to jail. She couldn't let it happen. She'd rather die.

She heard the door opening and closed her eyes. She couldn't take much more. Yesterday, Mother had slapped her face again and again until she opened her eyes.

"Wake up! Wake up, you slut. Eat!" She'd tried to force some bread into her mouth. "This is getting tiresome, Felicity, watching you sulk. Are you going to agree now? The arrangements are already made. You'll be leaving soon. Think of it as the best thing for your little boyfriend. Imagine Tess's face when the Guards come to take him away. That should help."

No, she'd rather die.

If she were dead, Mother couldn't hurt her any more. She'd be with her baby and she'd never be alone again. No more food now, no more water.

It'll be over soon, she thought, keeping her eyes closed as Mother grabbed her hair and yanked her head backwards.

Felicity Montgomery

Then – November 1987

Florrie wasn't sure why she'd come. She didn't feel up to it at all. Perhaps she'd leave before the others arrived. She quickly gathered her raincoat and bag from under the chair and made her way back outside. She usually loved playing bridge with the girls on a Friday evening, but her mind was elsewhere and she'd be no use to anyone in this mood.

Why hadn't Felicity contacted her yet? It had been almost two weeks. Perhaps the young fella had rejected her, or maybe she hadn't had a chance to tell him yet. Whatever was happening, Florrie was starting to get worried.

"Give her time," Jim kept saying, but it had been time enough now and she couldn't rest until she knew Felicity was safe.

She dreaded the thought of seeing her sister, but she'd just have to do it.

"Another couple of days, Jim, and then I'm going up there, and you can come with me," she'd said sharply.

"Patience is the ability to countdown before you blast-off," he'd said, leaving the room.

"Florrie? Are you coming or going?"

She'd just made it to the car, ready to make her getaway

303

without having to face twenty questions, when she saw Tess Maguire waving at her. Shite! she'd been spotted.

"Ah, Tess, I'm going. I'm just not in the humour tonight," Florrie said, opening the car door.

"I'm not much in the humour myself, to be honest. Are you all right, pet?" Tess asked, knowing Florrie well enough to know that she never missed a bridge night.

"Sure, I'm grand. A few things going on is all, you know." Florrie looked at the ground.

"Listen, what do you say we bunk off and head to the pub? I could do with a chat and a drink, Lord knows!" Tess said.

"Ah, I'd better not."

"You'd be doing me a favour. Come on, my treat," Tess said, putting her hand on Florrie's.

"Go on, then," Florrie smiled, pulling the car door open. "Hop in before the others see us."

Florrie hadn't intended to tell Tess anything. But then again, what harm could it do? The news would be out soon enough anyway and she knew Tess cared for young Felicity, too. And maybe little Lucie knew something that might help.

Tess's eyes were wide as she sat opposite Florrie in the pub and listened to her story.

"And there she was on the doorstep. You could have knocked me over with a feather. I mean, I always hoped she'd find me, but I never really thought she would. And then when she told me why she'd come . . . Oh, Tess." Florrie took a sip from her drink and rested it back on the table.

"Is she all right? Did Margot hurt her? Why didn't she come to me?" Tess asked, a little hurt.

"I don't know, Tess. I know you two are close," Florrie said, shaking her head.

"Well, what happened?"

"Oh, Tess . . . " Florrie paused. "She's pregnant."

"*What*?"

"She's pregnant. I took her to have it confirmed with the doctor in Ballinstill and she's terrified. It's a terrible mess." Florrie rubbed her hands down her face as she spoke. "Jim says it's a problem because she's still only seventeen. If she were eighteen, I'd march up there now and bundle her into the car. Anyway, she wanted time to tell the fella, but he's obviously told her he wants nothing to do with it. Otherwise, I'd have heard from her and, oh, Tess, I'm worried."

"Sweetest Jesus above! Felicity, pregnant? But how? When? Did she say who it was?" Tess stared at her in shock.

Florrie shook her head. "She wouldn't say, said she'd got out for a night and met him – in love, she told me, and . . . " She stopped when she saw Tess's face. "What?"

"Oh, Jesus." Tess's hand shot to her mouth. "Oh, God, no," she whispered as the pieces of the puzzle gathered in the air above her. "I think I know," she said finally.

The night at her house. The knowing stares between them. Her now sullen son. The whispered conversations between Lucie and Sammy. The odd comings and goings. There it was, all laid out for her.

"It's Sammy," Tess whispered.

Florrie looked at her. "Sammy?"

"I'm sure of it. Oh, God, forgive me. What have I done?" Tess put her face in her hands and started to cry. "I've something to tell you, Florrie."

It was a different set of cards that were laid on the table that night in place of bridge and by the end of it, the two women were shocked.

"What now?" Florrie asked.

There was no reason to point the finger of blame – what was done was done.

"I need to talk to Sammy. How could he reject her? I'll kill him with my bare hands – that poor girl. And him going around like he's heartbroken? How dare he!"

Tess was annoyed, furious that she'd raised a son who'd balk from his responsibilities, angry that he'd slept with her in the first place. But if he'd rejected her, it was far worse. Tess had told them all their lives that any problem could be dealt with but never run from. She'd practically drilled it into them.

"I'll call you in the morning, Florrie," Tess promised before making her way home to face whatever music was blasting from that darn stereo.

Tess had to hand it to him. He looked devastated all right, as if his world had ended. She'd thought the whole way home how to handle this and decided she'd let him tell her, give him the chance to show his side of it. It was how she'd always parented – ask first before accusing. Even though she'd have liked to kill him there and then, she held back.

"Sammy, are you okay?" Tess asked, peering around the door of his bedroom.

He sat up suddenly, wiping at his eyes with the back of his sleeve.

"What is it, son?" Tess sat down on the bed beside him and put her hand on his leg.

"I'm fine, Mam. Just fine."

But the tears in his eyes told another story and she put her arms around him. It was the age-old rule that a little affection administered at the right moment could break the toughest and Sammy was no exception. She waited.

"Mam, please don't be cross, but I've something to tell you."

For the second time that evening, Tess listened to a different version of the same story with the added twist of unrequited love and rejection.

"I fell in love with her, Mam. She's amazing and it was all going well, and then it just stopped, with no explanation. I don't know if I did something, it just ended. She won't answer my letters. She's even stopped going to the meetings with Lucie. Not even Lucie has heard from her now. I don't know what to do. I'm worried."

They both looked up as the door opened slowly.

"I'm sorry," Lucie said, coming into the room. "I don't mean to earwig, but I'm worried, too. There's something not right. Felicity said she needed to tell Sammy something important, promised that she'd be there on Saturday, that she needed to talk, and then she never showed up. They said she was sick in Brownies. It must be serious. Is she okay? Do you know something, Mam? Is she sick?"

Tess looked at them both. "I do know something." She looked from one to the other.

"Oh my God, what is it? Is she hurt?" Sammy stared at her.

"Sammy, love. There's no easy way to tell you this – she's pregnant."

"*Pregnant*?" Lucie shouted. "Oh, Jesus Christ. Sammy, you idiot. What have you done?"

Tess looked at Sammy. "Yes, love. Pregnant. And I'm

not a bit happy with you, but we'll talk about that in a moment. She went to Florrie Hughes and told her. She wouldn't tell Florrie who the father was, but I'm assuming it's yours. Three months gone. Would that make sense?"

Sammy looked at his hands and nodded. "I'm sorry, Mam, yes. But pregnant? Oh my God! Pregnant? Is she sure? Is she okay? I need to see her. I need to tell her it's okay . . . I . . . I love her, Mam. I'm sorry, so sorry I've let you down, let her down, but I won't let her down now."

He looked like a little boy at that moment and Tess thought her heart would break. He hadn't known and even though she still wanted to wring his neck, she felt proud of him.

"But why didn't she tell me?" Sammy asked.

Tess saw all the pieces once again arrange themselves in front of her. There was just one piece of the puzzle still suspended in the air that slowly drifted down as Lucie caught her mother's eye and they both whispered, "Margot."

Felicity Montgomery

Then – November 1987

Had she slept? Was she even awake? It was hard to tell now. Even when Felicity tried to open her eyes, everything appeared black. She was sure she had slept. She remembered the girl in her dream, just like her. Her blonde hair almost white in the sunshine. She was in the orchard, digging in the ground by the oak tree, her hands covered in dirt, but she was smiling.

"I found her," the girl said. "I found her. Let's go." She held out her hand to Felicity. "Let's go into the tree."

Felicity reached out, but something was holding her back.

"My baby. I can't find my baby."

She wished she could go back, take the girl's hand and go now. Why was it taking so long?

"How is she this morning?" Michael looked up as Margot swept into the dining room.

"She's on the mend, still weak," she lied.

Margot would have to tell him tonight about Felicity and the baby. Felicity wouldn't touch any food and looked very unwell. She'd always been a dramatic thing, though.

She'd bring her something now and force her to eat. It would all be over soon.

"Perhaps I'll call the doctor again," Michael replied. "Seems quite a while to be unwell. I'll go and check on her now, in fact." He stood up.

"Sit down, Michael!" Margot said impatiently. "I'm afraid I've something rather distressing to tell you," she started before hearing a loud bang.

"What in the blazes is that?" Michael looked up.

They both stopped, hearing the loud hammering again on the front door. Michael stood immediately and headed to the hallway, flinging open the door.

"What's going on here?" The reverend stared at the small crowd of people gathered on the doorstep. "I say, can I help you?"

They looked back at him. It was the same crowd who'd met early that morning in Station House, where they'd knitted the story together for Sergeant Hughes. They'd all had plenty to add to it, right back to when Felicity was a child. Sammy told the disgusting story of the puppies while Tess and Lucie stared on, aghast.

"There were always unexplained bruises, always silent pleading in her eyes," Tess added, crying as she guessed at the torture Felicity must have endured. "I didn't help her – I didn't do enough."

"We didn't know, Mam. She kept it from everyone." Lucie hugged her, only now realising how brave her friend really was.

They'd all known a little, but only now as they'd all laid the pieces out were they able to stitch together the real story, the reality of what had gone on inside the reverend's house for all those years. It had been there all along, all the little clues, pointing clearly to the fact that there was a madwoman in the vicarage, watching over a child, and she was still a child.

"Please, Jim. Please. Have you been listening? She's in danger. Margot must know about the baby and you've heard now what she's capable of. Isn't it enough?" Florrie pleaded with her husband.

Sergeant Hughes sat silently, shaking his head. He'd been listening all right, heard the whole sorry story. He was a man of few words, aside from his much-loved quotes, but for the life of him he couldn't come up with a single quote that would do this mess justice.

"Please, Jim," she begged.

"Fuck this!" Sammy stood up. "I'm going to get her. Arrest me if you want, Sergeant Hughes, but I have to try."

"Easy, lad." Jim stood up slowly and lifted his hat from the table, still shaking his head in disbelief.

"Say something, Jim, for Christ's sake." Florrie was on her feet.

"Jesus, woman, calm yourself." He held up his hand, still thinking. "Always so many words." And then it came to him, the thing that had been on the tip of his tongue. "There's a time for words and a time for action, and now is the time for action," he said, heading for the door.

They all stood here now, taking in the reverend's shocked face at the unlikely group who'd come to visit him.

"What's this about?" Michael pressed.

"What on earth?" Margot emerged from behind him. "This is quite the collection of degenerates!"

Margot looked them up and down, her eyes settling on Florrie. What on earth was her stupid sister doing here? That little liar. Felicity must have told them all she was pregnant.

"I need to speak to you and Mrs Montgomery as a matter of urgency," the sergeant delivered. "Alone." He turned and held his hand up to Tess, Lucie, Sammy and Florrie, who were all by now worked into a frenzy.

"Well, I should think so!" quipped Margot. "Whatever cavalry you've brought with you, you are now trespassing."

Jim walked through the door, leaving the troops behind.

"Now, Reverend, I'm going to hazard a guess that you have no idea what's going on here."

The reverend responded by shaking his head nervously. He couldn't even meet the sergeant's eyes, but he was almost relieved. He'd lived every day, for close to ten years, in fear of their secret making its way into the open and now here it was.

"And I'm going to assume, Maggie, that you *do* know what's going on here?" Sergeant Hughes regarded her, remembering Florrie's words: "And you can tell when she's lying, Jim. You'll see it. That was one thing our Maggie never learned to control."

Margot appeared calm, her defiant eyes fixed on his, but the tell-tale nervous blotches had started to flower on her chest, inching up her neck, and crawling towards her face.

"Yes, Sergeant, unfortunately, I do," she replied evenly before turning to Michael. "You see, Michael, Felicity is pregnant. I was going to tell you today, but I only just found out myself and I'm sorry to tell you, but I believe she was raped by that *thug* outside. I'm glad you're here, Sergeant, as I'd like to press charges."

Michael could hardly speak. "Pregnant, Felicity? I don't understand."

"Yes, but you should, Michael. It was your idea to give her all that freedom, let her consort with the likes of *them* . . . " Margot gestured at the window. "So really, Michael, this is all your fault!"

"Felicity? No." Michael put his head in his hands. "That boy, I've seen him outside before, at night."

"Yes, he's been stalking the house for the last week – Tess Maguire's boy. I believe you brought that onto us as well," she added smugly.

"Now hold up here, let's not run away with ourselves." Jim knew darn well what the old bitch was up to. "And there's been a fair few accusations made against you, Maggie, come to think of it. There's been a report about you murdering puppies, abusing Felicity, unexplained bruises, withholding food from a child, shall I go on?"

"How dare you! You disgusting man!"

Margot's face was puce, while the colour had entirely drained from Michael's, who looked as though he were about to faint.

"Bit of truth in that, is there, Reverend?" the sergeant asked.

"Michael, tell him to get out of our home. Tell him it's nonsense."

The reverend was clutching tight to the edge of table now and even the sergeant looked concerned.

"Help! Help!"

They all turned.

Lucie had grown tired of waiting. She needed to see Fliss. She didn't care now what happened to her or what trouble she'd be in. While everyone else waited, she'd sneaked off around the back of the house and found the back door open. She'd run through the house and up the stairs, not caring who heard her. She had to get to her friend, her blood sister. She had to see if she was okay. Sergeant Hughes was right – this was a time for action. Lucie had tried the handle of Felicity's bedroom door. It was locked. She'd turned the key, left brazenly in the door, pushed it open and screamed.

The cavalry outside pushed through the front door as soon as they heard Lucie screaming. Sergeant Hughes, Michael and Margot emerged from the parlour. But it was Sammy who got there first and without hesitating, he scooped Felicity up and ran down the stairs. Sergeant Hughes followed him out of the front door, starting the engine of the car as Sammy gently lay Felicity on the back seat.

"Go. Drive. Quickly," Sammy shouted as the others watched open-mouthed.

But they'd all seen it – the trail of red, spilling from Felicity's opened wrists onto the parquet floor, right down the stone steps of Knockmore House.

Felicity Montgomery

Then – November 1987

It was Sammy's face Felicity saw first, looking down at her, smiling through his tears. She smiled back then he leaned over and gently kissed her.

"I have to tell you something," she whispered, suddenly remembering.

"It's okay, I know everything," Sammy smiled tenderly.

"But the baby! Oh no, the baby! I hurt the . . . " Felicity grew distressed.

Florrie flew to her side and gently took her hand. "The baby is fine. You lost a lot of blood and it's early days, but you need to rest. We're all praying for the baby."

"No praying." Felicity shook her head. "Just hoping."

"Okay, pet, we're all hoping. And we're all here. Right here. And we're not going anywhere."

"What happened?" Felicity asked, looking up at Sammy. "I can't remember."

"We'll talk about it again when you're better. I love you," he mouthed.

They were all here. Florrie and Tess and Lucie. Sergeant Hughes had left to *tidy up* a few things, but they were all here – they'd always been here. She looked at them all.

She'd felt so alone for so long, but they were all here – right where they should be.

"Where are *they*?" Felicity's eyes shot open, suddenly terrified. "Where is *she*?"

"They're gone," Tess told her. "All gone now. You're one of us now, love. Sleep, little one."

PART THREE

Ann Fitzgerald

Now

Ann had waited for hours, sitting alone, staring into space, wondering. It was well after 9 p.m. and for the third night in a row, she'd sat waiting and thinking, trying to order her thoughts as well as she'd organised her wardrobe the day before, clearing out the old, making room for the new. What was wrong with her? Before they were married, Dom had told her something that still played on her mind. She hadn't thought of it too much at the time, but now it seemed huge.

"You know I'm a carrier for cystic fibrosis, do you know if you are?" Dom had asked her casually one day after they'd made love.

"Really? What does that mean?" Ann rolled onto her side to face him.

"Well, if you're a carrier as well, then we have an increased chance of having a child with the condition."

"Oh. I have no idea. I really have no idea," Ann said, trying to think.

"Is there any history of it in your family?"

"I don't know. I never heard of anything." There was no one to ask.

"Well, you can have a test. Maybe you should," he suggested before gathering her into his arms and kissing her.

She hadn't, of course – it had gone right out of her head, the plans for the wedding consuming her. But she wondered about it now. Maybe she should have the test. But what else would she find out? What other skeletons were nestled in her dark closet, waiting to make an appearance? What else didn't she know?

Ann heard the front door and sat up.

"Well, did you make a dent in the credit card?" Dom asked, breezing in through the door. He kissed her on the forehead and flopped down on the sofa beside her.

"Yeah, I got a dress. Not too expensive – just a little chip in the card, not exactly a dent."

She was always worried about spending money and from a lifetime of being careful, it didn't come easily to her.

"I told you not to worry about money, Bella, especially once this deal I'm working on goes through," he smiled. "And hey, sorry I missed dinner. I just grabbed something at my desk. But it'll all be worth it. One step closer to the goal."

He yawned and she nodded. She'd rushed home from town after her shopping trip with Sophie earlier to make another dinner, only for it to be scraped off the plate and straight into the bin.

"I've been thinking," she started, following Sophie's lead. "Maybe I could get another job. You know, just until I'm pregnant, anyway. I'm just a bit bored at home on my own. Sophie's off on a Monday, but the rest of the week is long and . . . " She trailed off when she saw his face.

"Ah, don't start, Bella," he said impatiently. "We talked

about this. I need you by my side in the support role and you'll be pregnant soon enough. Maybe *Big Bad Dom* could come out tonight."

Ann cringed. The first time he'd used the analogy, she'd laughed, not sure why he'd be referencing his manhood to a bottle of Domestos, but he continued to use the little joke and it got under her skin – just like, well . . . bleach.

"I've got my period, sorry," she lied.

"Oh well, that'll explain your little mood." He held up his hands to her in defeat before softening. "Look, Bella, everything will settle down soon and you'll feel different once there are loads of little Doms running around to keep you busy." He put his arm around her.

"I suppose. Oh, listen. I booked a dinner for us on Friday in that new restaurant you said you wanted to try. Just the two of us. I thought we could catch up properly."

"Sorry, sweetheart, no can do. I've got the annual boys' dinner that night. Fitzgeralds are hosting and you have that charity lunch with the girls, remember? Did you un-sync our calendars again?" he said, standing up. "I'm gonna grab a beer – you want one?"

Ann shook her head and watched him cross the kitchen to open the fridge. She knew that even if she stood in her knickers and bra at the door, it wouldn't keep him away from the lads. She also knew very well that he'd told her about that lunch. She'd conveniently chosen to forget. Ann hated those lunches. It was like a full-on fashion show, complete with bobbing heads and scanning eyes, ready to look you up and down. They all looked the same – smooth foreheads and plumped cheeks, like hamsters storing nuts for winter. She was going with Dom's best friend's wife. Issy was lovely, but she stared at Ann so intently when she spoke that Ann was always convinced there was something in her teeth so spent much of the conversation trying to remove the imaginary piece of lettuce.

That was the weekend gone now. When they first got together, there were constant lunches out and romantic walks at the weekend, followed by hours of making love. Ann had to admit that Big Bad Dom knew his way around the bedroom all right – he was fantastic in bed, always had been, and he made her feel like the most beautiful girl in the world. Back then, Dom was happy to be with just her and she loved the intimacy they shared in their little bubble. But they rarely had those days any more, they hadn't for months, and now he'd have a giant hangover for Saturday and possibly most of Sunday after the annual dinner. Last year he'd turned up on the doorstep at 5 a.m., vomiting into the topiary tree and slurring at her, and she knew this weekend would be no different. She wondered what had changed . . .

It was after they'd got engaged, she supposed. Suddenly, they were continually having dinner here and there with all of his friends in whatever restaurant was deemed to be *the* eatery of the week. She liked them all, but the boys always sat at one end of the table and the girls at the other. She always came home from a night out feeling as though she hadn't seen him at all.

There were six couples, all married or soon to be, and the conversations were an endless Ferris wheel of bridal dress designers, venues, flowers, bridesmaids and hen nights. Ann was only thankful that the chat hadn't yet turned to babies, all still enjoying their freedom too much. Ann had no interest in it all, but she nodded along, her reserved demeanour often mistaken for exotic knowledge, which made them crave her opinion even more. The girls all had hair extensions, nail extensions, eyelash extensions – literally anything that could be extended was. She wouldn't have been surprised if one of them arrived one day with leg extensions. There was Botox and Baby Botox – "Prevention is better than cure" – so they all shared the same expression of permanent shock.

They couldn't be more different from her if they tried. She was devastated when they added her to their WhatsApp group, which was practically a full-time job. It pinged at any hour of the day, much to her annoyance, forcing her to switch it to snooze and quickly back again after she was left with seventy-eight unread messages about – nothing.

All of their friends had been shocked when she'd revealed she didn't have a wedding planner. Instead, she'd organised it all with her mother-in-law.

"He landed on his feet the day he met you, love," Patricia Fitzgerald told her, delighted that their son had selected someone not driven by his fortune.

Ann had purchased her dress online. "I'm sure it's a Temperley gown," she'd heard the girls whispering on the day. They'd scoured websites afterwards looking for the price tag. They just hadn't thought to look at the Monsoon Bridal collection from the high street store. The wedding had been perfect. All she'd seen was Dom as she'd walked up the aisle. For her, it was just about marriage. She'd have married him in a drive-through.

"I know you're not from this life, and I know you don't care much for it, but accept it, don't fight it," her father-in-law told her on the way to the wedding after agreeing to give her away. "We're all just the same underneath it all, just people wanting to be loved. Dom will grow up soon and learn it's all just frosting, remember that, but he loves you very much," he'd said.

And she loved Dom. She was sure she did – she just didn't feel like herself any more. She'd enjoyed working, loved the buzz of the office and the banter she had with her co-workers. When she was working those long hours and out with Dom at the weekends, having Sunday dinner with his family, she was always too busy to think about the past. And for a while she'd been so swept up in her life that she'd forgotten about it.

"There's nothing we can do about the past. We only have the present," Dom told her whenever she got upset. He knew a little about her previous existence, but not enough. Ann found it awkward to discuss it with him and he'd never pressed her on it, except for that one time. "Would you like to take a drive back there and look around?" he'd offered.

"No. No, there's nothing for me there now. Nothing at all."

Once upon a time, her world had been *there*. Everything she'd ever wanted had been in one little house, in one small town, in one tiny family. There, she'd felt safe. There, she'd felt like she was in exactly the place she was supposed to be. She wanted to feel like that again. She wanted to feel like herself.

There, she'd been plain old Ann Maguire.

Ann Maguire

Then – 1995

"Time for bed. Come on, little one," Mam called from the kitchen.

Ann snuggled back into the sofa and pulled the blanket up around her chin. "Just one more, Daddy, please," she begged.

Mam put her head around the door and smiled. "One more," she said. "And then bed."

She disappeared again, leaving Daddy and Ann laughing together. He picked up his guitar, singing softly he as strummed along.

"I love this one, Daddy," Ann whispered, joining in.

They were always singing together, her and her daddy. He'd even started to teach her to play the guitar, showing her how to make chords with her fingers and strum the strings. She was good, too. Daddy told her so.

"Your get your looks from your mam, but she sounds like a drowning cat when she sings," he'd laugh. "The singing is up to you and me, kiddo. Someday we'll sing together onstage. You get the music from me. That's my contribution!"

She loved singing with him. He'd taught her loads of duets.

"I could listen to you two all day long," Mam used to tell them.

Mam would sit on her chair and close her eyes. When they weren't singing, the radio was always on, or the television.

"Silence is golden, but I prefer noise," Mam always said.

Dad used to come in from work in the evening smelling of oil and diesel, with splodges of grease on his clothes, and immediately pick up his guitar. Mam often had to prise it out of his hands to get him to sit down and eat dinner.

"The three pals" – that's what they called themselves. Ann loved it when they took their dinner into the living room and sat on the soft carpet, eating and talking and laughing together. Daddy was the best singer in the world.

"Could have been famous," Mam said. "I remember the first time I saw him, standing up there on the stage, all the girls staring at him."

Ann loved hearing the story of how her parents met. She remembered the first time Mam told it.

"But he sang only to me and I thought my heart would burst open when I heard his voice," she said.

Dad listened as she told it, leaning on the doorway, his hands tucked into his pockets, smiling at her, the kind of smile that came all the way from his toes.

"Afterwards, he bought me a Coke and asked me lots of questions – very nosy, he was – and then he kissed me and well, the rest is history," Mam finished.

He started singing then – some song from the olden days.

"Dance with me, Felicity," Sammy said, holding his hands out, taking Ann's mam in his arms.

Ann watched them twirling around the living room. "Yuck, stop kissing!" she squealed from behind her hands.

Dad chased Mam around the room then until they all collapsed on the floor laughing.

"Sure, I'm only a failed musician," Daddy said at last when they could laugh no more.

"Maybe," Mam replied, smiling at him. "But you're an accomplished father and that's even better."

They lived in the apartment above the garage, where Dad worked as a mechanic. He fixed cars and Mam worked in the little shop they had, which sold bread, milk and all the essentials. Mam even baked cakes and sold them fresh. People would say that Felicity Maguire made the best cakes in all of Knockmore.

"I learned from an exceptional old lady – she made the best apple tarts in the world. Mrs Walsh was her name, but I called her Nelly," Mam would smile sadly.

Everyone loved Mam. She was beautiful and friendly and happy. "Always smiling," that's what they said.

Ann once heard two ladies talking about her mam outside the shop. "What a lovely girl! Hard old start in life. All the same, it's all forgotten now, thank God. But there was something not right up in that house – everyone was glad to see the back of them – quite the mystery. Some say they separated. Imagine a reverend separating!"

Ann asked Mam about it later that day.

"Where did you come from, Mam? Was it a big house?"

"What do you mean, little one?" Felicity asked.

"Before here, where did you live, when you were little, like me?"

"Well, here in Knockmore. But my life started the day I met your daddy," she said, kissing Ann's nose.

"But where are your parents?" Ann asked, unsatisfied.

"They passed away," Mam said quietly. "Now, little

one. The past is the past and the present is a gift, and we have everyone we need in our lives."

Mam always knew what to say to make Ann feel safe and she always felt protected. She had her mam and dad and her best friend, Ciara. She had an aunty too, who was a nurse in Australia. Aunty Lucie used to send her letters and postcards and big parcels for her birthday. She'd sent her a kangaroo cuddly toy for her eighth birthday with a baby roo tucked into its pouch. It was Ann's most prized possession. No one in school had one. Then she had her nana Tess and her grandpa Paddy, and another aunty called Florrie, who used to live nearby but moved away to Cork.

On the weekends, Daddy played in a band and they'd wait at home for him. He always came to tuck her in afterwards – he was never late.

"As soon as I finish, I can't wait to get back to my girls, my two blondies," he always told her before kissing her goodnight.

Ann wished she could sing on the stage with him. Mam said she could be anything she wanted when she grew up – it was okay with her that it was more important to be happy, that was all that mattered.

"I think I'd like to be a singer in a band and do sums for my work."

"Oh, I hated maths when I was little. I never got it right, but if that's what you want, that's what you must do, my love. You certainly have the talent to sing in a band. The little voice of an angel. And keep practising that guitar!"

"What did you want to do, Mam?" Ann asked.

"I used to think I wanted to be a vet, but what I truly wanted was a family, and I have that now. I have everything I ever wanted, right here."

Ann Maguire

Then – 2001

"It's not unusual for couples to die so close together," Mam told her, hugging her tight. "It happens, little one. Sometimes it's hard for people to carry on when they lose someone so close."

Ann still couldn't believe it. When Grandpa Paddy died last year, the day before her thirteenth birthday, she'd been so sad. She'd had nightmares for weeks, thinking about him lying in the coffin and being lowered into the ground, all alone. Nana Tess didn't want to leave him there, either. "He'll be cold," Nana Tess kept saying. "Paddy hates the cold." She'd wanted to sit there for hours with him. In the end, Dad and Lucie had taken Tess's arms and led her away.

The only good part of it all was that Aunt Lucie had come home from Australia for the funeral. Ann loved spending time with her. Aunt Lucie told her funny stories about when Mam was young and the games they used to play. Ann loved hearing it all. Aunt Lucie had mentioned the big house again, but Mam shook her head, warning her to stop. Ann asked about it again and this time, Mam walked her up to the other side of Knockmore and pointed out a big mansion.

"That's where I lived, before you, Ann, before you were born." Mam looked up at it and shivered.

"Wow! it's huge. Were you rich?"

"No, little one. Not rich," Mam laughed. "Not at all. It was a nice house, but it was cold and there wasn't a lot of love in there," she said sadly. "That's all you need to know. It just goes to show that you can't judge a book by its cover. Big houses aren't always what they seem." Ann had wanted to ask more, but Mam seemed sad looking at it. "Someday I'll tell you more when you're old enough. Let's get home."

They moved in with Nana Tess a few months after Grandpa Paddy died. Dad didn't want her alone in the house, so they gave back the lease on the garage and moved out of their little apartment. Dad took a workshop nearer home and Mam gave up working altogether, and they started a new life back in the Estates. Mam said it was the best place in the world to live and it was like they'd all come full circle.

Ann loved living there. She was near all of her friends from school, and she could come and go to the town as she pleased. She loved living with Nana Tess too, even though she was quieter nowadays and cried a lot. "I've lost my spark, little Annie. Paddy and I were like peas in a pod, but I have you now." Ann could listen to Nana Tess for hours. She loved all the old stories about when Dad and Aunt Lucie were growing up and when Mam came to live with them. It was a happy time – until it wasn't. Mam went to wake Nana Tess one morning, but she didn't wake up.

"A broken heart, that's what they said. Almost romantic in a way," Mam told her. "She just couldn't live without Paddy."

Aunt Lucie came back over from Australia again and

all too soon they found themselves back in the graveyard, with Nana Tess's coffin being lowered on top of Paddy's.

"Together again, for ever now," Daddy said.

Ann liked the thought of them together for ever. None of them wanted to leave Nana Tess there this time, the day of her funeral.

"She was the glue that stuck us all together," Aunt Lucie told Ann. "It'll never be the same again."

She'd seen Aunt Florrie and Uncle Jim, too – they'd come from Cork. Uncle Jim used to be a sergeant and he told her all about it when he wasn't coughing.

"Lung cancer," she heard Aunt Florrie tell Mam.

"When your time is up, it's up," Uncle Jim said. "Pass me another few biscuits there, Ann. May as well make hay while the sun shines. God help me, you're the image of your mam. Thank God you didn't get the looks of your other grandmother – face like a slapped arse that one had!"

"*Jim*! Sick or not, watch your mouth." Aunt Florrie winked at her. "Ann, you know your mam was sent straight from heaven. You come and visit me whenever you like, love, I'll tell you all about it."

When it was all over Aunt Lucie had to leave. It had been all right when she was there. She'd stayed longer this time, but she had to get back. Ann had sat at the bottom of the stairs listening to them talking in the kitchen.

"I've only gone and found myself a doctor. I think I might be in love," she heard Aunt Lucie say.

"I knew you'd find someone special. And a doctor no less. Margot would have approved!"

They'd both laughed.

"Sure, if you can't laugh, what else is there?" Mam had said eventually.

"I'm glad you can see the funny side now. Doesn't bear thinking about it all. Do you ever hear anything?" Aunt Lucie had asked.

"Not a thing. I do wonder, though. So much time has passed and I'm happy. But it gets you thinking, can people change?"

"You're too soft, Fliss. Leave it alone, won't you?" Aunt Lucie had said.

Ann had wanted to ask about it, but then Aunt Lucie was leaving and she never got the chance. Mam said every time Aunt Lucie went, she took a little piece of her heart with her, back to Australia. Mam held Aunt Lucie tight when she was saying goodbye.

"No reason for you to come back now, is there?"

"I'll come back. We're blood sisters, for ever linked. Remember?"

Mam had pulled back from Aunt Lucie then, holding on to her two arms. "Start a life now, Lucie, do you hear me? Marry that doctor and don't look back. Make the life you always wanted. Don't be worrying about us. We have each other."

"Hush now, Felicity. If you need me, I'm here. Well, if I can ever afford to come back again," Aunt Lucie had laughed.

It took Mam a long time to feel better after Nana Tess was gone. Ann would often come home from school and find her crying in the kitchen, looking at old photos that she kept in a battered old tin box. Daddy was sad too, but he hid it better. There were lots of whispered conversations between her mam and dad for a while. Ann caught snippets of them here and there.

"It just has me thinking about the past, Sammy, and

everything that happened. I feel like I don't know everything. Don't have all the answers. Maybe I should try to find—"

"Felicity, we talked about this before. No good can come of dragging up the past and I can't ever risk you feeling so low that you'd hurt yourself again."

Ann had peeked over the banisters and saw them hugging. He was smoothing her face with his hand.

After that, everything got better. Dad said they needed some sunshine, so he took them on their first holiday the next month. They went to France on the boat. It was the best time ever. Mam used to throw off her sundress and run straight into the sea. She looked so young and free.

"I'm the envy of every man here," Dad said, nuzzling her neck.

"Get away out of that; sure, I'm practically middle-aged!"

"Felicity, you're thirty-two, with your whole life ahead of you. There's still time for you to do whatever you want to do."

"I forget sometimes. Maybe that's what happens when you have kids young. You forget."

Ann knew her mam had only been seventeen when she'd had her, just three years older than she was now.

"I'd never let that happen me. I'm going to live ten lives before I have kids," Ann told her parents as they listened, smiling. "I'm going to travel the world. Imagine being married at eighteen. What *were* you thinking?"

"Real-life love story, that's what we are," Dad laughed. "Ah, if you saw her on our wedding day, Ann, you'd understand why I couldn't wait another minute to make her mine."

"And you, my love, are part of that real-life love story, better than the ones in books," Mam told her. "Like Romeo and Juliet."

"You should pick a better love story, Mam. We all know how that ended."

"Oh, I don't know, love. Ours is pretty perfect, isn't it, Fliss?" Dad winked at Mam. "I remember the very moment I saw her coming down the aisle towards me," he grinned.

"Not the wedding story! Please, God, not the wedding story," Ann laughed, knowing there was nothing she could say to stop him once he'd started.

Instead, she sat back and listened to him tell the story she knew so well, of how he'd never seen anything so perfect walk towards him in all of his life.

"No fuss, no regalia. Just me and your mam, our closest friends, a dress from a charity shop, me in my leather jacket and you, Ann, in Tess's arms."

"Yes, Dad, I know, I know. There's not every girl in Knockmore who can say they were the guest of honour at their parents' wedding! You pair of hippies!"

"Oh no, we were much cooler than hippies. We were hippies in leather and lace."

Ann Maguire

Then – 2002

"Girls, the mess! Have you not decided what to wear yet?" Mam peered into the bedroom at all the clothes strewn across the bed and laughed.

"Mam! We'll be down soon – I'll clean up, don't worry," Ann answered. She'd settled on a little black dress and her favourite boots. "Ciara has her eye on someone and she needs to look perfect."

Ciara was sitting on the bed, red-faced, looking entirely flustered, with three different tops in her hand.

"Oh, I see. Let me see if I can help," Mam smiled, remembering the time she was getting ready for her first disco with Lucie all those years ago. "I'd pick that red top and those jeans you have on. Whoever he is won't be able to resist," she winked, grinning at the pair of fifteen-year olds, their greatest worry being what to wear, exactly as it should be.

"Thanks, Mrs Maguire. I think you're right. Less is more," Ciara answered, pulling on the red top.

"Girls, you'll be gorgeous whatever you wear, I promise you that. Now, come on down. I have pizza and treats for you, and the other girls will be here soon."

335

"Your mam is so cool," Ciara said to Ann as Felicity left. "My mam would have me going out in my uniform if she could."

"Yeah, she's not bad," Ann smiled.

They always gathered at the Maguires' before going out anywhere. The door was always open, and Mam loved the hustle and bustle of a full house.

"Why didn't you have more kids if you love everyone coming round so much?" Ann asked her once.

"I might yet – you never know what's around the corner. I'm only thirty-three," Mam had said, sticking her tongue out at Ann.

"Ugh, gross, the thought of it!" Ann had squealed.

"Hey, less of that. Some women haven't even had their first by my age and here I am with a big hairy teenager," she'd laughed.

But Ann knew she wouldn't. Mam always said she was happy with her lot. "You can't improve on perfection."

"Yes, I suppose. You couldn't get better than me," Ann had said, winking.

Lately, everything seemed perfect. Dad was doing well in the garage and was busier than he'd ever been, and Mam was doing a night course in veterinary nursing at the community college. Ann was in Fourth Year in school and loved the easy year after the Inter Cert exams. She'd aced it and enjoyed the time out before she had to put her head down again for the final two years in school.

Dad was still doing the odd gig here and there with the lads. I get to sing without the pressure of hoping to be the next *big thing*," he used to say. All of his band members had families of their own now and the dream of taking Ha-yeah on the road was over, but they still played at the odd pub gig and wedding. "Makes me feel young. I'd give some of those younger lads a run for their money, but I've enough going on with you pair, trying to keep you in the lap of luxury!"

"Now, girls, let me get a picture of you all before you head off to break all the hearts of the Knockmore football team," Dad said now.

"Dad, do we have to?"

He insisted on taking pictures of everything and always had them lining up at every occasion.

"Yes. There are memories in these snaps. You'll thank me in years to come. Ciara, can you take one of the three pals? Felicity, didn't you have a dress like that black one once?" he asked.

"I did. Well, it was your sister's, but I wore it once. I met some fella that night – I can't remember his name," Mam joked, referring to the night she met Sammy.

"Come here, you!" He grabbed her and kissed her while the girls giggled.

"Guys, please. Stop acting like teenagers." Ann rolled her eyes.

"Ann, get into the picture. It's not every day I have two fine-looking ladies on my arm."

They stood on either side of him and he smiled proudly for the camera.

"There now. That wasn't so bad. Now, I must be going. I'll collect you two on the way home from the gig. No funny business now, do you hear me? I was a young lad myself once, I know all the tricks," he warned.

"Okay, Dad. Yes, we know. We'll be out at eleven thirty sharp. Please don't come in. We'll meet you in the car park of the football club," Ann said, nudging her friend.

"I might come in for a dance. I'll be on a high after the gig." He wiggled his hips and Ann squirmed. "Fliss, are you sure I can't twist your arm to come with me? You could witness the enchanting stage presence of Sammy Maguire. I promise I'll sing to you," he said, hugging her.

"Nah, love. As tempting as that sounds, I have study for my course to catch up on. I'll be reading about tending to sick kittens while you're all out dancing. But I'll have everything ready here, fear not."

Felicity would make tea and sandwiches for later, and they'd all sit around like old times, dissecting the evening and listening to all the gossip.

"Are you sure? Or are you afraid you'll get all hot and bothered again?" he asked.

She blew him a kiss and shouted, "I love you, Sammy Morten Harket. Always have, always will, and 'I'll be right here waiting for you'." Mam attempted to sing the last bit of the song to him.

"Murdered it! Ruined it!" he laughed. "See you soon, Fliss."

"Not if I see you first."

Afterwards, they'd both replay that moment over and over on repeat. They'd close their eyes and see it again and again. It was a moment like any other over the years in the Maguire house. There was nothing out of the ordinary and yet . . .

Sammy sang his heart out at the local pub, thinking of his wife and daughter all the time. Ann kissed a lad during the slow set and afterwards comforted Ciara when her *someone* went off with another girl. Felicity finished her assignment, took a shower, set the table and waited for them all to come home. She waited well past the time they were due back. When she heard the car pull up outside, she rushed to the door, excited to listen to the evening's events, then stood frozen watching the two blurred faces speaking.

It was a head-on collision. Felicity couldn't take in the list of injuries. But she heard the doctor at the hospital say, "He didn't stand a chance. A miracle he didn't die there and then." But Felicity knew Sammy would never have left without saying goodbye. He was right there waiting for them – waiting for her and Ann to arrive. He smiled at them before he closed his eyes. Sammy waited to see them one more time before he went for ever. One more smile for his Felicity. His life.

No. There was nothing out of the ordinary that evening and yet afterwards, they couldn't help but wonder if they'd known what was about to happen, would they have done anything differently, said anything different? There were no clues – no warnings issued that night as they all went about their plans. But for the rest of their lives, it would remind them how life can change in one instant and never, ever be the same again.

Ann Maguire

Then – 2004

"I'll fight it. We'll fight it together. I'm not going anywhere," Mam said defiantly, smiling through the tears.

But Ann knew half of her mam was already gone well before she got the diagnosis. Half of her died with Sammy and she knew the day they buried Dad that Mam would never be the same again. Ann wondered if it was how Nana Tess felt after Paddy died. No – this was worse.

At first, Mam was brave – Ann realised that. After Aunt Lucie left again for the third time in so many years, Felicity pulled herself together as best she could. Mam stopped the veterinary nursing course she was doing, instead focusing everything on Ann. And it hadn't been all bad. They'd had some nice times together, just the two of them, curled up watching movies, holding each other tight. But at other times there was an all-encompassing sadness that hung over them, a cavity that nothing could fill.

The music that once played ceased, replaced by a somewhat eerie silence – one that Ann couldn't bring herself to interrupt by picking up her father's guitar, which sat untouched in the corner of the kitchen, gathering dust. That part of their lives ended the day he'd left. Now, all that could be heard in their home was the clock ticking, the hissing of the kettle that took forever to boil, muffled sobs, the sound of life going on outside while they waited for theirs to begin again. But it was as if the light had gone out in their house. They'd experienced perfect times and then far too much sadness, all packed into such a short space of time. Was that all they would ever know?

"I can't bear any more. We're owed only nice things now, Ann. You and me against the world," Mam told her.

But the next news had been too much to bear. It was more than anyone was due in one lifetime. Somehow, she wasn't surprised when her mam sat her down to tell her. It was as though she'd been waiting for something else to happen, never being able to settle, always prepared for the worst.

"It's not good news, love."

They'd managed the breast cancer diagnosis, just about. They'd been optimistic at first. Ann had spent her final year in school studying and praying for everything to turn out all right. But it hadn't. She'd finished her exams and then Mam told her.

"The cancer's spread – it's in my liver. There's nothing they can do."

Mam didn't want any more treatment. It made her too sick, only prolonging the inevitable.

"You've kept me alive for the last two years, Ann. I'd do anything to stay with you, but I've been thinking a lot lately. I've experienced enough happiness in my life. There's been sadness too, but what I had with Sammy and with you, it was enough. I've made my peace with it all. Laid old demons to rest."

"What do you mean, Mam, what are you saying?" Ann asked, shaking her head.

341

"It's in the past now. All that matters now is your future. And I know you have a bright future ahead of you. Brighter than you could ever imagine. But I need you to listen to me now."

"Mam, you're scaring me."

"You, my love, set me free. The day I found out about you was the first day I started living. You were the best thing ever to happen to me and I've enjoyed every moment being your mother. But you listen to me now, my love." Felicity paused, tried to hoist herself up in bed so she was looking into Ann's eyes. "There's nothing here for you now – nothing at all. You need to leave Knockmore and make a life for yourself. There's too much sadness in this place now, so I want you to go and never look back. Never. Do you hear me?"

"Mam? What are you saying? I can't leave. I won't leave you, ever." Ann was crying now, unable to be strong any longer.

"I'll be gone soon – you must know that as well as I do. You've heard the doctors and I don't want you here alone, watching me die. I can't bear it. The nurse will be here for me. Ann, there are things here that can hurt you. It's hard to explain, but you must believe me. You have to trust me, please," Felicity begged, out of breath now.

"I can't just up and leave. What are you saying? What can hurt me?" Ann pressed, gripping her mam's hand tight.

"It's too late to explain it all to you. I've left it too late and there isn't time. But you must go, Ann, tomorrow. I've made all the arrangements. There's a lady in Dublin. She has a room. I've written it all down for you. She'll make sure you're looked after.

"There's adequate money for you to start with. You're

a clever girl. You can do this. I've lived enough of a life for anyone. It's been enough for me and I got my fairy tale in the end, Ann. I did. Now, you go and make yours. Find your great love and when you do, hold him tight, love him and he'll love you in return." She lay back on the pillows, exhausted.

Ann was terrified. She didn't understand what it all meant or what could hurt her, but she trusted her mother, knew she was doing what was best. There was nothing here for her any more. The house would be gone. Felicity had remortgaged it to pay the medical bills. All that remained was the sum of money that she'd stuffed into her hand.

"Dad and I'll be watching over you, for ever. You can do this – this is your freedom, Ann, take it."

So, she did.

Ann Maguire

Now

Ann left as soon as she could, staying just long enough so as not to appear rude. The other girls were going to make a night of it and headed off to the bar in The Shelbourne Hotel as soon as the charity lunch finished. But Ann didn't have the energy to stay and continue the same boring conversations that she'd listened to all day.

"Oh, would you look at her! She's had her teeth done. Like looking at a porcelain toilet bowl in her mouth when she smiles."

"Have you heard of the new restaurant in Ranelagh? We must go."

"Oh, he's been knocking her off for years behind the girlfriend's back."

"She wore that last year. You'd think the way she goes on she could afford a new dress."

Ann had wanted to scream. It was all such bullshit. She was only grateful that Dom's best friend's wife, Issy, had peaked too early on the champagne, having eaten nothing for days so she could fit into her bandage dress. She was so pissed by the main course that she was unable to focus her eyes on Ann like she usually did. At least Ann wouldn't have to search for imaginary lettuce in her teeth this time. Ann had excused herself as soon as the meal finished, jumping into a taxi to make her escape.

Ann curled herself into a ball on the sofa and pulled the blanket around her. She was exhausted. Maybe she'd try to wait up for Dom. He'd promised he wouldn't be late. She hated it when he was. It always made her think of Dad. She could still see it all so clearly. That night he never come home. She'd known, though. As soon as she saw Mam pulling up in the police car outside the football club, where she and Ciara were waiting for him to pick them up after the disco, she'd known. She remembered Mam holding her.

"There's been an accident. We have to go to the hospital. We have to hurry, love, we have to get to him."

All Dad ever wanted was to be with them: his two girls. They'd all been so close – their own little family, a perfect union. She could still see the way he looked at Mam as if he couldn't bear to peel his eyes away from her. She could picture them so clearly. Mam's body curling into his, her head resting on his chest, his head leaning on her. They fit perfectly together, as though it were destiny, written in the stars. There was nothing that mattered outside that. No fancy restaurants, no expensive clothes, no diamond earrings, just love. Did she have that with Dom? Did they fit together like the missing piece of the other?

She tried to think of anything else, closing her eyes and breathing slowly. It had always worked before. She was nearly always able to change the reel of the past in her head before it consumed her. But tonight, she couldn't stop it. Her dad lying in the hospital bed. Her mam's face. The sound of the machines. Another funeral. Her mam getting sick. It all flew at her – a thousand flashing images. Tears, laughter, sadness, bliss, like a mirror shattering.

Then there was Mam, frail in her bed, cancer visible on her face, holding her hand, telling her to leave and begging her to trust her.

So she had. She'd left. She'd boarded the train to Dublin, all of her possessions packed into a bag, and she'd gone. It seemed so strange now when she thought of it. Her Mam had died the next day. She felt it as sharply as if she'd been there – knew the exact moment without being told. No one had come looking for her to tell her, presuming that Felicity Maguire had sent Ann away to relatives to save her from the pain of burying another dead relative.

Mrs Crowley had been kind to her when she'd arrived. She'd sat her down and told her that her mam had answered an ad in the paper for a room to rent. She cared for Ann during those first few years, went above and beyond the call of duty. She wiped her tears when Ann cried, cooked her dinner, helped her to find a job. But Mrs Crowley never asked why she was there or what had happened. Mam had told her very little.

"I only spoke to her the few times, love. I knew from what she said, though, that she loved you. Wanted you to be safe. I've learned not to judge over the years, not to pry. But I believe she answered my ad for a reason and I was glad to help you. I'm all alone too, and you're a good girl. I like having you around."

At first, Ann had worked as a waitress and then eventually, when she'd proved herself, she found a job in the accounts department of a marketing company. After that, everything moved fast. She'd used the money Mam had given her to study accountancy at night and graduated top of her class. She'd loved her time at night school. It had opened her eyes to a different life and it was where she met Sophie.

Suddenly, everything started to fall into place. As soon as she was earning enough, she moved in with Sophie, leaving behind her room in Mrs Crowley's that she'd begun to outgrow. By that time Mrs Crowley, too, was ready for a change. She'd grown older, frailer, and was ready to move to a nursing home, for her final phase. It had all seemed so natural, progressive and unforced.

Then she'd met Dom.

Looking back on it all, it was as though she were looking at someone else's life. Was it possible to feel like that? Like a spectator in your own life? She'd experienced so much pain, tried for so long to block it all out, to survive. She'd spent twelve years on the outside alone looking in, battling her demons, fighting her grief, hiding from her past, carrying this guilt that never seemed to leave her. Now, when she should have felt like she was firmly on the inside, all she could do was look out, or back, at the past.

Ann didn't know who she was any more, or what she was running from, but she was sure that she'd landed in the wrong life and could never settle until she resolved her past. For a time, she'd wanted to become *Bella Fitzgerald*, the woman her husband wanted her to be, but something was stopping her. It was time to stop running, to face the music, to the find the security she'd once had before everyone had left her. Ann couldn't be a mother yet. Not until she'd said goodbye properly to her mam and made peace with it all. There were things she needed to know, her medical history at least.

She'd tried to outrun the past, but it had finally caught

up. She thought of Aunt Lucie in Australia and wondered if she was still there. Why hadn't she come for her? She was sure that she'd arrive one day and make it all better. But after a while, she'd stopped waiting. Maybe she could try to find her. Perhaps she could try to find Florrie – was she even still alive?

Ann sat up suddenly, finally realising what she needed to do. She could close her eyes to reality but not to the memories. The memories would never stop haunting her until she let them go.

"I have to go back."

Ann Maguire

Now

"Big and bouncy, darling? Have to make you look the part!" her hairdresser said, setting the cappuccino in front of her, along with a bunch of magazines. "Are you sure I can't get you a glass of fizz?" he offered. "Or a gin?"

"No, thanks, I'll save myself for later. And yes, big and bouncy is perfect, thanks. Work your magic."

Ann smiled at the hairdresser before opening a magazine to avoid conversation. She was nervous about the party tonight and didn't think she could manage the usual small talk.

"Are you going anywhere nice on your holidays this year?" he attempted as he took out enough round brushes to blow-dry twenty heads.

"No plans yet," she answered, not looking up.

Getting the hint, he commenced the job in hand, dragging her head in every which direction to secure the best root lift.

The caterers were already at the house setting up and the bar was fully stocked, all the cocktail ingredients laid out ready for the onslaught of guests. Aside from collecting the balloons on the way home and slipping on her dress, she was all but ready. Dom was playing golf with the lads and had sworn on his mother's life that he'd be on time.

"Please do. I hate it when you're late. I worry," she told him that morning before he left.

She'd worked hard, planning the perfect party to mark his third decade, and she'd had a tough few days.

After her revelation last week, knowing she had to look into her past for answers, she'd decided to try to find her aunt Lucie in Australia, trawling through Facebook and Instagram looking for leads. At first, she'd hit a brick wall, but then she'd come across an Association of Nurses Abroad website and sent them an email. She'd received a call the next day. They weren't at liberty to give out personal details, but the lady told her that there was a Lucie from Ireland on the database, but the surname was different.

"The unusual spelling of the first name though, and the date of birth, leads me to believe it might be the same person. Could she have married?" the lady asked her.

"Yes, she was going out with someone when I last saw her, but I don't know his name. It was a long time ago," Ann said, trying to think of anything more that might help.

"Perhaps if you send me an email addressed to who we think might be your aunt I can forward it to her. Then if it's the right Lucie, well, I'm sure she'll get in touch," she suggested, swept up in the excitement of finding a missing person.

"That would be great. Thank you so much," Ann said, touched by her kindness.

"I hope it's the right girl. Maybe we'll all end up going on TV on *Surprise, Surprise*! Be sure to let me know if you find the missing relative," she laughed.

Ann smiled, wondering should she reveal that it was

herself who was actually lost – and finding herself would be a nothing short of a miracle. She hoped the email she sent wasn't too matter-of-fact, but she hadn't known what to say. Ann still hadn't heard anything back, but at least she was taking action and it made her feel better. She hadn't even tried to find Florrie yet, sure that it would prove impossible. She didn't think Florrie was of the generation who'd succumbed to Facebook, but you never knew. She'd try next week.

"Okay, darling, all done."

Ann looked up. Even she had to admit she looked good. She'd taken Sophie's advice and had her make-up done too, and it was perfect – just enough to make her feel a little more like the other girls. She was enjoying being pampered for the day, seeing a new, more polished Ann emerging before her eyes and feeling excited for what the future might bring.

Ann let herself into the house, ran upstairs and quickly slipped on the black backless dress that had been hanging in her closet for the past few weeks. She took out her new shoes and giant earrings then looked appraisingly at herself in the mirror. Her reflection twisted and twirled. She looked just like them – elegant and glamorous – and she liked it, suddenly remembering her father-in-law's words. Maybe it was time to give in and enjoy what she had, instead of continually fighting against it.

"Coming," she shouted, hearing the doorbell ring and hoping it was Dom. She'd have liked for them to have a drink together first before the others arrived.

"Holy cow, look at you!"

It was Sophie.

"You look a million bucks, too," Ann said, hugging her friend tightly.

Sophie was wearing a black-and-gold lace dress that revealed very little flesh but left little to the imagination and impossibly high black suede ankle boots.

"I know," Sophie giggled, doing a twirl and shaking her hips. "And you look stunning," she said approvingly. "Just stunning. A real proper trophy wife, Ann, like it or not. And knock me over with a feather, but are you wearing fake eyelashes?"

"I sure am. If you can't beat 'em, join 'em," Ann laughed.

"Come on. Let's grab a cocktail before the others get here and we can watch the girls trying not to vomit when they see you." Sophie led Ann over to the cocktail bar. "Eh, if Dom's friends don't work out, I'll take *him* with a slice and ice," Sophie whispered, taking in the particularly hot barman.

It wasn't long before the house thronged with guests. The music was pumping, and Ann spent much of the evening running backwards and forwards answering the door, taking coats and trying to find out where the hell Dom was. By 9.30 p.m., she was sick with worry and still couldn't get through to his phone.

"No one knows where he is, Soph, and nor do they seem to care." Ann looked around at everyone enjoying the party, even in the absence of the guest of honour.

"Relax," Sophie told her. "Dom's always late. His phone is probably dead – he's had a few drinks. I bet he's in a taxi. I'm sure of it."

"I don't know. Something isn't right. I'll try him again. I'll be back in a sec."

Ann made her way out to the hall, pushing the front door open for some air.

"Dom! Where have you been?" she exclaimed when she

saw him standing by the side passage of the house looking like a deer caught in headlights. "What are you doing?" she asked. "Are you okay? I was worried. Oh no, are you pissed?" She looked him up and down.

"No, no, I'm fine." His words were slightly slurred. "I just needed the loo," he said, pulling up his zipper.

"Out here!" she laughed. "You could have come inside. We do have six toilets."

"Yeah, sorry. I was bursting," Dom said sheepishly.

"Come on inside – everyone's waiting." She put her hand out to lead him in. "I'm glad you're here. I missed you," she said, kissing him.

He kissed her back and she pushed open the door.

"Hey," she said, turning back. "I have something to tell . . . " She stopped. "Dom?" she said, seeing him glancing back towards the side passage.

"Come on, Bella, let's go in," he said, taking a step forwards.

"Wait." She pushed past him and walked to the side of the house.

"Hello, *Bella*," Sabrina smiled sweetly just as Ann reached the corner.

She was standing with her back to the wall, adjusting the strap of her dress, smoothing her skirt and brazenly wiping her mouth.

"Sabrina? What the hell? What's going on here? Dom?" Ann looked from one to the other.

"Bella, come back inside. Sabrina was upset. We were talking," he said, trying to take her hand.

"Why are you even here?" Ann asked her.

"Dom invited me," Sabrina smiled, flicking her auburn hair over her shoulder. "We go way back, you know that.

Well before you arrived from whatever hicksville you came. And we weren't just talking, were we, Dom?" she smiled at him.

Ann thought she was going to throw up. Dom grabbed her hand.

"Bella, I'm sorry," he pleaded. "You've been so distant lately – I thought it was me. Come on, baby, I love you. She means nothing," he said finally.

Ann stared at him. He wasn't even going to deny it, was ready to admit it and then move on. Her blood ran cold.

"That's not what you said last Friday," Sabrina chimed in. "All those late nights working on that deal. What was it called again, Dom? Oh yes. *Me*," she added, grinning.

"You bitch." Ann stepped forwards and smacked her hard across the face. "And you? You piece of shit." She stood up as tall as she could in her heels until she was towering over him. "Fuck you. Fuck you and all of your notions about yourself. All you are is your money. Without it, you're just a pathetic little—"

"Short-arse," Sophie finished. She'd come looking for Ann and had witnessed enough to gather what was going on. "Come on, Ann. Let's go upstairs while Dom clears the room. Think you can manage that, lover boy?" Sophie looked over her shoulder. "And Sabrina, that dress is two seasons old and two sizes too small for you," Sophie spat, pushing Ann back into the house and straight up the stairs.

It took Dom an hour to get everyone out of the house, citing a family emergency.

"I'm going to Sophie's for a few days. I need to think," Ann told him once she'd calmed down.

"Please, Bella. I'm sorry. I love you," Dom begged. "Don't go; my Dad'll kill me."

"Pathetic!" Sophie started to laugh and Ann shot her a look. "I'll wait downstairs," she said, leaving them alone.

Ann looked at him, the disgust clear on her face.

"You know, Dom, you never really cared who I was. All you wanted was the trophy wife by your side. You don't know where I come from, or who I was before, or how hard I had to work to make something of myself, by myself. You just want me here, so you can do whatever the hell you want, while I'm always left waiting for you. I spend my life waiting for you.

"I'm sorry I didn't turn out the way you wanted me to. I have some things to sort out. I should have sorted it before I married you, maybe then things would have turned out differently. But I can't be with you, Dom. This is *not* how I pictured my life." She picked up her bag.

"Bella, please, don't leave me alone."

"I'm sure Sabrina will keep you company."

"Bella!" he shouted after her.

She stopped in the doorway and turned towards him.

"It's not Annabella or Bells or Bella," she shouted, picking up the picture of them on their wedding day in the antique silver picture frame and firing it at him with all of her might. She heard it smash against the wall and closed her eyes, taking a deep breath. "My name is Ann. Ann Maguire. Don't forget it."

Ann Maguire

Now

Ann couldn't believe it. How could he? How could she have been so stupid?

All she'd ever wanted was someone to love her, to make her whole again, to replace what she'd lost when her parents had died. But she hadn't found it – not with him, anyway. She was hurt and humiliated, devastated. No one here really knew her or cared about the person she was before. She'd come from a world where she'd been wrapped in love, from the day she was born, right up until her mam died. She'd known nothing but love and warmth all those years. Even when there was sorrow, even when Dad died, even when Mam got sick and then . . . it was gone. One day she had a family and the next, she was alone. And here she was – alone again.

"What was he thinking?" Sophie put her arm around her. "Of all nights."

"I don't know." Ann shook her head.

She couldn't stop the tears. Try as she might, they just kept coming. But Ann wasn't just crying over Dom. She was crying for them all, for Tess and Paddy, for Dad, for Mam. Ann missed them so much, especially now. She missed what her life could have been, should have been. How she'd survived in Dublin alone at just seventeen she'd never understand.

There must have been someone or something driving her on, making her breathe, forcing her to put one foot in front of the other all that time. She knew what it was. The love of her parents had buoyed her along in those early years when she'd first arrived here, keeping her above the surface. When she met Dom, she thought he was enough for her to be able to let go. So she had. She'd let go. She'd dropped the rope that held them all tethered to her and now she couldn't find it – couldn't feel it any more.

She was scared now and angry for what he'd done to her, furious at herself for letting it happen. She'd wanted to experience love, like that of her parents. The purest love – the kind you'd die for rather than go without. Ann imagined them together now, just the two of them, so beautiful, so young, suspended in time for ever. And she longed to be with them, to escape this physical pain that reached into her heart, squeezing it, deadening her limbs and suffocating her lungs.

"Breathe, Ann. It's going to be okay," Sophie said, rubbing her back in circular motions, soothing her like a baby.

Sophie had been with her all evening, back at the apartment in Grand Canal Dock, where at least she could be herself again, reverting to Ann just as quickly as she'd become Bella. She'd peeled off the fake eyelashes, replaced the backless dress with a baggy old T-shirt and kicked off her shoes, immediately crawling into Sophie's bed and allowing the years of sorrow consume her, the memories and pain to pour from her eyes and roll down her cheeks.

She cried until there was nothing left. Little hiccups escaped her now, like a child. She looked up at Sophie, her earlier smoky eyes now smeared all over her blotchy face.

"You look fab. I told you the earrings would work," Sophie said and despite herself, Ann laughed.

Ann wiped at her face, looking down at the smears left on her fingertips – the only remnants of the celebration. Well, not forgetting the famous earrings that still dangled unsuitably from her lobes.

"He's ringing my phone now, won't stop. You want me to tell him to piss off?" Sophie asked. "Your phone's out there – shall I get it?"

Ann didn't want to talk to him. She wasn't ready but she nodded.

"Here," Sophie said, throwing it on the bed. "It's hot to the touch. I'm going to make you some tea. Don't do anything stupid," Sophie warned.

Ann picked up the phone – thirty-two missed calls from Dom and two from his dad. His sisters had tried, too – they must all know by now. She wondered what he'd told them. There were six voice messages and two text messages. He was persistent if nothing else, but she knew it was probably more about his reputation than wanting to fix things and it was only a matter of time before he showed up here.

Ann opened the email icon, looking at all the online offers that she regularly received but never remembered signing up to. She almost missed the name. But there it was: Lucie Woods.

She wiped at her eyes and stared at the name and the title: Ann?

Ann clicked it and watched the text appear.

Florrie folded FelicityAnn,

Oh my God! Is it you? Is it really you? I nearly fell over when they sent me the email. I almost didn't open it. They're always sending me all sorts of subscription rubbish and I nearly deleted it. I can't believe it! Are you okay? Where are you? I need to see you . . . to explain.

I did come. I came for you, but they told me you were already gone. I shouldn't have listened. There's so much I want to say to you. Call me. Call me right now. Please. Or answer this at least. I won't sleep ever again until I know you are safe.

Lu

xxx

Ann looked at the number. She should call her. But how could she tell her everything that had happened? Ann felt ashamed. She'd left her mother to die alone. She hadn't even been there for the funeral. What *had* she been thinking? But Mam had insisted, said it was her dying wish, and Ann would have done anything to please her.

She'd call Lucie. But not now. She needed a few days to catch her breath, and she needed to get out of here by morning before Dom arrived and convinced her to get back with him. She couldn't. Not now. She wasn't even sure if she ever wanted to see him again. Ann knew where to go, somewhere he'd never find her but somewhere she hoped she might find herself. She typed a quick response:

Dear Lucie,

I can't believe I've found you. I'm okay, really. I'm fine. I'm having a few problems, but I'll tell you

about it in a few days. I'm living in Dublin. I'm going to go back to Knockmore for a few days and I'll call you when I'm back. I leave tomorrow. I promise I'm okay. Please don't worry.
Ann
x

"I'll come with you. I'm not letting you go alone – please let me come," Sophie pleaded.

"I'll be fine. I'm used to being on my own," Ann assured.

Ann stuffed the clothes that Sophie had lent her into the bag. Sophie threw a baseball cap and sunglasses at her.

"If you're sure, at least wear these. You look like a hot mess. And please keep your phone on so that I can contact you. I'll deal with *him*, but please come back. You have a room here for as long as you need. Promise me. Don't go doing another Houdini. Make your peace and come back."

Sophie handed her the car keys and Ann hugged her friend tight. Ann was so grateful to have her in her life, knowing she'd lost too many people to lose another.

"Thanks for the loan of your car. Now I have to come back. I just need to be there for a while. I need to be home."

There were very few cars on the road so early on a Sunday morning. Ann took her time on the journey, lost in her thoughts. It took only a few hours on the motorway before she took the turn-off that would lead her back to where it all began. It was twelve years since she'd been on this stretch of road and she marvelled at how little it had changed. It was a twisty wonderland of overhanging trees that over time had grown towards each other, meshing together to form a tunnel of greenery. The road became narrower as the trees grew denser along the final stretch. She felt an unfamiliar calmness wash over her upon reaching the brow of the hill, quickly followed by panic.

She pulled in and stopped. There it was. Funny that you can live in a place for more than half of your life and not really see it, but from up here she could see everything and she looked at it now as if seeing it for the first time. It was a town in a valley, nestled away from the outside world, a tiny universe in itself. She looked at the two churches on either side – one on the crest of the far hill surrounded by big old houses and the other deep in the town – the two schools, the main street and behind it, the rows and rows of houses of the Estates, within which her life had started before it ended.

Inside the walls of those little houses were families having breakfast, getting ready for football in the club, mothers hanging out washing, fathers reading the Sunday paper, girls laughing after the disco in Lennon's and lads snoozing off their Saturday night pints. There were children already out playing on the road, people walking up to Mass, and she smiled. It was just how she'd left it. Nothing had changed and yet everything was different.

Ann looked up at the two magpies that had come to rest on the gatepost beside her – two for joy. Her mam was always counting magpies. She told her once that three magpies had given her a sign that changed her life. Ann knew she'd come to the right place. It was precisely where she needed to be.

She started the engine and drove down into the town. There were some new shops on the main street and she recognised some of the familiar old ones that had battled proudly through the recession and would continue to battle, despite the new shopping centre built at the other side of town. There was even a hotel now. It was a small modern building and it would do perfectly.

Ann checked in with ease, not seeing any familiar faces, and was thankful not to have to make small talk or answer questions to which she didn't know the answers. She wondered if people would recognise her, suddenly grateful for the baseball cap and dark glasses that Sophie had given her.

Not realising how tired she was, she flopped down on the bed and fell asleep. She woke up starving and decided to take a bath and order some room service. It was already late and there would be time tomorrow for her to look around. She glanced at her phone: twenty-four missed calls. Dom must be getting tired. She turned it off and threw it into the bottom of her bag, not wanting to talk – she just wanted to remember.

Ann closed her eyes in the bath and let her mind drift. Backwards. Back to the times living above the garage and their little shop. Back to singing with her dad before bed. Back to the snippets Mam had told her over the years and the stories Tess had whispered to her about when Mam was little. She wished she'd listened harder. It was hard to imagine your parents in another life other than the one you are. She knew her grandfather used to be the reverend. Maybe she could ask them in St Patrick's Church, perhaps they'd know something.

She started to hum one of the songs she used to sing with Dad and for the first time in for ever, she could almost see him when she closed her eyes. He wasn't much older than Dom was now when he'd died. So very young, so dreadfully unfair. Mam said he died doing something he loved at least. Ann just wished it hadn't been so soon.

* * *

Ann pulled her coat around her and shivered against the wind that suddenly gathered. Wasn't that always how it was in graveyards, as though the sun couldn't manage to break through the grief? Ann knew she'd be here, but it didn't ease the pain that engulfed her, turning her legs to jelly. She kneeled in front of the grave, tracing their names with her fingers, etched into the marble headstone, and once again let the tears fall. There they were, right beside Tess and Paddy – exactly where they belonged:

Sammy and Felicity Maguire.
Together in life and now in Eternity. For ever young.

Lucie must have arranged the shiny black memorial, to mark her parents' grave, to announce to whoever passed that they once existed, once mattered – that it hadn't all been a dream. It was hard to imagine Mam buried in the earth, gone from this world.

"I'm here now, Mam. I'm sorry I never came. I should have been there," she whispered. "It's all gone wrong, Mam. I thought I had it all figured out, but I was wrong. I miss you so much. I never stopped missing you."

It was too hard to be here, looking down at where beautiful Felicity Maguire was finally laid to rest. Perhaps this was the reason Mam hadn't wanted her to see all this. If it was still difficult now, it would have been far worse to make sense of it all at seventeen. It was better to choose to be alone, maybe that was it. Twelve years and it still didn't seem like she was gone, but here was the proof – her name right beside Sammy's, where it was always meant to be. Ann placed the little bunch of flowers on the grave and stood. She'd come back again tomorrow – maybe by then it would have sunk in a bit more – but it was too painful to stay here any longer.

Ann left the graveyard and made her way up through the town towards St Patrick's Church. She'd never spent any amount of time up this far as a child, except the time Mam had shown her Knockmore House. She looked about now at the big granite houses, the imposing doorways and the immaculate gardens. The houses slanted up the hill to the church. It was like something from a postcard – the perfect location for one of the many country weddings she and Dom had attended. It would have sent the WhatsApp group into overdrive.

She stopped when she reached Knockmore House and looked up the driveway. It was beautiful. There was no denying it. The door was painted red in stark contrast to the grey walls. The sash windows shone in the sunlight and the three granite steps leading to the door were very grand. She wondered, did they point to the answers she so craved? The gravel that covered the driveway was practically snow-white and the gardens so perfect they almost didn't look real. Everything was just as it should be: perfection.

You'd never have guessed that her mother, so unassuming in every way, had come from this. Dom would have killed for this house, his Range Rover sitting proudly in the drive. Ann almost jumped out of her skin a moment later when that was exactly what drove up beside her and stopped. The window rolled down and a man in his early thirties leaned out.

"Can I help you?" he asked, smiling broadly.

"Oh no, not at all, sorry. I was taking a walk, admiring the house, sorry," she stuttered.

"No problem at all."

She nodded politely.

"Eh, could you move a little so I can get past?"

"Oh, God, yes. Sorry."

Ann moved to the side of the gate, allowing him to drive the mammoth car through the gateposts, waving apologetically as he passed and swept up the driveway, parking in front of the red door. Ann started back down the hill.

"Sorry, do I know you?" she heard. "It's just you look familiar," he asked.

He stood with his hands casually tucked into the pockets of his jeans. He didn't look as if he was from Knockmore and she was sure she'd have remembered him if he was.

"Eh, no. I don't think so. I'm not from here, or at least I am but I'm not. I was. I used to be, but not any more," Ann said.

His face broke into a wide smile.

"Well, that clears that up!" he laughed.

"Sorry," she flushed. "That made no sense. See, I grew up here when I was a kid, but I moved when I was seventeen. I'm just down for a few days."

He was tall and fit-looking with short sandy hair and the biggest smile she'd ever seen. She couldn't help smiling back.

"I'm Mark," he said, holding out his hand.

"Ann." She took it. "Nice house you have there." She gestured towards the gate.

"Oh, it's not mine," Mark laughed. "I'm just down for

a few days, too. It's my parents'. They bought it a few years ago, had it all refurbed. It was a bit neglected to say the least. Used to be the—"

"Vicarage," Ann finished.

"Yeah, right, you're from here but not."

"So, you're from Dublin?"

"No, no way, hate the place. I'm from Wicklow. A bit quieter but still with access to the city when I need. I took over the folks' old house and they moved here to get away from us all. Well, just my sister and me. Mum loves it here," Mark told her. "They're away at the moment. I was just checking up on it."

"Oh, right." Ann looked towards the house again.

"Hey, would you like to grab a drink?" Mark asked, looking at his watch. "Or a coffee? Yeah, a coffee," he corrected, realising it was far too early for a drink. "Sorry, I'm not very good at this." He screwed up his face, waiting for her answer.

She laughed. "I'm sorry, Mark, it was lovely to meet you, but I'm just here for a few days and well, my life is currently under construction – a refurb, so to speak. Sorry."

"No probs." Mark held up his hands. "It was just, I don't know, I thought I knew you." He looked embarrassed. "Hey, it was nice to meet you, Ann. See you around. You know where I am if you change your mind. I could show you around the gardens sometime," he said awkwardly.

She waved as she walked away before turning.

"I might take you up on that sometime," she said.

His face broke into another smile. God, he was handsome and tall. It was a welcome change to be looking up while talking to someone. But today wasn't the day to complicate matters further. Not when she had so much to do here still. She had yet to work up the courage to go to the Estates, knowing it would be the hardest journey of all. She'd leave it until tomorrow. There was also a phone call she needed to make – one that she'd been putting off. She'd been able to get a phone number for Florrie from the local sergeant. Ann had known his son when they were children and he was more than happy to help her.

"She's still in Cork. I know I have it here somewhere," he told her, rooting through the big grey filing cabinet. "Lives with her daughter there. You know Jim died? A long time ago now. He was some man. 'The true measure of a man is how he treats someone who can do him no good,' as he used to say himself," the old sergeant laughed.

"Yes, I knew Jim was sick all right. It's been a long time since I've spoken to Florrie. She must be in her mid seventies now."

"She surely is, and still as bright as a tack, I'm sure," he said. "It's good to see you, Ann. You're the image of your poor mother. Thought I was seeing a ghost when I saw you walk in. I don't mean to pry, but where did you go after . . . you know?"

"I went off to Dublin, to relatives," she lied. "Mam thought it was for the best. There was no one here for me, Sergeant," she said quickly before he could ask anything else. "Can I ask you? Do you remember much about my mam when she was growing up?"

"Not a bit, Ann. I only arrived in Knockmore when you were a little one. My young lad was about four when I was posted here and took over from Jim," he said, shaking his head. "Ah! here's the number. Tell her I was asking for her, won't you?"

Ann sat on the bed now in her hotel room, took out the

piece of paper and dialled the number. Florrie answered on the second ring and Ann almost hung up, suddenly not knowing what to say.

"Florrie?"

"Yes, this is Florrie."

She sounded the same.

"It's Ann. Ann Maguire."

There was silence. "I'm sorry, did you say Ann Maguire?"

"Yes, it's me, Ann, Felicity's daughter."

"Oh, Ann! I can't believe it. Is it really you?" Florrie said.

Ann could hear her smiling.

"It is. I . . . I'm sorry. I got your number at the Garda station."

"Well, I'm so glad you called. How are you? I think about her all the time, you know? I never made the funeral. Jim was so poorly then. So very poorly. I couldn't believe it when Lucie called me to tell me she'd died. My poor Felicity. Gone too soon. A tragedy. She was a real lady – born that way," Florrie said.

"Yes, I still miss them both. I'm so sorry about Jim."

"He was a good man. He had a good life."

"He was, Florrie. I'm so sorry to disturb you, but I wanted to ask you some things about the past. It's hard to explain, but Mam sent me to Dublin after she died," Ann told her, again not wanting to admit that she'd left before she died. "There was so much she never told me."

"Well, yes, that was Felicity. After it all, she never wanted to speak of it again. You could hardly blame her," Florrie said sadly. "It was all too much." Florrie coughed loudly and then caught her breath. "Did she tell you anything at all, dear?"

"Very little – just that it was an unhappy childhood and that she was happy to escape it. She told me after her parents died that she was set free."

"Died? Did you say died? Well, I'm not sure about Michael. No one ever saw him again, but Maggie only died last year."

"Maggie?" Ann was confused.

"Well, Maggie, Margot, whatever she was calling herself then. Felicity's mother – my sister. She died last year."

"Are you sure?" Ann was shocked.

"As sure as I'll ever be. Didn't I get a fit of conscience! And I went to see her. She was in a nursing home. Not that I got much sense out of her – dementia, the doctor told me. The same thing our mother had, God rest her."

Ann couldn't believe it. She'd been alive all along.

"Funny, she was in and out when I saw her. She made very little sense at all. But I do remember she kept asking for Felicity. She said more than once that there was something she needed to tell her."

"What was it?" Ann asked, hoping this was it.

"I couldn't get it out of her and I didn't have the heart to tell her Felicity was already dead. Much as she was the greatest wagon that ever walked the earth. I'm not a cruel person and Maggie was confused. Still," she laughed, "she managed to tell me that I had an arse the size of a bus before I left. I never went back. Imagine, she had my number as her next of kin! I don't think she ever spoke a kind word to me my entire life.

"There was nothing else to say to her and it was too far to keep visiting. Before that, she'd been only an hour from Knockmore, living on her own. Lord knows where Michael ended up." Florrie stopped. "Come to think of it, Felicity contacted me once, looking for the address. Said she wanted to send Maggie something. I didn't like to pry, but I couldn't understand why she'd give her the time of day, after everything."

"What do you mean, Florrie, after everything? Can you tell me about it?" Ann asked.

"I can, love, but right now I have to go. I have an appointment with the doctor. This old-age business catches up on us all, like the past, I suppose. Could you visit?" she asked. "Some stories require a drop of gin, if you know what I mean?" Florrie laughed.

Ann promised she would. Sooner rather than later. She couldn't believe that her grandmother had been alive all that time. Whatever happened all those years ago must have been awful for Mam to lie about it. Ann lay back on the bed and closed her eyes. She'd have to be patient. Florrie would tell her everything.

Ann Maguire

Now

Ann was still in her clothes from the day before when she woke the next morning, even more exhausted and still replaying the conversation she'd had with Florrie. Ann couldn't understand why her mother had lied to her and was more eager than ever to get to the bottom of it. She'd already decided to drive to Cork later that day and speak with Florrie, knowing she'd met a dead end here. Aside from one quick call to Sophie to let her know she was all right, she hadn't bothered to look at her phone. She wasn't ready to talk to Dom yet, not until everything else was settled, but there was one more place she needed to visit before she left.

She quickly showered, grabbed a coffee from the hotel lobby and set off towards Farmleigh. Every step she took brought her a little closer to the past and the memories flooded through her as she walked. She pictured herself walking to school with Mam, dashing up and down the green with her friends, waving to her dad as his van rounded the corner. She could hear Nana Tess laughing, see her parents sitting at the dinner table, holding hands, and it hurt so much.

As Ann approached the house, she was reminded once more of the difference it bore to the grandeur of Knockmore House. She stood for a moment, replaying it all, imagining the last time she'd seen her father at this door, with Mam waving at him and her father bursting with pride. She could see them all returning to the house after each funeral, the family diminishing a little after each one. And finally she pictured herself leaving that day, her bag over her shoulder and the envelope of money tucked into her inside pocket: seven grand in cash, just enough to get her away from Knockmore and to start a new life. She'd been nothing more than a child and was suddenly angry at her mother, furious for what she put her through, with no explanation, no reason. How could she send her away like that? How could she ask her to leave?

Ann walked away. All that remained here was bittersweet memories that were too painful to revisit. It wasn't going to change anything – she was still alone.

"Annie, Annie, is that you?"

She heard the voice and turned, the sight of her alone enough for her legs to give way. She'd fought too long, been too brave, and she fell into Aunt Lucie's arms.

"You came," Ann said, sobbing into her hair, barely able to catch her breath.

"I'm so sorry, Ann. I'm so very sorry. I've so much to tell you," Lucie soothed. "I left as soon as I got your email. I've been travelling for days. Hush now. My poor Ann. It's okay."

Ann clung for dear life to her family member, to the only person who knew her before, who could connect all the dots for her.

"I can't believe you're here! You must be exhausted,"

Ann said now, sitting in the chair beside the bed back in her hotel room and staring with disbelief at her aunt.

Lucie stretched out on the bed. "I am tired, but I knew when I got that email that something wasn't right. What is it, love?"

It hadn't taken long for the years to melt away between them and Ann felt ready to talk.

"I've made a bit of a balls of everything," Ann said finally. "Seems I married a complete idiot."

"You're married?" Lucie was shocked. "Oh my God. I've missed so much. What happened? I'll kill him."

Ann laughed, delighted that her aunt hadn't changed, still as feisty as her hair, and started to tell her the story of the birthday party.

"What an asshole!" Lucie shook her head as Ann finished. "Mind you, there are plenty of them out there."

"I just wanted to find someone like Dad, I suppose," Ann laughed. "Does that sound weird?"

"Sammy Harket!" Lucie giggled. "That's what we used to call him before . . . before Fliss," she said sadly. "I still can't say her name. I miss her so much. I miss them both."

Ann nodded. "Me too. That's why I came back. She told me not to, you know. Did you think I ran away?"

"No, Ann. I knew."

"You knew?" Ann was shocked.

"Yes. But let's start at the very beginning before we get to that. There are things you should know. I'm not sure why they never told you. Maybe they were protecting you."

Ann listened as her aunt began to roll out the past, revealing the fabric of her life. Lucie told her everything she knew, in the order it happened, from what she'd seen herself and from what her mam, Tess, had told her, starting with Margot and her evolution from the Estates, with her cruel treatment of Mrs Walsh and then of Tess. Lucie spoke of how Felicity was abused, neglected, unloved. She spoke about the night Felicity met Sammy and how it was love at first sight.

"We were just kids, Ann, but I knew even then that the connection they had went far beyond their years."

Lucie told her of the friendship the girls had nurtured all through their lives. Ann heard the secrets of the oak tree, the puppies and the weak reverend.

"Fliss never let on to any of us. She always hid it. But that woman was pure evil and I suppose he wasn't much better. Her father did nothing to protect her in the end. Then Fliss met Sammy and everything changed for her, but Margot tried to stop that, too," Lucie said.

Felicity stared at her aunt, hardly able to take it all in.

"I can't believe it. So how did she get away? What happened?" She needed to know.

"Oh, Ann, it was so awful," Lucie continued as she proceeded to tell her all about the discovery of the pregnancy and Margot locking up Felicity. "But we all pieced it together in the end. It was me who found her. She'd slit her wrists open on broken glass. I thought she was gone. Thank God we got to her on time."

Ann shook her head, unable to believe what she was hearing. "My God, it's like something from a book."

"God, they loved each other, though. Sammy and Felicity. It was that real-life love that's very hard to find and you were born out of that – you were her happy ever after," Lucie smiled.

"Yes, I always knew they loved each other. They

couldn't keep their hands off each other! It was so embarrassing when I was a kid, but I'd do anything now for them to be here. It would be a privilege to feel embarrassed now."

"I can imagine. It was just so unfair though, wasn't it? After everything they'd been through. Sammy killed and then Felicity getting sick. I wish I'd come sooner. But I suppose she never changed. She always wanted to fight everything alone," Lucie said, no longer able to hold back the tears. "It took me a long time to come to terms with it all – how life can be so fucking unfair." She looked up at Ann. "I was all alone, too. I lost everyone too, and then you."

Ann looked at the ground before asking the only question that she needed to be answered. "But why did she send me away?"

Felicity Maguire

Then – 2004

It hadn't been difficult to find her in the end. She'd been close by, this whole time. One phone call to Florrie was all it took, though she hadn't told Florrie why – just said that she needed to send Mother something. She didn't want to bother Florrie with her own problems. Florrie had enough going on with Jim and they'd lost contact over the years, through distance and life, she supposed.

Mother almost slammed the door in her face when she saw Felicity standing on the doorstep, but Felicity quickly stuck her foot out, jamming the door. Mother turned and stalked back into the kitchen, sitting in an old floral chair that had seen better days, and continued to stare at the television. Felicity closed the door and followed her, looking about as she walked through the tiny house that was almost as miserable-looking as she was.

Felicity noticed a stale smell as if no air was ever allowed filter through the dank room and bitterness clung to the atmosphere. She almost laughed when she saw where her mother had ended up, but it suited her, better than Knockmore House ever had. She looked different – frailer, more wizened, like she often forgot to eat – but the same steely look fixed her face.

"I was wondering if you'd come some day. You were always sticking your nose where it wasn't wanted," Mother said, not looking up.

Felicity sat down across from her, close enough to smell the drink that lingered from the night before, or perhaps from that day, it was hard to tell.

"I see you're still drinking," Felicity said, turning up her nose.

Margot laughed. "Well, whatever numbs the pain of this place," she said, still not meeting Felicity's eyes.

"Yes, quite the drop from Knockmore House," Felicity said. "That's all you ever wanted, wasn't it, Mother? The grandeur. You never wanted Father or me. All that talk for all those years about being better than everyone, looking down on people, and look at you now! What a load of shit!" Felicity spat.

Margot looked up and smiled smugly. "Ah! I see you've stooped to their level at last. All you were good for, really," she said coldly. "What do you want, Felicity? I did what they asked, left you be, allowed you to stay with that scum, why did you come?"

Felicity remained quiet, stunned that Mother could still manage to make her feel so small, like a child begging to be loved.

"I wanted to know why," Felicity said at last. "Why were you so cruel? What did I ever do to you?" Her voice broke.

"Still sniffling away, Felicity, really?" Margot turned her nose up before glaring at her. "I wanted you to be better. I wanted you to have a nice life like I never had. But your father was a weakling and you turned out to be a whore!"

"You used to hit me. You used to lock me up. You almost killed me!" Felicity shouted.

Margot laughed again. "There's that wild imagination again, running away with you. Always making up stories."

"It's all true. It all happened, you know that."

Margot stared blankly ahead again. What was the point? The woman was delusional. She'd never get the answers she wanted. Felicity stood up to leave.

"Still the same, Mother. Well, you can't hurt me any more. I grew up. You can't hurt me. And you're right, I am one of them now – and proud of it."

"You'll never be one of them," Margot replied. "You are Felicity Montgomery until the end. Oh, I see what this is about." Margot narrowed her eyes. "You don't look well, unless living the hard life doesn't suit you? Hmm? Or are you sick?"

Margot looked Felicity up and down, taking in her grey pallor and noticing the almost blue circles under her eyes. Her clothes hung from her already ravaged frame and her once thick hair was sparse, revealing scattered slices of her scalp.

"Is this the final tick on your list?" Margot asked.

Felicity sat down again, exhausted from the game, tired of the charade.

"Yes, Mother. You were always so observant. You're right. I'm dying."

Margot said nothing, the silence of the years hanging between them before she finally spoke.

"If you're looking for money, you've come to the wrong place. Your father made sure of that. Did you ever find him? Did he stay in touch with his dearest daughter?"

Felicity shook her head. "I don't want your money.

Can't you see, that never mattered to me." She paused. "No, I never saw him again. He never tried to see me and I didn't want to see either of you, not until . . . "

"Until what? The end?" Margot laughed. "What do you want then, Felicity?" She was growing impatient.

"I came to make peace, to tell you I have cancer and not long left," Felicity said, her voice not more than a whisper. "Sammy died two years ago," she continued. "He was killed in a car accident. And Tess before that and Paddy. They're all gone." The tears flowed freely now, she couldn't help it. "Lucie's in Australia, set to marry this year, and Florrie and Jim moved away long ago, and—"

"And you're all alone! Poor Felicity."

Felicity shivered, the words catapulting her back to the time she'd been enclosed in her room for the day after referring to her father as Poor Michael.

"Well no. I have Ann. My Annie," Felicity said.

"Annie?"

Margot's face dropped. That name. There it was again.

"You have a granddaughter. Her name is Ann – seventeen years old."

Margot looked as though she were going to be sick. Felicity opened her bag, took out a photo and handed it to her.

Margot took it. That same face. That same hair – three generations of them. She couldn't look at it. It still haunted her. She didn't want her here any more – she didn't want to remember. She needed to get rid of them, once and for all. Make sure they never darkened her door again. Felicity still didn't know. She still didn't know the truth. Margot thought that's why she'd come, but Felicity really didn't know.

"They told me you lost the child." Margot handed the picture back. "How long do you have left?"

"I don't know. Not long. Weeks, maybe."

"And the girl? She's only seventeen. Not an adult. No other family, except me, of course." Margot's eyes narrowed.

"She'll be fine. I'll make sure she's fine."

"But you can't live alone at seventeen." Margot smiled sweetly. "Remember? That was your problem too, Felicity. She could come here and live with me. I could teach her a thing or two. Make sure she doesn't make the same mistakes you did."

"There's no need. No need at all." Felicity shook her head.

"Now, Felicity, don't be rash. What are you afraid of? I should call the authorities. Yes, that's what I'll do. You can't leave a child alone. Even you must see that. She must be with family, with me. Let's be sensible here."

"Don't you dare, Mother!"

"It could be my parting gift to you, dearest. Little Annie, right where she belongs, with her grandmother." Margot was serious now. "Doesn't that feel like history repeating itself?"

"You wouldn't dare."

"Oh yes I would. It's only right. Bring the girl to see me. I have enough room."

"Mother, leave it."

"I'll take extra good care of her. It would just take one phone call. I'll see to it immediately. I was never comfortable with losing control, was I, Felicity? It would feel right to have a focus again."

Felicity was on her feet then.

"One phone call," Felicity heard as she slammed the door behind her.

She had to get out of here. She shouldn't have come. Margot could still hurt her and Felicity knew she would, given half the chance. Felicity had to get Ann away from here as soon as she could. She couldn't take the risk of Ann ending up with that manipulative evil bitch. She'd protect her from that pain, make sure she didn't end up in the wrong life as she had. She'd get Ann far away. Her Annie. Her life.

Margot sat back in the chair, satisfied. Imagine Felicity thinking she'd want anything to do with that girl! She shuddered at the thought. It was over now. Felicity would be dead soon, buried like the past, the secret safe. She'd never liked looking back. What was done was done.

Margot got up, poured a drink and sat back down, suddenly feeling confused again. What day was it? Lately, her mind was twirling all together, making it hard to think, difficult to focus. Better that way. Best to forget.

Ann Maguire

Now

"Felicity rang me, you know. The week before she died. She'd been to see Margot. She couldn't trust that she wouldn't try to harm you or take you to live with her – claim custody somehow. I told her I wouldn't let it happen, but she said not even I knew the full extent of what she could do.

"I begged her, Annie, but she knew best. She wanted to set you free, even though it broke her heart in two. But she knew you'd be okay, that you were strong like she was in the end. She'd taught you well and she knew you'd find me when you were ready. She knew you'd come back here when it was time . . . " Lucie's voice trailed off.

"It's so hard to imagine," Ann said, still unable to understand how her mother had kept it all from her.

She thought about all she now knew and all she hadn't known. The life her mam had lived before her – a life that had almost killed her, a life from which she'd sheltered Ann.

"I wish I'd known."

"She thought she was protecting you. I couldn't have taken you to Australia. I'd never have been allowed. And she didn't want you ending up with strangers. I understood it – I'm just not sure I agreed with it. And I said I'd come back, but she wouldn't hear of it." Lucie paused. "Was it okay in Dublin?"

Ann talked then, telling her aunt everything that had happened to her right up to now. She left nothing out. She had nothing to be ashamed of any more now that she knew the truth. They spoke all night until morning.

"Let's take a walk," Lucie suggested. "Let's go and see it together. All of it."

They revisited all the old places, with fresh eyes and a new understanding. They laughed and cried and held each other. Then they walked through Knockmore, right up the hill to Knockmore House.

"I want to see it with my own eyes," Ann said.

Lucie took her hand and led her up the driveway.

"Let me show you. Let me show you the Felicity I knew," Lucie said as they knocked on the red door and waited.

It was Mark who swung it open and smiled so widely at Ann that Lucie couldn't help laughing.

"Do you two know each other?" she asked, glancing at Ann, who immediately blushed.

"Well, no. I mean yes. No."

"You never give a straight answer, do you?" Mark laughed. "Would you like to come in?"

"This is my aunt Lucie. I wasn't entirely honest yesterday, Mark. My mother grew up here. She was the reverend's daughter and, well, I'm not sure how to explain it all," Ann said, looking to Lucie for help.

"Maybe coffee and some cake might do the trick. Come in," he suggested and Ann stepped through the threshold to the past.

He led them inside and went off to fetch the coffee while Ann looked around, trying to picture the story Lucie had told her. Lucie helped her to explain it to him and Mark listened sadly to the unexpected history of the house.

"It's hard to imagine," he said at last. "How times have changed. I'm so sorry, Ann, so sorry for your loss. Would you like me to leave you to look around for a while? Please. It's the least I can do. Take your time. I'll be in the study if you need me," he said, gently placing his hand on her arm.

With Aunt Lucie at her side, they walked through the house, pointing out little things here and there, and Ann was finally able to visualise it all. They walked through the gardens, pausing briefly at the outhouse, shaking their heads in disbelief. Then they continued to where the orchard had once been and stopped at the oak tree, no longer hidden by the apple trees, now long gone. Aunt Lucie put her hand on the trunk of the old tree and closed her eyes.

"All of our secrets were in here once, in an old tin box," she said. "Felicity used to say she wished she could escape through this tree. Drink a potion to make herself small so she could disappear."

Ann kneeled beside the tree and placed her hand in through the fairy door, hoping to feel her mam's presence there. She patted the earth, suddenly feeling something rustle in her hand. She reached deeper inside and pulled out a small plastic folder.

"What's that?" Lucie asked.

They both stared down at it.

Michael Montgomery

Then – 1987

In the end, it hadn't taken long to wrap everything up. The archdeacon had been quite the sport about it. He'd pleaded the case to the bishop on Michael's behalf, but Michael already knew what the outcome would be. Michael was immediately deemed unfit to continue as reverend after he concocted a story that he'd had an affair with a member of a neighbouring parish and he wanted to leave the priesthood. It had been far easier than revealing the truth.

Michael was relieved. After everything, he was only too glad to wipe the slate clean and see the back of this place. He didn't deserve happiness. No, he'd settle for peace. Anything would be better than what had happened here. He didn't regret the lie he'd told the archdeacon. Lord knows he had greater regrets to occupy him for the rest of his days.

The archdeacon had been surprised but not in the least bit shocked. Poor Michael had put up with a lot over the years from that wife of his, filled with notions about herself and not an ounce of warmth in her heart. His own wife called her "Margot with the Marbles". He'd nearly called her Marble to her face once.

Of course, there was that terrible scandal with the daughter to consider as well. She'd got herself into "trouble" and was now shacked up with the boyfriend – such a bright young girl with so much promise. Michael told him that the family was very supportive and she was still going to sit her exams. The stress of everything had left Margot a little *weathered*. That was the word he'd used – weathered.

Margot didn't argue too much. She'd tried to, but once Sergeant Hughes explained the alternatives to her, she'd sat there tight-lipped. Felicity had almost died. The sergeant mentioned a string of words to them that day, all as terrifying as the next: abuse, neglect, manslaughter, proof, evidence, witnesses. It was enough to convince them both that it was time to move on and leave Felicity behind.

"Now, it appears I don't know the half of what went on in this house, but a pregnant girl, locked in a room, suffering from severe dehydration, says a lot to me, don't you think, Reverend?" the sergeant had said.

Michael had hung his head in shame. What had he done?

"You should be ashamed of yourselves. You know, she smashed a glass and cut into her wrists to escape this torture, and for what? Because she was pregnant! Shame on you both!" Sergeant Hughes lectured while Margot sat listening calmly as if listening to the Sunday Scriptures. "I strongly suggest you leave her be now. She has people who care about her, she's almost eighteen and let me remind you, if you don't agree, there will be consequences, serious ones."

They'd had no choice. It was over. The past had finally caught up. Michael wondered if he should he tell the truth now. But it was too late.

"I'll make the necessary arrangements, Margot. I think you've done enough. I'm going to go to London, to my brother. Start over," Michael told her. Perhaps he could teach and he'd be more accepted there.

She hadn't argued. There was no way she would go with him. They'd remain married in name, at least until Michael could arrange annulment papers, but what did it matter any more? There was never a marriage in the first place. It was all one big lie. He'd for ever regret the day he met her, the lies she'd told, the crimes she'd committed, how he was too weak to fix it. But most of all, he'd regret how he let Felicity down, time and again. He *was* pathetic. Margot was right about that.

He hoped Felicity now had the family she always needed. He'd prayed for it all, he supposed – prayed that it would all work out somehow and she'd be free. Felicity would make a wonderful mother. She was the kindest, most forgiving person he knew. He told Margot that Felicity lost the baby – the less she knew, the better.

He sat at his desk and finished writing the letter he'd started the day before. It was hard to write, to see it all down on paper, but he'd left nothing out, put it all down in black and white. When Margot finally told him about the oak tree and the way Felicity used it to communicate with the outside world – or those scum, as she'd put it – all the hairs on his arms stood on end and he knew what he needed to do. He had to try. He owed it to her.

He tucked the letter into a plastic folder and dug into the earth. Perhaps she'd find it one day and discover the truth – or maybe it would remain there for ever, buried inside the tree that held all of their secrets.

He didn't know what would happen to Knockmore

House – perhaps it would pass to the next reverend. Margot was already gone. She'd left the day before. For the life of him, he still couldn't understand how she thought she was going to be staying on there. He'd burst out laughing in her face. She honestly didn't know that the house belonged to the parish. All those years of playing at nobility or whatever she thought she was, all down the tube when she realised where she was going.

No, Michael had arranged a fine house for Margot, in the next county, a small town called Kiltimon. But it was practically identical to Knockmore in many ways. Well, they just had the one church there – the Roman Catholic one – four pubs, a post office and a butcher's. But yes, that was pretty much it.

"Rows and rows of terraced houses, with great big washing lines that stretch the length of the gardens and a wonderful sense of community," Michael told her. "And you won't have to worry much about money, I'll see to that. But you can always get a job in the butcher's."

"How dare you!" Margot fumed.

"Whether you decide to call yourself Maggie or Margot is really up to you," he continued.

"You bastard."

"Maggie it is, so. Anyway, it's number 56 Gertrude Terrace, but no one calls it that. No, I believe they call it the Estates. I'm sure you'll be happy there, in such familiar surroundings, just like where you came from."

December 1987
My dearest Felicity,
I don't know where to start or how to tell you everything I want you to know. But I needed to tell

you how sorry I am. I assume if you're reading this then you've found it, which means that you've come looking for the truth, and I hope you find it here.

I was weak, so very weak. I knew nothing until that day, that dreadful day when she disposed of the pups. I told her then that she'd to leave and that I'd care for you, but then she broke my heart. She told me the truth. The truth is that you were never ours. She stole you from a girl in the Estates who was pregnant and afraid. She was only fifteen. Margot found out about it somehow and arranged it all with the parish priest, threatened him.

She tricked me into believing she was with child herself. She discovered she was "pregnant" after she crashed the car and injured her back. As a result, she was placed on bed rest for the duration and I never questioned it.

She was clever, Felicity, so very clever. She fooled me many times, but this I could never forgive and what she did to you I will carry with me all of my life. I couldn't look at you after I knew. Not because you weren't mine, I always loved you, but because I'd let you down. I should have done more. I should have spoken up, but I was afraid of what would happen. I was afraid I'd be blamed and you'd be left with no one. I should have come forwards and faced the consequences – I know that now.

When they found you that day, almost dead, I knew she'd never stop. I made her leave you alone then. I wanted to set you free from us all, from this awful family that you became part of, through no fault of your own. I saw the love in that boy's eyes that day as he carried you out, almost dead.

I knew the love that Tess and Lucie had for you, and I knew you'd be better off with them. I hope you are. I hope you have a family of your own and you're back where you belong. Forget Margot. She'll never change. Forget me. I wasn't good enough for you.

Hold tight to love. It does exist, Felicity. I saw it in you, every day. Your real mother's name was Annie Slaney – that's all I know. But she died too, right after you were born. She couldn't carry on without you when you were taken from her. I hope this sets you free somehow. You are better than us, you always were. I'm so sorry for all the pain I caused you. I will never forgive myself. But know that I pray every day that you will find the peace you deserve.

I hope you always have your freedom – to do with it what you wish.
Michael

Ann Maguire

After

So much had happened and Ann found it difficult to leave Knockmore again when all she wanted to do was stay. She knew everything now. There was no stone left unturned, no question mark looming over her. They couldn't believe it when they found the letter and discovered the truth. The truth had been there hidden in the oak tree all this time. Felicity had been stolen.

It was almost too far-fetched to believe and yet it explained everything. Lucie knew straight away who Felicity's birth mother was – she put it together in an instant. She'd have been Felicity Slaney. Well, maybe not Felicity. What a different life she'd have had if she'd been left where she was. She wondered if she'd still have met Sammy. But she already knew the answer. Nothing stood in the way of destiny.

Ann's mother had been through hell, but she'd found her way out and ended up exactly where she was supposed to be, right where she'd started – full circle. Ann would never forget her mother's words: "I've lived enough of a life for anyone. It's been enough for me and I got my fairy tale in the end, Ann. I did. Now, you go and make yours."

After such hardship, such grief, she'd appreciated more than anything the small bit of happiness she had had.

For Felicity, it had been enough. She'd deserved so much more, but she'd never complained. She'd done everything to protect Ann from experiencing pain, sacrificing so much for her. Ann hoped her mam was at peace now, with the love of her life, with Sammy. Ann supposed she'd take an ounce of happiness too, if that happiness was true love, like the kind she'd witnessed as a child. Ann would never settle for less again, especially not for a husband who didn't respect her. She owed it to her parents to live life now, proud of who she was, to have the life they'd wanted for her. And perhaps some day, if she was lucky enough, to experience a love like they'd known.

Ann wasn't ready to think about Margot, to believe that there could be that much evil in one person. It was too much. Margot had ended up where she deserved too, right back where she'd started – alone and unhappy. Margot's life could have been different if she'd been brave enough to right her wrongs. Ann would learn from that. She'd take that lesson.

It was up to Ann now to find the right life for herself, but she knew now that she could. Especially now she knew the truth. The secret had damaged them all, affected all of their lives, but she wasn't going to let it ruin hers any longer.

Aunt Lucie made Ann promise that she'd to come to Australia and meet Hamish and her kids, Declan and Bella. Ann nearly spat her drink out when Lucie revealed her daughter's name. Ann would go, knowing she'd need a holiday, especially after what she was about to face in Dublin.

Ann had rung Sophie before she left, who'd been dying to tell Ann all about Dom. Apparently, his father was furious with him and Dom was still hell bent on making amends with Ann. Ann knew for sure that she wouldn't be working things out with him. Dom wasn't her ounce of happiness.

She was going to wipe the slate clean and start again. She was young. She had plenty of time to find the kind of love worth fighting for. Ann was going to stand on her own two feet – well, with a little help.

It turned out the house in the Estates hadn't been remortgaged. Lucie had got a local estate agent to manage both it and the tenants, but if she ever wanted it, the house was Ann's. They'd gone to collect the few boxes of belongings that a neighbour had stored for her – things that Lucie couldn't bring herself to part with. Ann and Lucie had spent hours poring over the contents the day before. In them, Ann rediscovered her past. All the photos Sammy had taken over the years, Felicity's wedding dress, her wedding ring with the word "Always" engraved on the inside and finally, Sammy's beloved leather jacket. Without hesitating, Ann had slipped off her pristine 2.5 carat solitaire diamond wedding band and replaced it with the thin gold band, which fitted her as well as it had fitted her mother.

There was still Florrie to visit so she could reveal the final piece of the puzzle to her. Perhaps Ann would try to find Michael Montgomery and set his mind at rest, if he was still alive. She might also have other family out there she didn't know about – Felicity's real birth family. Or maybe she'd leave the past in the past. There was still so much to think about. But whatever she decided, she knew where she'd come if she wanted to try – back to Knockmore.

Ann removed her baseball cap and sunglasses and flung them in the boot of the car. She grabbed Sammy's leather jacket from the box and pulled it on, hugging herself, feeling her dad's embrace. She ran her fingers around the gold band on her finger – a perfect circle. Then she inhaled and smiled to herself, looking around once more. Ann started the engine and then paused when a small white feather drifted from thin air and landed on the windscreen in front of her.

"You know what they say . . . " She could her Tess's words so clearly – the same words Tess had once used to comfort a frightened little girl, sitting alone on the steps of Knockmore House. "Feathers appear when loved ones are near."

"Goodbye, Mam. Goodbye, Dad," Ann smiled, before putting the car into gear and making her way out of the town, past the two trees and on to the winding road that would once again take her away.

Only this time, Ann realised, she knew her way home.

The End . . .

ACKNOWLEDGEMENTS

It takes an army of people to write a book they say, and it's true. I didn't stand a chance of ever completing *When Destiny Sings* without my army of people. Those who prevented me from throwing my laptop out of the window, those who fed and watered me when I refused to step away from the screen, and those who didn't let me to quit. The very same army who's with me through any venture I undertake and the very same army that you can sometimes fail to see until you go to acknowledge them. Here's my army . . .

To all at Poolbeg Press, in particular Paula Campbell, for taking a chance on me when I needed it the most. I wish you could have witnessed my face and the tragic dance moves when I opened *that* email from you. I am for ever indebted. You have made a dream a reality. I could never express how much it means to me. Well, I could, but it would be long and require editing. Talking of which . . .

To my wonderful editor, Claire Dean, for polishing this book to a level I never thought possible. For your encouragement, patience and efficiency. *And*, you got my sense of humour. Mission accomplished. I understand now why people thank their editors profusely. It's deserved. Thank you. I look forward to working with you again. Perhaps for ever, but not forever! (Ah! the things I've learned, not learnt!)

To my husband, Malcolm, to whom I dedicate this book

– my childhood sweetheart, my own personal Sammy Maguire, the love of my life, there aren't enough words. Through thick and thin, through every up and down, you'll always be my happy ever after.

To my children, Martha-Lily, Bruce and Gertie. For putting up with substandard catering for the duration of the journey, for giving me a reason, for making me laugh. Thank you for understanding how important this was for me.

To my parents, John and Amy Small. For helping me to believe I can do anything. I love you. And my siblings, Gillian, Sharon and John. The Originals. x

To my very early readers. Lucie, for lending me her name and being as good a friend to me as Lucie Maguire was to Felicity. For minding the kids to let me write and for making me go to the gym. Your support has been legendary. Susan, my sister from another mister, for inspiring me through your descriptions of growing up in a small town in Ireland. You gave me the visual for the fictional Knockmore but opened my eyes to a bigger world, which we've travelled together. Nicole, for endless hours of picking apart the story and piecing it back together again. For walking through graveyards with me to find the perfect names for "our" characters and for finally helping me to reach "the end . . . " I am forever indebted to you all.

To my later readers, Audrey, Suzanne, Joanne, Catherine and Jen. Your feedback was invaluable, your friendship even more so. To all of my school friends for everything – you know who you are.

To Yvonne, for twenty-eight years of much more than a friendship, which started with four little words: "I like your shoes." For those horrendous voice messages, for being way funnier than I will ever be and for believing in me, always.

My proofreaders, Lucie, Nicole and Anne-Marie. Please email them with the typos! Thank you.

To Eoin Dempsey, author extraordinaire, who slipped (or was forced) into the role of mentor, IT support, adviser, cheerleader and finally, friend. Without his advice and encouragement, you wouldn't be reading this book.

To anyone who cheered me, pushed me, believed in me, thank you from the bottom of my heart. I felt your presence. *When Destiny Sings* is my first novel. It was originally called *Evolve* and there's no doubt I evolved with it. I've loved every moment of this process. I hope you enjoyed it, too. I will write more, I know that now.

Destiny is a matter of choice.

Judith Cuffe

x

Printed in Great Britain
by Amazon